Interpretation for Preaching and Teaching

AN INTRODUCTION
to Biblical Hermeneutics

Stanley E. Porter

Baker Academic
a division of Baker Publishing Group
Grand Rapids, Michigan

© 2023 by Stanley E. Porter

Published by Baker Academic
a division of Baker Publishing Group
Grand Rapids, Michigan
www.bakeracademic.com

Printed in the United States of America

Library of Congress Cataloging-in-Publication Data
Names: Porter, Stanley E., 1956– author.
Title: Interpretation for preaching and teaching : an introduction to biblical hermeneutics / Stanley E. Porter.
Description: Grand Rapids, Michigan : Baker Academic, a division of Baker Publishing Group, [2023] | Includes bibliographical references and index.
Identifiers: LCCN 2022046586 | ISBN 9781540966377 (paperback) | ISBN 9781540966551 (casebound) | ISBN 9781493441709 (ebook) | ISBN 9781493441716 (pdf)
Subjects: LCSH: Preaching. | Bible—Hermeneutics.
Classification: LCC BV4211.3 .P67 2023 | DDC 251—dc23/eng/20221223
LC record available at https://lccn.loc.gov/2022046586

Baker Publishing Group publications use paper produced from sustainable forestry practices and post-consumer waste whenever possible.

23   24   25   26   27   28   29   7   6   5   4   3   2   1

Contents

Preface

I was honored when I was asked a number of years ago to deliver talks on hermeneutics to some missionary pastors serving in a major European non-English-speaking country. I have long been interested in questions of hermeneutics—that is, in questions regarding human understanding and interpretation, especially of written texts. I gladly accepted the invitation and set about developing the initial form of the book that you have in your hands (or, in this day and age, on your device). As one might expect, I took the opportunity so enthusiastically that I developed far more material than I would be able to discuss with my eager colleagues. While I was in the country, I also was asked to preach, and so I had the opportunity to use in my own sermon the approach that I had been modeling for my colleagues (although I have to admit that the use of consecutive translation is not something that I have grown fond of). In the course of developing these materials, I consulted with one of my closest and most trusted intellectual friends. He assured me that many of the things that I had to say were helpful, but he also did not hesitate to tell me that some of the things I said needed further thought and refinement. I took him seriously and have been in the lengthy process of revising the materials I first presented over the course of many years. I have drawn on a number of the individual ideas and sections in various ways as I have returned to the topic of hermeneutics. In the course of preparing the original lectures and then later transforming them into a book manuscript, I am embarrassed to say that I lost track of some of the sources that I used in their writing. I have done everything I can think of to try to ensure that I made appropriate reference to the sources I used, including doing internet searches and enlisting the work of numerous graduate assistants to provide suitable documentation throughout. If I have missed some sources, I apologize profusely and profoundly.

Hermeneutics has, in fact, become an area in which I have tried to establish expertise. My interest in hermeneutics probably began with my study of literature and language, especially English literature, for both BA and MA degrees, and then during my time in seminary where I focused on the study of Greek for an MA and then doing a PhD in both biblical studies and linguistics. I was privileged to study with Dr. Grant Osborne and be his teaching assistant. I took his course in hermeneutics, for which he prepared extensive notes, and have appreciated his major book on the topic. I readily acknowledge Dr. Osborne's influence on me, and that influence will be apparent throughout this book. My initial doctoral supervisor was Professor Anthony Thiselton, who pioneered the teaching of hermeneutics within the British university system, as well as writing abundantly and significantly on the topic. I also attended his lectures on hermeneutics and have been greatly influenced by him in my own scholarship. I even framed my doctoral dissertation as an exercise in hermeneutics, because I realized the importance of hermeneutics—questions of understanding—as framing even the study of Greek grammar and linguistics. While this book was being finalized, I was saddened to learn of Professor Thiselton's death. He will be greatly missed. The ideas of both Osborne and Thiselton no doubt infuse the content of this book, with their legacies remaining after their passing.

Through my continued research and writing in the area of hermeneutics, I have had the tremendous opportunity to co-author two monographs on hermeneutics with the philosopher Jason C. Robinson. The first, *Hermeneutics: An Introduction to Interpretive Theory* (Grand Rapids: Eerdmans, 2011), provides a critical appraisal of the major figures in the field of hermeneutics. The second, *Active Hermeneutics: Seeking Understanding in an Age of Objectivism* (London: Routledge, 2021), proposes a virtue hermeneutics in the light of our scientific age. I have also had the opportunity to write articles and edit several books on hermeneutics. Along the way, it was a great privilege to be able to refine my thoughts on the field of hermeneutics in many ways through my interactions with a host of different people.

This book is not a technical monograph on the subject. It is an attempt to make hermeneutics accessible and useful to those who perhaps more than any others need to be sure that the work they do is hermeneutically sound. Hence, this book is titled *Interpretation for Preaching and Teaching: An Introduction to Biblical Hermeneutics*. I envision my primary audience as pastors (and those studying to become pastors) and others who are regularly involved in interpreting and understanding God's Word, so that they can deliver a message of truth, relevance, and pertinence to the people who rely on them to be faithful interpreters.

In the course of preparing this manuscript, I have benefited from the helpful work of a number of my students and former students. Each of them has taken this manuscript upon him- or herself as a major task, and I sincerely thank them for their efforts in a variety of ways. I wish to thank Dr. Karl L. Armstrong, Dr. Woojin Chung, Dr. David Fuller, Dr. Zachary K. Dawson, Dr. Cynthia Chau, Solomon Umazi, Vinh Nguyen, Jackson Theune, and Jihyung Kim, my excellent indexer. I have benefited greatly from having this book on understanding read and improved by such a diverse group of people. Each has made a significant and worthwhile contribution to this volume. Their multiethnic perspectives and multicultural insights have definitely made this a better and much more useful work. It began its life as an attempt at multicultural communication, and I hope finds a home in a similar environment. I vividly remember the day that my graduate assistant, Jackson, came into my office and said that he had decided to see if my approach to hermeneutics works, so he had used it to prepare his teaching that week—and he found it did! And he committed to using it in his future preaching and teaching. My hope and prayer is that some of the things I have said in this volume will help others, pastors and other interested interpreters, in their ministries of preaching and teaching.

I try to provide examples from both testaments, but since I am a New Testament specialist, I inevitably revert to that area in most instances. I especially draw on one small book, Philemon, often neglected in theological studies, to provide instructive extended examples. I hope that the principles I lay out and the examples I use will also be useful to those primarily interested in the Old Testament. I have used a variety of translations (so indicated), as well as my own translations, throughout this volume. The reasons vary according to context.

I am also very thankful to my colleagues at Baker Publishing, especially my good friend and editor Dr. Bryan Dyer, for welcoming this book—and for Bryan's unstinting work to help make it a better (and shorter) contribution to biblical interpretation. I also appreciate the attentive and meticulous work of my project editor, Melisa Blok.

As in all areas of my life, I am very thankful to my wife, Wendy, for her encouragement and support, manifested here in the transformation of this manuscript into something that I pray is useful to the church and those who serve it.

I wish to dedicate this volume to my dear friend, Rev. Dr. Dennis L. Stamps. I think that I have known Dennis longer than any other of my academic theological colleagues. We met at the very beginning of my time at seminary and have continued to share the adventure of biblical and theological study. He was one of my first encouragers in hermeneutics, and so I hope that he sees in this volume a suitable if belated realization of that interest.

Abbreviations

AB	Anchor Bible	MJTM	*McMaster Journal of Theology and Ministry*
BAGL	*Biblical and Ancient Greek Linguistics*	MNTS	McMaster New Testament Studies
BLG	Biblical Languages: Greek	NICNT	The New International Commentary on the New Testament
CBR	*Currents in Biblical Research*		
CD	Church Dogmatics		
CTR	*Criswell Theological Review*	NovTSup	Supplements to Novum Testamentum
EvQ	*The Evangelical Quarterly*		
GBS	Guides to Biblical Scholarship	NSBT	New Studies in Biblical Theology
HUT	Hermeneutische Untersuchungen zur Theologie	NTM	New Testament Monographs
JBMW	*Journal for Biblical Manhood and Womanhood*	PRR	*The Presbyterian and Reformed Review*
JETS	Journal of the Evangelical Theological Society	RBS	Resources for Biblical Study
		RE	*Review and Expositor*
JSOTSup	Journal for the Study of the Old Testament Supplement Series	SBG	Studies in Biblical Greek
		SNTSMS	Society for New Testament Studies Monograph Series
JTS	*Journal of Theological Studies*		
LBS	Linguistic Biblical Studies	WBC	Word Biblical Commentary
LNTS	The Library of New Testament Studies	WUNT	Wissenschaftliche Untersuchungen zum Neuen Testament
MBSS	McMaster Biblical Studies Series		

1

What Is Hermeneutics, and Why Are So Many Talking about It?

Introduction

This book is about hermeneutics. I recognize that that may not mean very much to some people, possibly even to some of my readers. The term *hermeneutics* is itself a technical term that has come to be used in a variety of ways and in varied circles of discussion. These are often circles that are concerned with philosophical issues regarding how humans know and understand the world around them. This does not make it any easier to understand, to be sure. Nevertheless, I believe that positioning hermeneutics within this larger area of discussion enables us to understand more fully both its limitations and its great significance for us as interpreters of the Bible. In this chapter, I begin with a discussion of what hermeneutics is and briefly trace some of its historical developments. A chapter such as this within a book of this nature cannot say all that could or even needs to be said about such an expansive topic. Nevertheless, some of this basic knowledge is required to set the stage for what follows in subsequent chapters as we plunge into hermeneutics and interpretation itself.

What Is Hermeneutics?

Whether we recognize it or not, we are constantly engaging in the process of hermeneutics. Every thought we have, decision we make, and conversation we engage in is influenced and driven by the process of interpreting the world around us. Hermeneutics, the name given to this process, is what we employ in order to make sense of our lives and how we choose to live them. Recognizing and beginning to understand the importance of hermeneutics is obviously important for our constant thinking and decision making. You may, up to this point in your life, have associated hermeneutics only with the task of interpreting the Bible—and, of course, that is the subject we will attempt to tackle and make sense of throughout this book. However, before we do so, it is important to first understand that hermeneutics is not limited to tasks such as understanding our daily devotional reading, creating a sermon, or writing a paper. Hermeneutics invades, permeates, and informs everything we do. For those who take seriously the call of Colossians 3:17 to do everything, both in our speaking and in our acting, in the name of the Lord Jesus, recognizing the role hermeneutics plays in informing all we do throughout our lives is crucial. Understanding hermeneutics in this way will, I hope, make us not only better readers of Scripture but also better human beings. Let's begin with a helpful illustration of both the necessity and the value of hermeneutics as it relates to our everyday lives.

Human beings are constantly required to interpret various sign systems.[1] Sign systems may consist of any number of different formal and informal indicators of meaning, and they all require various types of interpretation. If someone does not appropriately interpret these signs, that failure may cause problems. Let us consider one apparently simple sign system: traffic lights.[2] The green light indicating "go" and the red light indicating "stop" appear to be relatively straightforward, but even these signs require interpretation. If there is another car in the intersection, a green light does not mean "go," but the more complex sign system of the lights and the traffic in the intersection means "proceed when the intersection is clear," requiring the driver to interpret when the driving situation warrants safe travel. The red light means "stop," but it may also mean "stop and then proceed," such as on a right- or left-hand turn, at least in some situations (but not in others). Some traffic lights have flashing green lights, which may indicate that certain drivers are allowed to proceed but not others. In other words, green and red traffic lights require interpretation before one

1. The field of semiotics is concerned with the various sign systems that humans encounter, create, and use. See Eco, *Theory of Semiotics*, and the more recent basic introduction, Chandler, *Semiotics*.
2. Traffic lights are a common example used by semioticians (those concerned with signs and their systems of usage). For a discussion of traffic lights as a nonlinguistic semiotic system, see Nöth, *Handbook of Semiotics*, 205.

proceeds, with potentially dire consequences if one does not. Even if all the above is relatively clear (or is it?), the yellow light is certainly problematic. Many drivers appear to be unclear on the meaning of the yellow traffic light, with interpreters acting as if it sometimes means "stop," and other times "speed up," and other times simply "proceed as normal." A variety of other configurations are also possible. Traffic lights represent what most people would consider to be a relatively simple and straightforward sign system, yet it nonetheless requires various and constant acts of interpretation in regard to the different colors.[3]

The term *hermeneutics* is the general term used to encapsulate what goes on when we engage in such interpretation, whether it is of traffic lights or of a variety of much more complex sign systems, such as language. Languages, and more specifically particular language systems, are highly complex sign systems that involve complex hermeneutical issues. Language is used in a variety of ways. One of these is in written texts. The Bible is a written text and, therefore, requires hermeneutical awareness whenever it is read. Familiarity with the Bible tends to result in readers believing that the Bible is like traffic lights, an easily interpretable and basic sign system, when in fact the Bible is a complex set of written texts that requires hermeneutical interpretive sophistication that goes way beyond traffic lights.

Defining Hermeneutics

To begin, I will offer a preliminary definition of hermeneutics: *discussion of the principles of understanding found in various models used to interpret a written text.* While this definition could be much broader so as to include interpretation of all sorts of sign systems, I have narrowed it to focus on written text so that readers can build a foundation for their understanding of this field as they address the more complex issues to be introduced later in this volume.[4] The words of this definition have been carefully chosen so that I can elaborate on several of the more crucial words in order to call attention

---

3. The recognition that one has a sign, the object of the sign, and what he calls "the interpretant," was apparently first explicitly articulated by the polymath Charles Peirce. See Peirce, *Pragmatism as a Principle*, 98–119.

4. Stanley E. Porter and Jason C. Robinson provide the following broader definition that befits the field of philosophical hermeneutics: "In its most basic sense hermeneutics refers to the many ways in which we may theorize about the nature of human interpretation, whether that means understanding books, works of art, architecture, verbal communication, or even nonverbal bodily gestures" (*Hermeneutics*, 1). They propose a constructive approach to hermeneutics in Porter and Robinson, *Active Hermeneutics*.

to their significance and rightful place concerning how we, in biblical studies, approach hermeneutics, or at least should approach it.

The first term within this definition that I want to call attention to is *discussion*. For most, it would not take long to identify someone they know who tends to over-impose their opinions on others and/or who presents themself as having the answers to every issue, or, in other words, is quick to speak but slow to listen. I used to attend a church with a man who had definite opinions on most, if not all, of the theological issues confronting the Christian today, and he was more than willing to tell anyone who asked (and sometimes they did not even have to ask) what his opinion was on a given issue. Admittedly there were times when I agreed with him, at least in part, but other times I did not agree with him at all. I soon learned, however, that in either case trying to continue any sort of dialogue was hopeless, since this man would not enter into *discussion*. Discussion is not another way of saying that one does not hold to firm convictions. Discussion is, however, a way of saying that we willingly engage in dialogue over the issues at hand.

Discussion requires two elements: (1) an opinion, a thought, or even a question to *contribute* and (2) the ability to *listen* to and evaluate what others have to say. Offering an opinion, a thought, or a question is an assertive posture that is meant to move the discussion forward. It is vital that Christians formulate opinions they are willing to share, but listening is equally important. This is the reflective posture that weighs both one's own and the other's argument. Each element is important, though many Christians, regardless of denominational affiliation, fail to realize and practice this. For example, on the issue of whether women should wear head coverings, mentioned in 1 Corinthians 11:12–16, it has been argued that a woman's hair is to serve as the covering ("in place of a covering," as some translate; v. 15). I do not wish to debate the meaning of this verse, but I believe that a number of churches who maintain that a woman must cover her head have failed to enter into discussion of this issue and instead are working on the level of tradition alone.[5] This controversy provides a short example that speaks to the reality of the importance of hermeneutics.

The second term I would like to treat is *models*. Students of the Bible have only lately arrived at the importance of models for human understanding. A

---

5. Although few contemporary evangelical churches still struggle with the issue of head coverings, earlier in the twentieth century few women would arrive in church on a Sunday morning without wearing a hat. Within the twentieth century, it was not unknown for some churches to split over this issue. The predominant issue of hermeneutics today for evangelical churches is probably women in leadership, followed closely by LGBTQ+ matters (and they are sometimes linked).

very important book in this regard is the philosopher Thomas Kuhn's classic work in the philosophy of science, *The Structure of Scientific Revolutions*, in which he uses the term *paradigm* to refer to a scientific model that characterizes a given period in intellectual history until a new paradigm, or way of seeing the world, revolutionizes scientific thought by solving the puzzles that the old paradigm could not solve. There was once a time when scientists thought that the earth was the center of the universe, but the Copernican revolution—named after Nicolaus Copernicus, the Renaissance polymath who placed the sun at the center of the universe—instigated a paradigm shift, so we now understand that the earth revolves around the sun, and not vice versa, and this affects the way we understand the world. The term *paradigm* has become widely popular in reference to any way of thinking. However, to be truer to the Kuhnian usage, paradigms describe the various ways different observers view and make sense of the data they are analyzing, including the sets of theories and methods used to interpret the data. I take note here that the word *hermeneutics* is *plural* and is most often used in the plural: the field of hermeneutics houses multiple paradigms, ways of understanding and interpreting, some of which are complementary and some of which are more exclusive. They all, however, represent ways of viewing data. The old saying "a picture is worth a thousand words," then, can easily be applied to hermeneutics because what we experience can be viewed through any number of interpretive lenses or by means of a variety of pictures.

By way of illustration, consider the Statue of Liberty, which stands in New York Harbor—the celebrated gift from France to the United States. The Statue of Liberty can be viewed from several different angles. A paradigm or model can be likened to each of the various ways one might approach the statue. Some see it as they take a harbor cruise, others see it as they fly over in an airplane or helicopter, and still others take a boat to the island to stand right at its base and look up. Viewers used to have the option of going into the statue itself and looking out over New York City from the crown on the top of the statue's head. Although this analogy has clear weaknesses, it nevertheless illustrates the concept well for our purposes: any given object or set of data can be viewed in a number of ways, and each different angle provides a different picture, no matter how slight that difference may be. There is not necessarily only a single view from which the data may be observed. The same can be said for discussing a text like the Bible.

In the field of Christian theology, paradigms function on various levels and in different ways as means of characterizing perspectives on understanding. For example, it could be argued that every Christian shares at least one grand and large-scale paradigm in common with every other Christian, related in some way to the salvation of humanity through the redemptive work of God. On a slightly lower level, Roman Catholic and Protestant Christians appear to hold different paradigms of Christianity. Roman Catholics may emphasize in their paradigm that the church is the mediator of grace to the believer, and this is accompanied by certain other understandings—for example, church leadership. In comparison, Protestants may want to emphasize the doctrine that Scripture alone is the believer's authority, and that it teaches the doctrine of salvation by grace alone, unmediated by the church. At a slightly lower level again, Protestants would themselves divide along certain fundamental lines related to the doctrine of election. Reformed Christians interpret their Christian lives through the paradigm of God's sovereign election as taught by a person such as John Calvin, while the Wesleyan/Arminian tradition emphasizes in its paradigm the free will of humanity, a stance argued by Jacobus Arminius and proclaimed by John Wesley.

With this last example we can draw a link between our two terms under discussion here—*models* and *paradigms*. These terms are often used interchangeably, but I believe it is sometimes better to differentiate between them. A model is a means by which paradigms are made evident. In other words, models are the means by which we can say things about the paradigms we hold. So, with the distinction between Reformed Calvinism and Arminianism, we can point to the acronym TULIP (Total depravity, Unconditional election, Limited atonement, Irresistible grace, and Perseverance of the saints) as an example of a model. This acronym is a structured set of codependent theological beliefs about soteriology that shapes the way we can speak in a consistent and coherent manner about Calvinism, which is the paradigm that gives overall shape to the theological data and technical vocabulary.

Biblical scholars themselves employ many different models of interpretation. The rise of historical criticism since the time of the Enlightenment in the seventeenth and eighteenth centuries led to an emphasis on reason, rationalism, naturalism, and empiricism, treating the history and development of the text of Scripture as if it were the same as any other written text. This eventually led to the development of several models of interpretation that reflected these Enlightenment principles. The most important ones that continue to be used are form, source, and redaction criticism, which are all forms of historical criticism. Historical criticism had a huge influence on interpretation of the Bible for many years, even if less critical forms of interpretation continued to be used in more conservative circles. These are sometimes characterized as diachronic interpretive models because they tend to emphasize the origins, history, and development of the text.

Since the 1980s, a variety of other models of interpretation have been introduced into biblical studies, most of them borrowed from other disciplines and adapted to biblical studies.[6] These include, among others, literary criticism, in which various texts of the Bible are treated the same as if they were secular literature (e.g., the Gospels are examined as a literary type, such as a fictional narrative); social-scientific criticism, where various descriptions of social groups and their relations are drawn on to explain the biblical accounts, such as the various groups in Pauline churches and their relationships; and ideological criticism, in which various ideological frameworks influenced by major social, cultural, and political trends are used to read the Bible, such as feminist or gender-related perspectives or socioeconomic models (such as Marxism). There are other models as well, such as narrative criticism, theological interpretation of Scripture (TIS), and linguistic criticism.[7] Many of these models are characterized as synchronic, because they tend to emphasize the text as a thing itself, although some also contain diachronic elements. The point is that each model of interpretation brings particular questions to bear on reading a written text and hence identifies what counts for evidence in that particular model. For example, a literary model might pay attention to such matters as character, plot, and setting but not be concerned with questions of historicity or factuality. An ideological model might be concerned with issues of socioeconomics and not attend to issues regarding intricacies of language. No model can attempt to ask all the possible questions that one might ask of a text. Thus, there are limits to the various models that are used in interpretation. Interpreters must know both the potential and the limitations of the models they use and cannot expect a single model to answer all their questions.

I am aware that I may already be running the risk of stirring up some of my readers by suggesting that various models can be used to interpret Scripture or even formulate Christian doctrine, especially since many would claim that they are being led by biblical teaching alone. Before anyone objects too strenuously, I would ask that the following points be taken into consideration. First, I am striving to define by example what a model is. Although the term is slippery, it is helpful in discussing hermeneutics. In fact, it is a necessary term. Even those who would argue for a very straightforward approach to Scripture, such as using what is sometimes called the grammatical-historical

---

6. The following volumes on the history of biblical interpretation note this important divide. See Porter and Adams, *Pillars in the History of Biblical Interpretation*, vols. 1 and 2; Porter and Dawson, *Pillars in the History of Biblical Interpretation*, vol. 3.

7. For essays on the variety of interpretive models available in biblical studies, see the various entries in Porter, *Dictionary of Biblical Criticism and Interpretation*.

method, are using a model.[8] Second, I am merely pointing out that there are, in fact, different models of interpretation with distinct sets of assumptions being used in the Christian church today related to significant matters of scriptural interpretation and the related doctrinal issues. It seems rather pointless to deny this situation, especially when all one needs to do is pull up a list of the various installments in any of the several multiple-view textbooks and similar series, many of these published by major conservative evangelical publishing houses.[9] Third, recognizing the fact that there are different models of interpretation says nothing about which ones are correct and which ones are in error. That is a *different* question. I hope that by the time readers reach the end of this book they have a much better idea about how to adjudicate among various models of interpretation, as well as the interpretations at which these models arrive.

Before we venture further into our topic, it is necessary to recognize that there are ways of evaluating the validity of different interpretive models, as well as ways of evaluating the quality of different interpretations themselves. However, from the outset I think it is healthy and wise to admit that it is not always so easy to see which models are superior to others, and that the criteria for determining superiority are themselves complex. In fact, I think it can be argued that in a good number of places there is room for several different models, some perhaps better than others, depending on the *purpose* they fulfill. To draw from the transparency of the word *exegesis* (a close cousin of the word *hermeneutics*), each model can be used to *lead out* different things from the text. I will be presenting one model, and I have reasons for using it, though I would be the first to admit that there are others who prefer and arguably even successfully use other models.[10] All of this is part of what is involved in discussing hermeneutics, practicing and seeing various models of understanding and interpretation.

The third term I would like to single out from my definition of hermeneutics is the word *various*. As I have already mentioned, there is not a single method of interpretation, and there is no one method of interpretation for written texts in particular, even the text of Scripture. As I will note briefly later, many of the theological debates through the centuries have arisen over which model for interpreting Scripture has been used. My belief is that if we, as interpreters and guides of others in interpretation, were more sensitive to the models that are used in interpretation, as well as the paradigms they

8. For example, see Blomberg, "Historical-Critical/Grammatical View."
9. See, for example, Porter and Stovell, *Biblical Hermeneutics*; or Porter and Dyer, *Synoptic Problem*.
10. See chapters 4 and 5 for the level of textual analysis.

presume, we could clarify and advance discussion and debate significantly by at least being aware of the presuppositions of other interpreters. *Presupposition* is a rather faddish word that refers to the pre-understandings that any person brings to his or her attempts to make sense of the world. In 2 Samuel 12, when Nathan tells his story of the shepherd to King David, we can see a poignant example of how presuppositions influence our understanding. David interprets Nathan's account literalistically, reacting angrily at the suggestion that such injustice could be going on in his country, while Nathan applies the story allegorically to David himself. David's pre-understanding that Nathan is simply relating a state of affairs in the country and nothing more leads to David not understanding that Nathan's story is really about him, even if it also reflects a more general principle of justice.

The fourth term of significance in our working definition of hermeneutics is *principles*. To carry on rational discussion, it is helpful to talk in terms of various discrete principles that make up the system of interpretation employed by a given model. This is not meant to deny a genuine mystical element to the Christian life and even to scriptural understanding itself, but such understanding seems to me to be almost entirely personal. In other words, those ideas arrived at solely through a personal mystical experience, while quite possibly valid, true, and even trustworthy for the individual involved, are very difficult to discuss and evaluate objectively unless they are overtly expressed in a principled way. Imagine my frustration when in a recent theological "discussion" with a friend I found that I disagreed with him on several fundamental issues and pressed him as to why he held a certain view, to which he responded that he knew why but could not explain it to me. It is important to stress that the interpretation of Scripture is not simply a matter of unanalyzed tradition, though tradition certainly has much to do with what paradigm is in use. Nor is interpretation simply a matter of personal *feeling*, though personal commitment is a vital stage after rational appropriation and understanding. Further, interpretation is *not* simply a matter of random sampling or proof texting, since this inevitably leads to the selective defense of particular biases. Principles of hermeneutics may involve elements of all of these, but they are principles because they are communicable, analyzable, and assessable as part of the process of interpretation.

The final term I want to highlight is *written text*. Some may be surprised that I have not used the word *Bible* or *Scripture* here. I have done so consciously and for what I believe is a very good reason. For some readers of the Bible, the idea has grown up that interpreting Scripture is completely unlike interpreting anything else. While the Bible may be much more than just a written text, it is at least, and in certain important ways, *primarily* a written text like any other. In other words, as readers of the Bible, we must go through many of the very same processes of interpretation that we would go through when reading and interpreting a history text, poetry, a novel, graffiti, and the like. This does not denigrate Scripture, but it makes us aware of how important reading and interpreting any written text is. Interpretation is essential, not something extra, to understanding. Certainly, inspiration as a meaningful doctrine guarantees things about the trustworthiness of this particular text, the Bible, and says something about the conditions of its creation and the divine force that stands behind it. But these factors, significant as they may be, have little to do with the actual process of reading the text of Scripture.

A possible response to what I have said above might be that the Bible is different from some texts because it was written so long ago. It is certainly true that the Bible was written long ago. Any given text has its own horizon or limits of place and time in which it stands, and the interpreter has another horizon, in which he or she stands. Contained within the definition of hermeneutics I have given is the underlying concept of the two *horizons*,[11] one of the text and the other of the reader. Every text presents the problem of the two horizons, which is how these two different horizons—often separated by great differences, such as time, culture, language, and the like—can come together so that a contemporary interpreter with his or her horizon of understanding is able to understand a text written from a potentially very different horizon. This separation of horizons, however, holds true even for texts written today, since the horizon, or world of discourse of the text, cannot be identical with that of the reader, who stands outside of it, even if only a moment of time has passed. The text continues to exist independent of the circumstances that occasioned its production. This independence is just as true, if not more so, of a text that was written two thousand or more years ago.

The problem of the two horizons is true of all interpretation of texts, even if it is heightened and increased by the span of time between the writing and the interpretation of an ancient text such as the Bible. A classic example is the parable of the Pharisee and the tax collector in Luke 18:9–14. In this parable, the Pharisee is proud that he is a Pharisee and acceptable in God's eyes, while the tax collector does not raise his eyes but realizes his sinful condition. Today there is a tendency to shrug and say, "Of course the tax collector is forgiven; he is the good guy of this story." For the first-century reader, the opposite was the case; the Pharisee was the righteous person who was con-

---

11. Anthony C. Thiselton notes, "Although the word has now become a technical term in hermeneutical theory, even in popular parlance 'horizon' is used metaphorically to denote the limits of thought dictated by a given viewpoint or perspective" (*Two Horizons*, xix).

cerned to obey the law to its ultimate degree.[12] In interpreting this parable, therefore, we must attempt to understand it in light of both the original shocking impact for the first-century reader (the horizon of its origin) and our rather jaded reading that comes from a lifetime of hearing it in Sunday school with its same old villain (the horizon of our reception). In many definitions of hermeneutics, the locus of the text's meaning and authority is often recognized in terms of an explicit and recoverable authorial intention, which I will discuss later, but it is essential to stress from the outset that one's status as a reader is also of crucial significance. An essential part of understanding and preaching, therefore, involves bridging or fusing these two horizons of the text and the reader by means of interpretive models.

What I am trying to emphasize about interpreting the Bible, therefore, is really two important points. On the one hand, interpreting Scripture is one of the, if not the, most *difficult* activities that a human being can ever do, since it involves a complex process of reading, analyzing, evaluating, synthesizing, and expounding, all within the confines of certain structures and limits of human understanding. On the other hand, interpreting Scripture is one of the *easiest* processes to be involved in, since it is a process that everyone who reads a biblical text enters into, regardless of his or her knowledge of the Bible, faith background, age, and so on, if that person is capable of reading written language. The words of one commentator on the Gospel of John capture the wonderful paradox of biblical interpretation: Scripture is like "a pool in which a child may wade and an elephant can swim. It is both simple and profound. It is for the veriest beginner in the faith and for the mature Christian."[13]

For a long time, the common perception has been that interpretation or hermeneutics was concerned with only the difficult and troublesome—that is, the areas of Scripture that are particularly odd, usually on account of difficult language, the distance in time and culture that separates us from the biblical writers, or uncomfortable theology. However, I think it is healthier if we realize that interpretation, especially of Scripture, is actually a *contemporary* and *relevant* subject concerned not only with the puzzling or difficult but also with the simple and seemingly clear passages of Scripture. This is because one's interpretive model establishes the rules by which

12. For more detailed usage and explication of this example, see Thiselton, *Two Horizons*, 12–16.

13. Morris, *Gospel according to John*, 7. The word *veriest* might pose a problem for some readers, as it is now an archaic word in most contemporary English—a good example of how even modern English requires interpretation. If such is the case for modern English, then one can only imagine the possible challenges of reading ancient Hebrew and Greek, the two primary languages of the Bible.

interpretation takes place, and this can result in different interpretations of the same passage that vary in their degree of insight and compatibility, among other aspects.

Let us return to the example used at the outset of this chapter: traffic lights. Regardless of whether one walks or drives, for the safety of everyone, the interpretation of those lights is extremely important! Suppose someone is driving along and the light they come to is green. They go through the light. If it is red, they stop. Why is this? Is there anything inherent in redness that says stop, or in greenness that says go? Green has stood for many things in both literature and life through the centuries, such as fertility, greed, and environmental awareness, many of them having nothing to do with forward propulsion or *going*. In other contexts, red is actually the color that signals go, such as a bullfight! The fact that most people stop at red lights and go on green is because there is a widely promulgated code agreed upon. People stop and go on the appropriate colors because we have been trained to interpret these colors to mean certain things in a particular context. It works for everyone's safety and order in society if, in the vast majority of cases, we interpret these colors in a similar manner. However, one's model of interpretation for the yellow light illustrates how different people can interpret the same sign in significantly different ways. For the sake of the illustration, we can say that those who are cautious and have a good sense of their own mortality may well interpret a yellow light as a sign to slow down. But those who are prone to taking risks and do not like to be patient may well interpret the same light as meaning "speed up!" Moreover, the cautious person, under certain circumstances, may indeed interpret the yellow light as a need to accelerate, and this goes to show that the same sign, object, situation, text, and so on can be interpreted differently by different people, as well as differently by the *same* person because we are often responsive to the world based on the situation in which we find ourselves (our location in time, place, etc.).

From here, one should not go as far as to say that with Scripture there must then be endless valid interpretations, which are conditioned according to the context in which a biblical text is interpreted. Continuing with the same illustration, if a person is stopped by a police officer for running a red light, I would not recommend that person expressing to the officer the opinion that red and green are wholly arbitrary symbols in a wholly arbitrary system, or that a different interpretive code allows one to go on red. Such an interpretation would not "work" in that situation; it is invalid, and without a doubt would result in a ticket (and perhaps having to recite the alphabet backward or walk a straight line or touch one's nose!). Interpretive models perform the same function: they establish the "rules" of the particular interpretive game that is being played at the moment; they guide and set parameters around the interpretive decisions that can be made of a text.

A Brief History of Hermeneutical Models in Biblical Interpretation

Before discussing the individual items of interpretation that are most relevant to the twenty-first-century interpreter of the Bible, it is wise to consider a brief overview of and historical perspective on hermeneutics. Many think that hermeneutical questions are only the result of the modern preoccupation with philosophical questions. The history of biblical interpretation, however, reveals otherwise, showing that questions of understanding have been important throughout virtually every period of church history.[14] We stand at the end—at least up to this point—of a long history of hermeneutical thought.

The earliest examples of struggles with the interpretation of Scripture occur in the Bible itself.[15] These kinds of examples also have parallels in ancient literature much older than the biblical texts. For example, before Judah went into exile in 586 BCE, the law had been neglected and forgotten during the time of the kings, apart from occasional reformations, such as the one led by Josiah (2 Kings 23:1–28). Around 444 BCE, after Ezra returned to Jerusalem, Nehemiah 8 records that Ezra "opened the book in the sight of all the people. . . . They read from the book, from the law of God, translating to give the sense so that they understood the reading" (vv. 5, 8 NASB95). This example is significant because it points out that interpretation through translation was necessary since the meaning was not self-evident. The major reason was that the language of the text being read was Hebrew, and the people who were hearing it, as those who had returned from exile, were Aramaic speakers. The two languages, Hebrew and Aramaic, are related but different enough to constitute distinct varieties that require translation (and hence interpretation)

14. For a history of biblical interpretation, see Grant and Tracy, *Short History*, and Bruce, "History of New Testament Study," 21–59, who provide guidance and content for much of what follows; and Thiselton, *Hermeneutics: An Introduction*, esp. 76–205, for links to hermeneutics. There are many other, fuller histories of interpretation of the Bible available for those interested, several of them being multivolume for ambitious readers. See W. Baird, *History of New Testament Research*; Bray, *Biblical Interpretation*; Neill and Wright, *Interpretation of the New Testament*; Reventlow, *History of Biblical Interpretation*; and Yarchin, *History of Biblical Interpretation*.

15. For one major work whose main concern is to uncover the kinds of exegesis found in the Old Testament—that is, passages in the Old Testament that actually exegete and interpret older passages also from the Old Testament—see Fishbane, *Biblical Interpretation*. See also Reventlow, *History of Biblical Interpretation*, 1:5–18.

from one to the other. Out of this idea of interpretation came the Jewish oral tradition, which grew up as a "hedge around the law" to define and protect it.[16]

Some of the most important examples of interpretation of Scripture occur in the New Testament itself. The citation of the Old Testament in the New Testament is often debated by scholars.[17] Not only did Jesus cite the Old Testament, most importantly perhaps in Matthew 5:21–48, the so-called antitheses of the Sermon on the Mount, but some scholars have counted as many as 224 quotations of the Old Testament in the New Testament, and as many as five or six hundred allusions.[18] Several different theories have been suggested concerning the model or models of interpretation used by the New Testament writers. Many of these theories have arisen because the Old Testament text does not seem to be quoted "accurately"—that is, according to either the Hebrew Old Testament or the Greek translation (the Septuagint), either because the New Testament writers seem to have quoted the Old Testament out of context or because the Old Testament passage cannot be found at all. An example that shows this difficulty is Matthew 2:15, where the author says that Mary and Joseph stayed with Jesus in Egypt until Herod died, so that the Scripture might be fulfilled: "Out of Egypt I called my son" (NIV). In Hosea 11:1, this quotation quite clearly refers to the exodus of Israel from Egypt. So, what is the Gospel writer doing with this quotation?[19]

16. Later Judaism developed three major kinds of literature that were related to interpreting the Bible. The first were the Targums, which were interpretive translations into Aramaic of the original Hebrew Scriptures. Some scholars claim that the Targums lie behind some of the use of the Old Testament in the New Testament. The second were the Mishnah, Talmud, and Midrash, second- to fourth-century CE collections of oral tradition that record disputes by various rabbis over legal issues, and interpretive commentaries on the Old Testament. The third was the Septuagint, the translation of the Jewish Scriptures into Greek, beginning in the third century BCE and completed probably sometime in the first century BCE.

17. For brief introductions, see Reventlow, *History of Biblical Interpretation*, 1:47–104; Moyise, *Old Testament in the New*.

18. Andrew E. Hill and John H. Walton assert that "according to careful calculation, approximately 32 percent—nearly one-third—of the New Testament is composed of Old Testament quotations and allusions" (*Survey of the Old Testament*, 744). For more detailed statistics, see Hill, *Baker's Handbook of Bible Lists*, 90–91.

19. While referring to the broader context of Hosea 11, Scott Spencer here laments, "The dizziness all but knocks us out cold when we try and fit all this into Matthew's portrayal of the infant Jesus' migration to Egypt as a place of refuge" ("Literary/Postmodern View," 62). Spencer then proceeds in the essay to interpret Matthew's use of this text through a literary/postmodern hermeneutical lens. The other scholars in the same edited volume who interpret the passage provide other ways of interpreting Matthew's use of the same text, and these by no means exhaust all the possibilities. While these essays might in many ways be complementary in various respects, one can consult other volumes that demonstrate opposing models for interpreting the Old Testament in the New Testament that address Matthew's use of Hosea 11:1 (and other texts). See, e.g., the essays by Kaiser, Bock, and Enns in *Three Views*.

Without going into the specifics and complexities of this particular instance, I will simply introduce several of the various proposed explanations for how New Testament writers made use of the Old Testament. Some have suggested that each Old Testament quotation carries with it the wider context of the passage as found in the Old Testament. The New Testament writer, therefore, draws on this wider understanding, though this context may not be readily apparent in the small section he uses directly.[20] Others recognize that several of the Old Testament quotations are interpreted in ways one would find unacceptable today and argue that the New Testament writers, because of their unique position in the history of the church and the inspired status of their writings, were allowed a certain amount of latitude in their use of the Old Testament.[21] A third school of thought is that the New Testament writers bring out the spiritual implications of the Old Testament Scriptures in light of the later doctrines of salvation, whether the Old Testament writers understood the implications of a text or not.[22]

The patristic period of the church—from the second generation of Christians through to the eighth century—is often neglected, though its significance is not to be minimized. Two important developments touch directly on the issue of hermeneutics and hence understanding and interpretation. The first is the development of the biblical canon. Few people recognize the significance of this hermeneutical event for interpretation.[23] This applies to both testaments. In the early church, there was competition between two Old Testament canons: the Greek canon, sometimes called the Septuagint, and the Hebrew one.[24] Both were apparently widely used, even within Christianity. The vast majority of quotations of the Old Testament that appear in the New Testament, in those places where it can be determined, seem to reflect the Greek Old Testament or a form of it. Most of the books of the Greek Old Testament were translated from Hebrew (beginning in the third

20. Numerous scholars argue that biblical citations are pointers to the wider context of Scripture, although each varies in its own way. See Ellis, *Paul's Use of the Old Testament*; Hays, *Echoes of Scripture*; Wakefield, *Where to Live*; Watson, *Paul and the Hermeneutics of Faith*.

21. For example, concerning Matthew's use of the Old Testament, R. T. France notes, "What we have in these chapters, in other words, is not a random gathering of embarrassingly inappropriate texts, but the product of a sophisticated and probably lengthy engagement with Scripture in a way which goes beyond our concepts of 'scientific exegesis'" (*Gospel according to Matthew*, 45).

22. For a discussion of *sensus plenior*, see Lunde, "Introduction to Central Questions," 13–18; Moo, "Problem of *Sensus Plenior*," 188–90.

23. For a concise summary of the issues, see Beckwith, "Canon of Scripture," 27–34; chap. 13, "Origins of the Christian Bible," in McDonald and Porter, *Early Christianity*, 600–624.

24. See Jobes and Silva, *Invitation to the Septuagint*, for discussion. See also Ellis, *Old Testament in Early Christianity*.

century BCE and continuing at least until the first century BCE), but a few books were originally composed in Greek, and the number of books in this canon is larger than in the Hebrew Old Testament (it includes what is often referred to as the apocrypha, as well as possibly some other books). Christians debated their Old Testament until as late as the fourth century CE, when the Western church accepted the Jewish canon of Hebrew Scriptures as authoritative (the Eastern church continues to recognize the Greek Old Testament).

Whereas the determination of the Old Testament canon was directly related to the Jewish selection of Scriptures, the selection of books for the New Testament was more problematic, causing debates as late as the Reformation, when some of the books were considered of lesser value because they did not endorse the doctrine of justification by faith as strongly as others (e.g., Luther placed Hebrews, James, Jude, and Revelation at the end of his translation of the New Testament). There are a variety of views on the process by which the canonical books of either testament became authoritative—self-authentication, apostolic testimony, functionality within the early church, and others—but whichever view of the canonical process is taken,[25] the fact is that the final decision on which books to include, and the language of the testament, dictates which books are studied today. This is a crucial interpretive decision, since it indicates which books are recognized as inspired and which are merely for our possible edification and knowledge. In other words, it helps to establish one of the two horizons—namely, the horizon that deals with the text itself. Canonical criticism, a significant area of importance in academic biblical studies, not only investigates how the range of books was canonized but helps to define the range of interpretive models that would be appropriate if one interprets within the boundaries of the canon itself.[26] The Scriptures, in the form of varied traditions, played an early and formative role in the establishment of both Jewish and early Christian communities of faith, and the process of canon formation for each influenced how books were selected and interpreted.

The second crucial patristic event is the development of two significant schools of biblical interpretation: the Alexandrian and the Antiochian.[27] Alexandria, Egypt, was the leading intellectual city of the Roman Empire and had a substantial Jewish and Christian population. Hence, it was a center for Hellenistic Judaism and Christianity. Essentially, the Alexandrian school

25. Many of the different views are represented in Bruce, *Canon of Scripture*; McDonald, *Biblical Canon*; Metzger, *Canon of the New Testament*; and Kruger, *Canon Revisited*.

26. For works in canonical criticism, see especially Childs, *Introduction to the Old Testament*; Childs, *New Testament as Canon*. See also Wall, "Canonical Criticism."

27. For an informative summary, see Young, "Alexandrian and Antiochene Exegesis."

taught that all Scripture was symbolic, and so it must be interpreted allegorically (and hence anagogically or spiritually). The early third-century patristic writer Origen, this school's greatest exponent, believed that all Scripture had a spiritual meaning, even though it may not have a literal one, and that behind the words lies the ultimate mystery of the deeper meaning. So, the episode in Genesis 24:15–20 where Rebekah draws water for Abraham's servant means "we must daily come to the wells of Scripture in order to meet with Christ."[28] Origen devised practical guidelines for exegetes to guide them in determining the spiritual meaning of a scriptural passage: (1) compare the truth with other spiritual truths (1 Cor. 2:13); (2) compare a seemingly literal text to other similar but spiritual texts; and (3) let faith be the guiding impetus for interpretation.[29] Many believers are unknowingly familiar with Origen's three rules, since they have been adopted, in their essential characteristics, by many Protestant interpreters.

The Antiochian school developed both in opposition to Origen's method and under the influence of the Jewish synagogue in Syrian Antioch.[30] This school argued that every passage of Scripture has a literal meaning and that this is the *only* meaning, though it recognized that alongside this literal sense is a typological sense arising from it. This allowed the school to develop its doctrine that the Old Testament author himself foresaw—by means of a vision granted him by God—the future fulfillment of the prophetic word, though this sense was not at variance with the historical or literal sense. Thus Isaiah 7:14 was seen by Isaiah to refer to Mary as well as to the "young woman" of the prophet's time. Some might be surprised to see such radically different models of interpretation growing up so early in church history, but recognizing these competing models helps us today to appreciate the fact that the determination of the meaning of Scripture has not followed a single, unified path throughout the history of the church. There have been many starts and stops in different directions.

In the Middle Ages, the allegorical approach continued to develop and became even more complex, with various layers of interpretation constantly being added.[31] To keep to a brief summary of the history of interpretation, I will mention only one figure: Thomas Aquinas. Born in 1224, Aquinas was the paragon of the age and is most well-known for formulating a relationship between faith and reason based on the principles of the ancient Greek philosopher Aristotle. In other words, by using the insight of the Aristotelian

28. Farrar, *History of Interpretation*, 199.
29. Grant and Tracy, *Short History*, 60.
30. See Richardson, "Antiochene School."
31. See van den Hoek, "Allegorical Interpretation."

paradigm of philosophy, Aquinas caused a major shift in biblical interpretation when he postulated that knowledge was based on the senses or reason rather than on ideas having their own existing forms, a much more Platonic idea. Nevertheless, it was Aquinas who firmed up the allegorical interpretation of the church. Although he began with what might be called the literal sense, he also believed in allegorical, moral, and anagogical senses of Scripture. The legacy of Aquinas is great, for both Roman Catholics and other Christians. His model of interpretation has been used by many Catholics ever since, until Vatican II in the twentieth century, when Catholic scholars were given permission to pursue modern critical methods of interpretation. The legacy of Aquinas for Protestants includes his emphasis on reason and the senses, which contributed to the development of critical thinking regarding the Bible, and his attempts to find a cohesive system of Christian thought that led to development of dogmatic theology as endeavors to encompass all Christian theological knowledge.

Protestants, for the most part, are products of the Reformation model of hermeneutics, and so it would be unwise to underestimate the influence of Martin Luther and John Calvin on later hermeneutics in the Protestant church. One of Luther's major claims was the doctrine that Scripture alone is the basis of all Christian doctrine. Unfortunately, this formulation has been subjected to great and serious abuse by those who believe that this means "Scripture alone, apart from the serious work of interpretation," a formulation that Luther would have soundly rejected. As a product of the Renaissance, Luther stressed the importance of studying Scripture by means of the original languages, Hebrew and Greek. Luther translated both Testaments into German from Hebrew and Greek, and in the process became the father of modern German. He wrote extensively, including commentaries on many books of the Bible. Luther centered his interpretation around Christ, and faith in him alone, as the means for salvation.[32]

Whereas Luther was the dynamic, explosive force of the Reformation, John Calvin was a great systematician but also a visionary. Calvin, author of the rightly renowned *Institutes of the Christian Religion*, is certainly one of the most important people in Christian history, though, to be sure, his writings are also some of the most widely neglected by a good number of Christian scholars who would benefit greatly from reading them more closely. Whatever one's view of Calvin's individual doctrines, it must be noted with awe and respect that Calvin was a biblical interpreter of the first order and that his

---

32. For a brief discussion of how Luther's hermeneutics—which were more theologically centered—contrasted with the more explicitly author-centric views of the later Schleiermacher, see McLean, *Biblical Interpretation*, 35–36.

systematic theology grew out of the wholesome desire to formulate a consistent and entire doctrine of Christianity founded on the biblical text. For example, though Genesis 1:1 would have helped his defense of the doctrine of the Trinity, he refused to take *elohim*, a word translated "God," as plural in sense, although it appears to be plural in form; and he recognized that Mark 14:24 taught that Christ's blood was shed for the whole world and not just the elect, as Calvinists after him would sometimes deny in order to fit Scripture into their Christology.

Post-Reformation hermeneutics is a much more complex field of discussion, and to do justice to it requires a solid grounding in philosophy, as well as the sociology of religious thought. Four movements in particular stand out as paradigm-shaping in the history of post-Reformation hermeneutics. These movements can help us identify some signposts for how and why hermeneutical thought developed as it did. The first movement is the rise of rationalism, which grew out of the Enlightenment and displayed an optimism in the progress of humanity and a confidence in humanity's ability to solve the questions of an ordered world with scientific reasoning. In other words, rationalism stressed that the world functions according to wholly consistent, logical principles and that the human mind sets the standard for determining what is right and wrong, since it too functions by logical principles and thus has the ability to explain the order of nature. This movement continued with unabated force through the nineteenth century, and in many ways it continues in much hermeneutical thought today. We cannot downplay the significant and long-lasting impact of a great many results of Renaissance and rationalist thought: rationalism as a philosophical school represented by people such as René Descartes, Thomas Hobbes, and Baruch Spinoza, and the scientific discoveries of the scientists Copernicus, Kepler, and Newton. However, from the outset of this movement, the church seemed to fall back on the defensive and soon lost its sense of authority as greater emphasis was placed on human reason. As a result, the world saw a major worldview shift from Christian theism to deism, where God's workings in the world were restricted to the forces of nature. God became the divine clockmaker who created the clock, wound it up, and then left it to run. The church must share in the blame for its defensive posture, since it did not make a significant enough attempt to reassess which of its doctrines were truly called into question by the new science and did not adjust its practical teaching to new ways of thinking.

The second movement is the rise of romanticism. As a result of the Enlightenment, the eighteenth and nineteenth centuries became times of turmoil and unrest in religious thought. This opened up room in philosophical thought for romanticism. By no means was rationalism eclipsed by romanticism, but in response to humanity's weakened confidence in the all-sufficiency of ordered reasoning in a world where chaos exists, a need arose to believe in something more, to place faith in something, with the resulting embrace of abstract transcendence. Here it is necessary to mention the enormously important contribution of the nineteenth-century German philosopher and theologian Friedrich Schleiermacher, who is widely considered to be one of the most influential theologians of the nineteenth century. Schleiermacher also stands out as one of the most significant modern theorists of biblical interpretation for his novel hermeneutical approach, which stressed the individual human being's psychological makeup.[33] He believed that an interpreter must try to become psychologically linked to the thought processes of the original writer. By enacting this move in interpretation, Schleiermacher asserted that the modern reader must translate him- or herself back into the mindset of the first century, so that the interpreter might know the mind of the author (his intentions) better than the author knew themself. Schleiermacher's method of interpretation—despite its not being systematized—emphasizes the constant interplay between knowledge of the language of the text and psychological knowledge of the biblical author. The rise of both rationalism and romanticism, with its idealized view of the subject and its knowability, laid the foundation for the rise of critical thought and interpretation.

The third development is the rise of higher or historical criticism. Higher critical schools of thought, often linked to historically based criticism, were the philosophical offspring of the rise of rationalism and led to theological liberalism with its skepticism and rejection of transcendence. The major historical critical movement to note here is the rise in the early to mid-nineteenth century of the Tübingen school of the great and highly influential German scholar F. C. Baur.[34] The nineteenth- and twentieth-century critical schools arose out of the philosophical presuppositions of their age—that is, the belief that the supernatural is beyond discussion, since it cannot be scientifically analyzed, and that inspiration is a bankrupt concept, since the biblical documents arose out of conflict in the early church, especially conflict between the law-oriented Jewish Petrine school and the faith-oriented gentile Pauline school, thus fostering a dialectical development in the early church reflected in various New Testament books.[35] For example, James and Matthew are

33. For a good, brief survey of Schleiermacher's life, thought, and contribution to New Testament studies, see W. Baird, *History of New Testament Research*, 1:208–20; Porter and Robinson, *Hermeneutics*, 24–33.

34. See H. Harris, *Tübingen School*.

35. See Baur's major work on Paul in which he argues his thesis that earliest Christianity was divided according to the two major factions of Paul and Peter: *Paul the Apostle of Jesus Christ*.

examples of the legalists, and the Pauline Epistles of those endorsing a faith ethic (see Acts 15). This theory still has its advocates and respondents, who are now reviving discussion of the date of the book of Acts (the tendency in recent scholarship is to move the date to the second century, the date where Baur put it), and it continues to influence much of the discussion of early Christianity in many if not most scholarly circles.

A second significant figure to mention in this third development is Rudolf Bultmann, the German scholar who took nineteenth-century thought into the twentieth century and whose reputation has clearly suffered at the hands of more conservative Christians.[36] Bultmann published much significant New Testament scholarship, such as in form criticism, where his study of the synoptic tradition is still widely regarded. However, he is well known as an existential interpreter who promoted the notion of demythologization. Based on the rationalist-empirical and deterministic thought of the nineteenth century, Bultmann simply could not accept the biblical worldview, with its multi-storied universe and direct divine activity, except as a mythological account of the divine-human encounter. Hence, he demythologized the Bible due to his concern with what authentic human existence means in a modern worldview.

Bultmann found himself in a difficult situation for two reasons. First, he did not appreciate the controlling influence of the presuppositions of his own worldview; he was a dialectical theologian who dedicated his research to the historical-critical method. That he was concerned with issues arising from presuppositions is seen in a significant essay in which he noted that it is impossible to do biblical analysis without presuppositions, although—and in this lies the difficulty—he took it for granted that the historical-critical method was the approach most free from presuppositions.[37] Second, Bultmann had a genuine concern for establishing the relevance of Christianity, a first-century religious phenomenon, for the contemporary twentieth-century human. Bultmann realized that he, like everyone else, was quite clearly a product of his time. How does one believe in, for example, miracles in a consistently rational universe? His solution was to propose that the Bible uses mythological language. By this he means not that the Bible is full of fairy tales about misguided people but that the biblical documents record the genuine struggles of people confronted by God. The language they use, therefore, is not meant to be taken literally,

36. See Porter and Robinson, *Hermeneutics*, 226–9. Disparaging comments about Bultmann can still be heard in some circles.
37. One of the biggest challenges for any scholar is to set aside, or at least demonstrate a tempered self-awareness of, his or her own hermeneutical presuppositions in the practice of interpreting any given passage of Scripture. Bultmann speaks to this issue in his classic 1957 essay "Is Exegesis without Presuppositions Possible?"

since it records their personal spiritual experiences. Modern interpreters must demythologize it. In other words, they must go behind the myth—the serious account of individuals experiencing God—to see what these instances say about fundamental spiritual truths. Bultmann's method of interpretation is clearly limited, especially when seen from a later perspective that does not view the universe in the same rigid and mechanistic way as he did. Despite such problems, there is a lesson here related to several of the points I wish to make in this chapter: models are crucial for interpretation, but we must constantly be reevaluating not only our findings but the very models themselves.

The fourth important development in post-Reformation hermeneutics is the increasing concern with cross-disciplinary thought, in which various schools of thought began to interact with each other. In the humanities, for instance, and in light of some of the thought of the philosopher Immanuel Kant, there has been a much greater awareness of the way we view the world around us. This reassessment has been mirrored in the sciences. The sciences have come to realize that the idea of objectivity is not well-defined; that the observer is involved in the thing he or she is observing; and that the scientific method involves what is often called abductive thinking, requiring the scientist's intuitions rather than simply their inductive or even deductive thoughts. Such insights have had significant effects on the various disciplines in the humanities. Many books have been written plotting such developments as the rise of various literarily, ideologically, and culturally motivated models of interpretation (they go hand in hand). These criticisms go by a variety of names, including various types of literary criticism (such as formalism, reader-response, and deconstruction), social-scientific approaches, rhetorical approaches, and other forms of biblical interpretation (such as economic, post-colonialist, feminist, ideological, and philosophical, among others).[38] Some of these terms may be unfamiliar to pastors or seminary students, but the point is that this is a day and age of reevaluation in light of newer models of the traditional methods used for reading and studying the Bible. For better or worse, we are entering a time of shifting models as scholars begin and continue to ask new and different questions of the text.[39]

38. I realize that in this brief description I am lumping together a great number of diverse interpretive models, but they have in common that they are (usually) reacting to traditional historical criticism and motivated by more openly avowed presuppositional concerns. For an extensive overview of the current issues in biblical interpretation, see Porter, *Dictionary of Biblical Criticism and Interpretation*; and, more specifically, McKenzie and Kaltner, *New Meanings for Ancient Texts*.

39. While addressing the topic of new approaches to New Testament studies, Luke Timothy Johnson openly states, "We live in an age much fascinated by 'methodology,' and the currents move rapidly" (*Writings of the New Testament*, 547).

Study and Practice

This chapter tries to make us aware of the pervasiveness of semiotic systems in the world around us. As a practical exercise, observe as many semiotic or sign systems as you can identify. For example, in the discussion above we considered traffic lights, one of the most common sign systems. There are many others as well. Sign systems exist in all different spheres of human life. For example, gestures are a sign system, whether they are made with one's hands or with one's face or through some other means. Clothing constitutes a semiotic system. Most of us today are aware of the use of emojis. These constitute a sign system. What are some other sign systems that you notice? Once you have noticed a sign system, attempt to decode it by analyzing the nature of the signs and how these signs relate to each other. What is the potential for change within the sign system?

The term *hermeneutics* may be new to many readers. Keeping in mind the brief history of hermeneutical models within biblical studies discussed above, think about various interpretations of the Bible that you are familiar with. These may be from commentaries or other books, or from sermons that you have heard or written. Can you identify any of the hermeneutical models that appear to be operative in these various interpretations? Can you conceive of how the interpretation could have gone differently if another or different hermeneutical model had been applied?

Conclusion

As I conclude this chapter, I wish to set an agenda for what to expect in the succeeding chapters of this book. Hermeneutics, as expressed above, is concerned with the conditions by which understanding of a text is made possible, and so in this book I am concerned with the principles found in various models that may be applied to reading a written text. Over the course of the following chapters, I will discuss a specific model for interpretation that I believe is particularly fruitful for handling God's Word today. I will also apply this model to actual texts, which will entail interacting with other models that have been used throughout the history of biblical scholarship for various reasons and with varying degrees of success. From what I have said, it should be clear that hermeneutics is a serious business in which the church has been involved, in one form or another, since its earliest days. It will be to our benefit not only to understand this history of interpretation but to know the major questions being asked about interpretation today. In working through several important interpretive questions over the next several chapters, I would like to prompt my readers to keep three larger questions in mind:

1. What is the appropriate role for tradition to play in Protestant interpretation?
2. Some wish to affirm the doctrine of the clarity of Scripture, for more than simply matters of salvation. How clear is Scripture, really? Or rather, how can we talk about its clarity in helpful ways?
3. One of the major reasons for interpretation of the Bible is to make use of it in daily life. What is the *relation* among the Bible, the church, and the world?

There may be instances where the so-called natural or obvious meaning of the text of Scripture seems to stand out, but I would contend that, more often than not, most texts are more complicated than we would like them to be. I do not say this to discourage anyone from reading the Bible or to take away from the importance of reading Scripture devotionally. Quite to the contrary, I wish instead to stress the responsibility we have as interpreters of God's Word to interpret Scripture well. Possessing a grasp of hermeneutics is vital in this process.

2

Hermeneutics and the Authority of Scripture

Introduction

The first chapter addressed basic issues regarding hermeneutics, such as what it is, its importance, and its history in relationship to biblical studies. This chapter demonstrates the importance of hermeneutics as it addresses a central issue: the authority of the Bible. I will argue that questions regarding the authority of the Bible are, at their heart, hermeneutical questions. As a result, we must examine various views of authority. With these in mind, we will be able to appreciate the history of hermeneutics in relationship to biblical authority. In the previous chapter we discussed hermeneutics and the history of biblical interpretation, but here I focus more particularly on biblical authority in that discussion. I then turn to a discussion of the major contemporary hermeneutical issues regarding biblical authority. These issues result in the raising of some important questions regarding biblical authority. I raise some of these questions not with the intent of answering all of them but with the object of drawing our attention to their hermeneutical significance. These topics provide the platform for discussing interpretation of the Bible in the subsequent chapters.

How Hermeneutics Is Related to Biblical Authority

What is meant by the term *biblical authority*? What is not meant is that the Bible as a book has authority in itself as an object. Rather, the authority we are referring to is God's authority, and since the Bible is God's Word, his authority is mediated through the Bible and is exercised on us in some way. A big question, then, is how God's authority is exercised on us through the Bible. This is precisely where hermeneutics enters the discussion and the reason why hermeneutics is so important for questions of biblical authority. We will explore the complexities, history, and contemporary proposals for how hermeneutics relates to biblical authority in this chapter, but my answer to this question will unfold throughout the remainder of this book.

Every question we can ask of the Bible is a question that involves another set of larger questions about our knowledge, about both its certainty and its evaluation. Whenever someone asks whether one view on biblical authority is better than another, some set of criteria must be invoked. In other words, we are interpreting the data in terms of a model. Most of us maintain a model that tries to identify the authentic voice of God, but how can it be determined that an interpretation is the voice of God and not merely some personal thoughts, or the collective thoughts of a group of people, or the prevailing thought in our tradition? Consider, for example, when Paul uses the word ἱλαστήριον (hilastērion), often translated as "propitiation" or "expiation," in Romans 3:25. Is he referring to an ancient concept of propitiating a wrathful God or to a process of canceling or expiating the debt of sin?[1] Many evangelical interpreters have no problem believing that God can be wrathful, while some other interpreters find this view of God totally repugnant.[2] What criteria are most appropriate for making an interpretive decision about Paul's meaning by his use of this term here? Even after we determine what a biblical author meant to say, we must then determine what God is saying through that passage today. Is the teaching in 1 Corinthians 7 and 11 about the role of men and women merely Paul's response to particularly troublesome situations in the early church, or does Paul establish timeless truths that are still applicable to the church as a whole? These are questions of hermeneutics, to be sure, but our conclusions have wider implications.

The issue I wish to raise here is summed up in the following statement: *the questions about biblical authority are inextricably bound up with the fundamental questions of hermeneutics*. In other words, the interpretive models that we bring to the task of interpretation, along with our presuppositions and pre-understandings, have decisive implications for what we determine the

---

1. Is the ἱλαστήριον (hilastērion) the "means" or the "place" of expiation? See Porter, *Letter to the Romans*, 97–99.

2. That this is a significant point of contention among evangelicals today is noted by McDermott, "Emerging Divide in Evangelical Theology," esp. 365.

Bible means and thus reflect our view of its authority.[3] In this regard, biblical authority is directly related to hermeneutics, which, in turn, is related to both one's faith commitments and one's interpretive presuppositions. Even the most skilled interpreter cannot escape the importance of models of interpretation and along with them the presuppositions one brings to the interpretive task. One of the first discussions in the garden of Eden reflects the importance of interpretation within a context of, in this case, divine authority. In the first question posed to a human, the serpent in the garden asks Eve, "Did God really say, 'You must not eat from any tree in the Garden'?" (Gen. 3:1 NIV). God in fact had not said this, but the serpent is attacking the authority of God by misquoting him. One must be attentive to what God actually does and does not say, and sometimes determining this is admittedly a major undertaking (hence the numerous books on biblical interpretation—if interpretation were easy, we would not need all of these books), in order to respond appropriately and thus duly recognize biblical authority.

The many questions on the relationship between biblical authority and hermeneutics impinge on a wide range of other issues that cannot be discussed fully here,[4] but a couple topics warrant further consideration. First, apologetics, the task of defending the Christian faith, plays a significant role in questions of biblical authority. It can be argued, and the argument is an important one, that the Bible must be justified as a reliable document. It is not enough to say that "the Bible says," but the Bible must speak out of a justified wider context than merely the text itself.[5] There are two major approaches to apologetics: presuppositional and evidential. Presuppositional apologetics begins from a particular philosophical and theological predisposition regarding the authority of the Bible and uses this as the foundation for its apologetic arguments as logical entailments. Evidentialist apologetics attempts to establish the authority of the Bible by showing such things as its historical accuracy and attestation through archaeology and the continued reverification of the Bible—both personally and publicly—even during the increase of knowledge in our scientific age. Both approaches, while they often appear to be objectivist

---

3. A classic debate over biblical authority is between Rogers and McKim, *Authority and Interpretation of the Bible*, and Woodbridge, *Biblical Authority*. This debate reveals some of the need for a proper hermeneutical stance, as there is an apparent effort by Rogers and McKim to attempt to reread the Renaissance as if it were today, rather than recognizing and rejoicing in diversity, while there is an apparent attempt by Woodbridge to convey that ancient and modern disputes are necessarily about the same issues.

4. One could perhaps start with N. Wright, *Last Word*, and move on to any number of other works from there.

5. For a helpful survey of different ways to defend the veracity of Christianity and the authority of the Bible, see Cowan, *Five Views on Apologetics*.

in orientation, are heavily reliant on hermeneutical presuppositions. Simple appeals to apologetic arguments—especially evidentialist ones, where those with other opinions hold to different presuppositions—often accomplish very little because the disputants are talking at cross-purposes.

Second, the issue of authority also touches heavily on biblical ethics. Today many books are being written to answer the question of what constitutes a Christian ethic.[6] Most do not find it adequate any longer simply to transfer propositional statements derived from the Bible straight into modern practice. One example among many possible others, of course, is the practice of the Old Testament system of worship, including the offering of sacrifices. In fact, there is a small but vocal group in the United States that still argues that the Old Testament laws for the punishment of sin or crime should be applied directly in this day and age.[7] Many more examples of ethical dilemmas of application can be cited, including possible rules for church authority found in the New Testament, and, more specifically, rules for personal conduct. The most troublesome areas seem to be those where the Bible does not actually address the issue that confronts us today. We may be fairly well decided that the New Testament strictly forbids murder, but what about the death penalty, abortion, nuclear weapons, or even, more poignantly, assisted suicide?

As I hope is becoming clear, the authority of the Bible—and this includes whether it is inspired and how—is a hermeneutical and not simply an interpretive or textual issue.[8] Even though the Bible at a number of places attests to itself as having authority, it is not self-authenticating as authoritative since not all the biblical authors make such statements, especially the New Testament authors. Even if they did, such a claim to possess authority does not amount to proof for one who chooses not to accept it. In other words, one cannot simply arrive at biblical authority on the basis of interpretation. Even if interpretation is a part of hermeneutics, hermeneutics is a much larger category regarding the understanding of our world, including written texts and in particular the Bible.

Whereas interpretation is often confined to understanding what the text meant, hermeneutics must be concerned with both what the text meant and what it means, with the two being inseparable—that is, one cannot talk about

---

6. A still reliable and useful volume is Longenecker, *New Testament Social Ethics*, esp. 1–9, on different approaches to using the New Testament in ethics: propositionalism, universalism, spiritual encounter, and contextualism (most of these descriptors are mine, not Longenecker's).

7. The main proponents of this view would probably be Greg Bahnsen and R. J. Rushdoony (both deceased), along with Gary North and Gary DeMar. For critiques, see Barker and Godfrey, *Theonomy*.

8. The comments that follow are based on Porter, "Authority of the Bible as a Hermeneutical Issue."

the former without also speaking about the latter if one wishes to complete the hermeneutical circle. There is meaning found in the form of the original text itself, but there is also meaning found through the understanding of the contemporary reader in an interpretive context. As a result, within a hermeneutical framework, the authority of the Bible may not be demonstrable by interpretation or by exegesis, even if it is a plausible presupposition from which to do one's interpretation. We must recognize that both horizons are always relevant, that of the text and that of the reader. Hermeneutical awareness will not answer all interpretive questions, but it provides the basis for approaching matters of authority, so that one can have confidence in inspiration as guaranteeing certain things about the trustworthiness of Scripture and the nature of its creation and warrants of belief, even if these are separate from the interpretive process itself. However, such a stance also sets the parameters of interpretation.

To get a firmer grasp on the issue of biblical authority, I would like to take a few moments to discuss two troublesome areas. There are a number of others, but I will concentrate on these two.

Foundationalism

The first is the issue of foundationalism.[9] Theology has traditionally argued that the Bible has the primary, or foundational, place of authority but that one also must consider reason, tradition, and even experience.[10] Can any authority, in this case the Bible, be an ultimate authority if some other authority, such as tradition, reason, or experience, is also appealed to? Many would like to say that the Bible is self-authenticating in its language or that the Holy Spirit provides proof of the Bible's validity. This certainly may be true in an individual believer's life, though it would seem very difficult to make this a communicable generalizable principle. It is not difficult to see how potentially dangerous this self-authenticating or Spirit-attested hermeneutical position can be, since either requires a rare insight into both the human mind and the

9. The foundations of belief is a widely discussed concept in modern philosophy. Traditional foundationalism, as seen in philosophers such as Aristotle and Descartes and in empiricism, idealism, experientialism, and even logical positivism, among others, has largely given way to post-foundationalism and even anti-foundationalism, shifting from correspondence theories of truth (what we believe corresponds with reality) to coherence theories (in which our systems of belief cohere and form a network of intertwined beliefs). Post-foundationalism is represented by Willard Quine, while anti-foundationalism is found among the pragmatists, such as Richard Rorty and Stanley Fish. Many of these people and topics are discussed in Thiselton, *New Horizons in Hermeneutics*.

10. Some will recognize this as what is often described as the Wesleyan Quadrilateral, attributed in formulation, if not in terminology, to John Wesley.

present-day activity of God, an insight that gives few clues, if any, for objective or transferable evaluation. Why, for example, do not all Christians agree on every issue, even major issues, such as the mode and meaning of baptism or the significance of the Lord's Supper, if they are responding to the same Spirit? It is simply not enough to say that one tradition is correct when many different traditions appeal to the same criteria of verification. How does the fallenness of humanity come into play? If we grant that every person is a fallen creature, though many are redeemed by God, to be sure, they still run the risk of being in error, even if unconsciously. To say that the Bible is our ultimate authority does not in any way relieve us of using all the tools available to us—especially our minds—to interpret it responsibly.[11]

Others may point to 2 Timothy 3:16 or to the example of Jesus's view of the Old Testament as justifying biblical authority. These passages must be taken seriously, though their limitations in proving the full authority of Scripture must be noted. For one, the possible translations of 2 Timothy 3:16 are several. Not only can it be rendered, "All Scripture is inspired by God . . ." (πᾶσα γραφὴ θεόπνευστος, *pasa graphē theopneustos*), but it can also be rendered, "Every Scripture inspired by God is . . ." This second translation seems to be defining the character of those Scriptures that are seen as inspired and, therefore, is not helpful in answering the question of which Scriptures are inspired.[12] Also, the Scripture referred to is probably the Old Testament alone, since the concept of a "New Testament" was not existent when Paul wrote this letter (assuming he did so, as I believe). Regarding Jesus's view of the Old Testament, it is again true that he had a high regard for it, though it is not altogether certain how he is treating it in, for example, the antitheses of the Sermon on the Mount (Matt. 5:17–48), since some of his references are to the Old Testament and some are to extra-biblical statements.

The argument is correct, at least in part, that human qualities must figure into the issue of the authority of Scripture. As has been indicated in the discussion above, interpretation demands an interpreter, and hence interpretation requires involvement of the human self in interpretation. Because of its involvement in interpretation of the Bible, the human is necessarily a component of biblical authority. We may believe, and with good reason, that the Bible

11. The great Galileo Galilei, in a letter to the Grand Duchess Christina of Tuscany in 1615, made this revolutionary observation: "But I do not consider it necessary to believe that the same God who has endowed us with senses, and with the power of reasoning and intellect, should have chosen to set these aside and to convey to us by some other means those facts which we are capable of finding out by exercising these faculties, so that even in scientific conclusions which the evidence of our senses and necessary demonstrations set before our eyes and minds, we should deny what our reason and senses tell us" (Galileo, *Galileo's Selected Writings*, 68).

12. For discussion of the alternatives, see Porter, *Pastoral Epistles*.

contains all that God considered appropriate at a given time to reveal to humanity through a reasonably permanent form of human language, but this is different from the act of interpretation itself—a requirement for the exercising of biblical authority—which is the subject at hand. I am trying to emphasize that the human being has an indispensable part to play in understanding and that the biblical text, no matter how normative it may be considered, must be interpreted in order to be a living and functioning document.

Diversity and Pluralism

The second topic in biblical authority is the issue of diversity and pluralism.[13] Many have rightly noted that there is probably no such thing as a single biblical view on any given issue but instead a set of views, some of which appear difficult to reconcile. Ernst Käsemann, a well-known German New Testament scholar of last century, speaking on the issue of the church, says that one can prove any view one likes on the basis of what biblical book one uses.[14] He probably overstates his case. However, just because the Bible has a plurality of views on a given issue does not necessarily mean that every issue is subject to pluralism or that the Bible is simply pluralistic. Many scholars point out that the canon itself provides the limits of accepted diversity or what one scholar has called the "circumference of acceptable diversity."[15] In other words, there is a place for differences, but not all potential differences are acceptable.

We must admit that there are a number of issues where genuine diversity must be recognized within the New Testament. For example, in a classic and recurring instance, much has been made of Paul's and James's differing views on the relation between law and works (e.g., Rom. 3:21–31; James 2:14–24). More than one scholar has argued that Paul's apparent emphasis on justification by faith apart from works is incompatible with James's stress on the place of Christian works as a confirmation of faith.[16] When simple statements from each author are compared (e.g., "For we count a person justified by faith apart from works of law" [Rom. 3:28], and "You see that by works a person is justified and not by faith alone" [James 2:24]; my translation), plurality of opinion is often the result. However, Paul seems to be addressing the larger question

13. For select essays on several hermeneutical approaches to plurality, see Porter and Malcolm, *Future of Biblical Interpretation*.
14. Käsemann, "Unity and Multiplicity," 252.
15. Dunn, *Unity and Diversity*, 376.
16. For the relationship between Paul and James, see Nienhuis, *Not by Paul Alone*; Mitchell, "Letter of James?"

of Christian salvation and a believer's position before God, while James is concerned with the practical issue of a Christian in a church with members from varying socioeconomic backgrounds.[17] In all this, it is important to see that a contextual understanding of Scripture—a hermeneutical model that places understanding within certain sociological, cultural, and historical contexts recognized through a sensitive and attentive reading of the text—makes diversity less apparent and understanding more logically consistent.

Major Contemporary Views on Biblical Authority

I do not have space here to trace the history of biblical authority in the church, as interesting and informative as that history would be. I will instead focus on more recent views on biblical authority because of their contemporary relevance. A general tendency over the last several centuries has been a continued denigration of the Bible and with it a generally negative attitude toward biblical authority. Of course, this is not entirely true, since a good number of groups have continued to defend biblical authority. As a result, there are several major contemporary views on the authority of Scripture. Each of these may be seen as an interpretive community around which common views of scriptural authority revolve. Those within a given community tend to hold to similar views regarding Scripture, its interpretation, and its authority. It is impossible to treat any of these positions adequately, but I will introduce those with the most relevance.[18]

Conservatism, or Evangelicalism

The first is conservatism, or evangelicalism. This community is not univocal, but it has sufficient unity to be treated here under a single category. The conservative position was particularly strong during the Reformation, but despite the attacks of the Enlightenment and the rise of theological liberalism, this movement is still resoundingly strong within North American Christianity and, especially, majority-world Christianity. This perspective has several major characteristics: the New Testament speakers, especially Jesus but also Paul and others, believed that the Old Testament was inspired and authoritative for everyday life (e.g., Matt. 22:43; Rom. 3:2; 2 Tim. 3:16; Heb. 3:7; 10:16; 1 Pet.

17. See Porter, *Sacred Tradition*, 181–208, for fuller discussion but not necessarily the same conclusion. Cf. the philosophical hermeneutical interpretation of Thiselton, *Two Horizons*, 422–27.

18. For a helpful treatment of some of the issues raised here, see Marshall, *Biblical Inspiration*, esp. 31–47.

1:20). This view of authority incorporates the ancient interpretive principle of lesser to greater, whereby if the Old Testament was inspired (as of less importance than the New), then so was the New Testament, since it includes full revelation of the Christ that was only foreshadowed in the Old Testament (Heb. 1:1–4). In conjunction and consequence, the acceptance and endorsement of the Old Testament by New Testament figures like Jesus and the New Testament writers is then extended to the New Testament. This position also looks to the relatively united testimony of the entire Christian church until the Enlightenment on the nature of biblical authority and wishes to extend it to the present. Finally, this conservative view recognizes the inherent theological need for a reliable revelation of God to humanity.

Several criticisms have been leveled against this conservative/evangelical view, and here I will treat a few of them. First, critics argue that Jesus and the other early disciples and apostles were people of their times. As faithful Jews in the first century, they would have accepted the Scriptures as authoritative, simply as a matter of religious practice. This is true, of course, but it is not necessarily a criticism or a limitation. Jesus's opinion on the Scriptures seems to have been a pattern emulated by his followers. The biblical account shows that Jesus was much more than just a man of his times. His teaching is still unrivaled by any other teacher, as even his critics admit, and his resurrection is an event that still confounds critics who give the account more than passing consideration.

Second, critics say that Jesus contrasts his teaching with the Old Testament in the Sermon on the Mount rather than endorsing it.[19] However, "contrast" is perhaps not the best word to describe Jesus's invocation of the Old Testament, especially in Matthew 5:17–48. Jesus does not outright reject the statements from the Old Testament, but he reinterprets them in light of a new understanding, a form of progressive revelation.

Third, some critics contend that the composition of the New Testament is not dated from the apostolic period but is dated later, so most retreat from the idea of apostles to an apostolic circle or an even later composition. For example, the Johannine writings are often thought to emphasize the difference between the message that is proclaimed as having authority and the sacred books themselves. This has recently been attacked from all sides as being too sweeping a generalization about dating and the process of composition.[20]

19. See Worth, *Sermon on the Mount*.
20. See Carson, *Enduring Authority*, where an abundance of articles on various topics represent a strongly evangelical position regarding scriptural authority.

Fourth, critics argue that one can arrive at a sufficient truth through whatever needs to be the case. In other words, we do not need to believe all the items in the Bible, so long as there is general coherence, especially on matters of faith, rather than specific detail. We need merely some form of revelation, they say, not necessarily a completely authoritative revelation.

While serious objections have been raised to the conservative position on biblical authority, they have not proven fundamentally damaging to the large number of adherents who accept such arguments. In this brief discussion, I have tried to stress that whereas several of the objections have some substance, they do not account for all the data involved. In other words, the conservative/evangelical position raises issues that merit further hermeneutical consideration.

Neo-Orthodoxy

The second community of thought worth treating briefly is neo-orthodoxy, represented by Karl Barth and many others.[21] This community rejects conservatism as outlined above because it is considered an attempt at a false objectivism. Christianity, so neo-orthodoxy argues, is a witness not to the first-century faith but to God. Therefore, we should leave the realm of objective fact and move into the realm of obedience. God often wills to reveal himself in Scripture, not merely in the realm of rational discussion. Scripture, or what evangelical Christians call Scripture, then, is a possible locus of God's address, a vehicle for revelation. "The Word," not the words, carries authority, and so according to this view, Scripture, rather than being God's Word itself, is a witness to God's Word and becomes God's Word when the Holy Spirit speaks through it.

Whereas this position has much to commend itself in its concern not to become a form of bibliolatry and to leave open the potential for God to reveal himself, there are still several questions that might be raised. First, why has God chosen to use Scripture rather than other forms of communication? If he has chosen Scripture, what are the controls that might be used to know if an interpretation is actually God's revelation and not something else? The question of the control over this use of Scripture presents problems. Second, can revelation then be reduced to a matter of personal feeling? Again, what is to be used to distinguish among different personal beliefs, or is there no such

---

21. One of the best presentations of neo-orthodoxy is still found in Hordern, *Layman's Guide*, which treats Barth, Reinhold Niebuhr, Paul Tillich, Bultmann, and Dietrich Bonhoeffer in detail. On Barth more particularly, see the essays in Webster, *Cambridge Companion*, esp. Watson, "Bible."

thing as right and wrong theological interpretations? Third, if the biblical writers were merely attesting to God's work in their lives, which certainly is an important part of the biblical message, how do we know that their experience was in any sense authentic, informative, normative, and important for us? Does this view not make it impossible to formulate a normative theology on the consistent patterns in God's actions? Barthians have responses to these questions, but the subjective element remains troubling (as does the confusion over what exactly is meant by the Word of God)—not simply because it is subjective but also because it lacks clarity.

Historicism

A third community of thought is that of historicism. This group believes that the problem of authority is best defined as a concern with cultural change. In other words, one's frame of reference is very influential in determining what one experiences, so that a maxim for one culture may not have the same value for another.[22] Since historicism understands meaning according to and confined by one's worldview and by the time period and culture in which that worldview was created, the Bible must be situated within its own system of meaning. This implies that a contemporary interpretation of a biblical passage, understood in light of modern sensibilities, inevitably and *should* render a different meaning than that of the earliest readers of biblical documents. To believe in a miracle in the past is different from believing in a miracle now. Believers of the first century held to a worldview filled with spiritual powers, both good and evil, and this entailed the potential for miracles and even bringing a man back to life. People now are much more skeptical, to the extent that any foreign element present in the discussion is a category that a modern person cannot accept or even fully understand. This forces interpreters to take account of cultural change and to work out what the story would mean today, once the elements of the story unacceptable to a modern understanding of the world have been sufficiently explained. An example would include reinterpreting the exile of the Jews not as a punishment for sin, since this involves a view of God as vindictive, which is no longer believable, but as a series of political events. The "pastness" of the Bible is made evident: some passages still spark visions and faith, though certainly not doctrine.

22. For examples of proponents of this view, see Paul Tillich (*Systematic Theology*, 1:34–50), who in his discussion of the sources and norms for theology explains that everything derived from the Bible ultimately answers to the criterion of relevance; and Nineham, *Use and Abuse of the Bible*.

This third position offers some important insights, but, at the very least, it also overstates the difficulty of the historical gap or, to put it in hermeneutical terms, the issue of the two horizons. The problem of historical distance is not totally insurmountable; otherwise we could know nothing of the past apart from some apparently easily misguided, vague impressions. Most people believe they can at least passably understand Plato and other ancient literature when they read it. It is not so easy to split understanding into the idea of past and present meaning, as if interpretation occurs without an interpreter. This view is overly simplistic in its characterization of the past as a single conceptual perspective, overlooking pluralism even in the ancient world. The presence of Epicureans and Stoics (Acts 17) shows that there were multiple views of life, even in the ancient world. The continuity of the tradition of analysis and reanalysis that connects us to that past is effectively ignored by this approach, as is the generally agreed upon commonality of human personality, nature, and experience.

Functionalism or Pragmatism

To conclude this section, I will briefly address the functional/pragmatic view of scriptural authority. This community asks, How does the Bible function in the Christian community?[23] One scholar has said, "In Kantian terms involvement with the Bible is analytic in being a Christian: you can't first become a Christian and then consider whether, as an optional extra, synthetically in Kant's terms, some sort of involvement with the Bible might be added on."[24] In less Kantian terms, the same scholar states, "Being a Christian is not simply being a theist, believing that there is a deity; it is believing in a particular God, the God who has manifested himself in a way that has some sort of unique and specific expression in the Bible."[25] The strength of this argument is that it emphasizes that Christianity is intertwined with the Bible in an inseparable way, but what is meant by "involvement"? The Bible is not simply a book of true facts, according to this view, but more of a battleground, a set of competing attempts to understand what was done through Christ.[26]

Based on this view, there does not appear to be any compelling reason for one to become a Christian if, by becoming one, the new Christian is simply

23. One school of thought that would typify this position would be the so-called post-liberalism associated with Yale Divinity School. See Lindbeck, *Nature of Doctrine*; Frei, *Eclipse of Biblical Narrative*; Kelsey, *Uses of Scripture in Recent Theology*.

24. Barr, *Scope and Authority of the Bible*, 52.

25. Barr, *Scope and Authority of the Bible*, 52.

26. This attitude was also typical of what was known as the early Biblical Theology movement. See Childs, *Biblical Theology in Crisis*.

joining a battle to resolve further tensions between ideology and belief. Once one has become a Christian, is there any sort of reason to promote further study apart from a purely mental exercise? Whereas this fourth movement is right in showing that a view of Scripture must go along with the idea of Christianity, it is both possible and beneficial to retain a high view of scriptural authority, while having the Christian freedom to use critical tools to provide better understanding.

This survey of four major approaches to biblical authority points to a wide range of possible answers to the question of biblical authority. I am most comfortable within the evangelical community and find that on most issues evangelicalism can provide a model for answering what I perceive to be the vital issues of biblical authority. However, I would also want to argue that several of the other approaches offer insights that evangelicals should take into account both in formulating their own positions and in confronting others with differing positions. What then are the live issues in the discussion of biblical authority?

Major Contemporary Issues on Biblical Authority

Several major hermeneutical issues remain at the heart of the discussion of biblical authority and have direct implications for interpretation. In this section, I briefly discuss several of these as a basis for our further discussion of interpretation in the next chapter.

The Nature of Authority

What view of biblical authority do we have? We would want to acknowledge and perhaps even endorse the position that emphasizes a respect for knowledge, but this can be overdone. Knowledge of facts alone, without a strong personal commitment, results in sterile Christianity, the kind of Christianity condemned by Søren Kierkegaard and Dietrich Bonhoeffer. Others argue for obedience to the Word. If so, then it is important to be explicit about what is meant by "the Word." It is more than just words on a page, a new form of bibliolatry, but it is also more than a warm feeling we might get from reading these words. There must be a meaningful connection between the words we have in Scripture and the fresh word that God has for his people today. Still, others argue that the Bible, by its very obscurity, forces us to slow down and wrestle with it. This is not an unhealthy approach, no matter what one's view of biblical authority. As stated earlier, in any case, the interpreter must be a listener; they must come with openness since the most profound writings must be wrestled with before they can be appropriated.

Norms and Criteria

There surely must be a *via media* or middle way between those who argue that the Bible is a complete blueprint for life that only requires that one reads off God's specific will and those who say that the Bible offers nothing for today except general truths. I do not remember now where I read it, but I once read that the Bible is not a map to get us through life but a map to get to the pilot who will take us through life. In other words, the Bible not only reflects God's ways of addressing and dealing with humankind but includes exemplifications of the principles by which he does so. I hope that in the next several chapters readers will get an idea of how I approach this problem. It seems to me that the Bible is speaking on several different levels at once, or at least suggesting different levels of analysis, levels that I believe can be grasped and applied. We will explore these different levels from the ground up in chapters 3 through 8.

Truth and Life

Those who read and study Scripture may wonder why there is so much narrative in the Bible. This wonderment would especially be the case for those who incline toward the belief that the Bible is a blueprint or instruction manual for how to live the Christian life, because narratives do not easily translate into simple truth statements. Conversely, when we say the Bible is true, narrative texts can be dealt with if the Bible is turned into a book of facts, but this implies that the only way something can be true is if it actually happened. While this is one way to understand truth, and while the historical veracity of events in the Bible is vital to its integrity, the Bible can be true in several different ways. Let me explain some of those. What are we to make of poetry? The agonies of David expressed in the Psalms certainly appear to be truthful accounts of his experience, even if they are not propositional in nature. What are we to make of narrative texts, such as parables, that did not happen but that still communicate a message? These texts, we would want to say, are also true, but they are true in a different sense. Therefore, we must move beyond a myopic and rigid understanding of what it means for the Bible to be a book of truth. Wolfhart Pannenberg, a German theologian, says that the Bible has a universal message but that it is concerned with situational truth—that is, contingent truth situations and circumstances.[27] The problem is not a simple one. It involves taking situational documents and making them speak to our contemporary situation. This is the reason for the present work: to learn new and perhaps better ways to take a document written two thousand or more years ago and apply it to our modern circumstances. It will take the remaining six chapters to suggest how to do that.

The Christian God

At this point, the entire field of theology enters the picture. We must relate the Bible to our conceptions of God, Christ, and the Holy Spirit. In discussing the issue of biblical authority, it is easy to overlook the simple fact that the Bible must get its authority from someone or something. Though many if not most Christians would want to see the Bible as extremely practical for daily living, it is also in some way a divine book, and we must never overlook the divine element in biblical authority. It is not enough simply to posit that the Bible is divinely inspired. One's view of God and his purposes for humanity—if it is a meaningful belief—will have an impact on how one views God's revelation. This reciprocal relationship encompasses some large questions that can easily prompt extended and deep discussion, discussion that is outside the scope of this book.

The reality of the matter should by now be clear: the issue of biblical authority is a difficult one. Because of its importance for the wider discussion of hermeneutics, it seemed necessary to lay down some important basic concepts and major positions regarding biblical authority, as well as mentioning several enduring pressing issues, rather than to simply insist on a single resolution to the problem. I will suggest, however, a method for looking at the problem. The question of biblical authority involves at least four issues: the place of the Bible, the role of the church or tradition (especially as seen in various contemporary positions on authority), the nature and presence of God, and the interpretive process. These may form a square, with the center point representing the place where all of these are held in perfect balance. I doubt that any position can be found to be in such "perfect balance," at least for very long, due to the tendency of views to emphasize one or two of these elements out of proportion to the rest. For example, Roman Catholics tend to stress the role of tradition or the church in a disproportionate way, while many fundamentalist Protestant groups stress the Bible itself as the only "authority." As the many different proposals show, determining the perfect balance, if there is such a thing, is a task that requires much prayer and thought, and may well never be achieved.

27. See Pannenberg, "What Is Truth?," 20–21.

Study and Practice

This chapter has raised a wide variety of questions regarding biblical authority. Before thinking further about them, take time to think about the hermeneutical dimensions of the concept of biblical authority and how changes in one's hermeneutical perspective might affect one's view. Then, consider your own view of biblical authority. How would you define it, and where would you position it in relationship to other views of biblical authority? Once you have positioned your view of biblical authority, examine the major issues raised by questions of biblical authority as hermeneutical issues. Do you have other questions that you would like to raise regarding these issues? How would you attempt to solve them in light of the discussion so far?

Conclusion

In some ways, the content of this chapter may not seem pertinent to a book on hermeneutics. This is probably because hermeneutics is often thought of in the narrower sense of the techniques and methods of interpretation, which is how it is used in some other volumes. This book attempts not to be one of those volumes. In this chapter, I have instead endeavored to show that one's view of biblical authority constitutes one of the most important presuppositions of a biblical interpreter—that is, of one who reads and attempts to understand and apply the Bible to daily life. When one examines the history of biblical authority, one sees that this assumption has been important throughout the history of the Christian church as it in various ways has come to terms with the Bible, how to understand it, and how to regard its authority for the church and for human behavior and life. In that regard, one's view of biblical authority will have a vital influence on one's hermeneutical stance and hence on one's hermeneutical method and approach to fundamental questions of understanding and meaning. There are a variety of ways in which this authority may be viewed, both historically and contemporaneously. Even though I position myself within the evangelical camp, I recognize that this position has its limitations, whereas other views of biblical authority, although I believe more limited, also contribute to our understanding of the importance of the Bible, its foundations, and its authority. The subsequent chapters assume that the biblical interpreter has a view on biblical authority as that person comes to terms with the various levels of biblical hermeneutics and understanding.

3

Hermeneutics at the Level of Language and Linguistics

Introduction

The issues regarding language are diverse and complex, even for those who devote their entire professional careers to them. As the first step in our discussion of how hermeneutics might be borne out in the process of interpretation, we will consider a couple of fundamental topics that warrant suggestive comments, though they could demand much more space than we can presently afford. These subjects include the nature of language and the place of linguistics. This discussion will then lead into looking at the languages in which the Bible was written (Hebrew, Aramaic, and Greek), common word-study fallacies, the proper method for determining the meaning of words, different translations of the Bible, and other tools for Bible study. This chapter is designed to provide some of the basics for anyone who wishes to be a hermeneutically informed and faithful interpreter of Scripture.

The Nature of Language

The nature of language is widely disputed, even among linguists whose preoccupation concerns language. As a result, there are several approaches to talking about language. Some define language as an individual cognitive capacity, perhaps even originating in a particular language capacity in the human brain.

Such views of language have often ended up being more about the psychological language capacity of an idealized language user than about how people actually communicate. Others define language as a social phenomenon. This view understands language as an important social tool that not only enables humans to communicate ideas but allows them to do things with language itself. From a theological perspective, those who hold to the first view might posit that innate human language capacity is what it means to be created in the image of God—that is, with language as a human organ that reflects the divine language capacity. Those who hold to the second view, however, might point out that God creates by means of language and then instructs humans to develop and extend their functional language capacity through the task of naming the animals. We do not necessarily have to decide how to define language to realize that questions about the nature of language may have important implications, even theological ones. I take a functional view of language and so endorse the second view. Regardless of one's view, it is important to recognize that humans use language for various purposes and in varied ways. Some of these areas have also been misunderstood in biblical studies and so warrant some clarification.

Metaphorical language is an important subtopic in a discussion of the nature of language. A clear-cut distinction is often made, whether in interpretation or in translation or in any number of other areas, between metaphorical language and literal language. Usually the accompanying statement is that literalness is a good quality, akin to clarity and ease of understanding, while metaphorical language is subject to suspicion, since it is more difficult to grasp, trickier to determine its exact meaning, and less easily applied. I, however, would want to dispute that such a distinction can, in fact, be made. How often can one expect to come across a cow in a book? I do not mean a picture of a cow, since that is not a physical cow. I mean a cow in the literalistic sense: How often does one come across an actual mooing, milkable cow inside a book? The answer would probably be never, but when we use the language of reading about a cow in a book, we are merely referring to a symbolic representation of what one particular cow looks like to the author who wrote about one. Unless someone has had a particularly odd experience in their past, they, like me, have never seen a cow in a book, but, instead, have seen on numerous occasions the black marks on the page that form letters, which when put together spell out the word *cow*. There is both a sign, the word that we read as *cow*, and what that sign indicates—that is, a particular kind of animal.[1]

---

1. Many will recognize that this is the arbitrary relationship between the signifier (sign) and signified (its meaning). This is one of the fundamental principles of modern linguistics. See Saussure, *Course in General Linguistics*.

Given this simple, somewhat humorous description, would a reasonable person say that the phrase "I saw that there was a cow mentioned in that book" lacks clarity and is difficult to understand? The meaning is probably reasonably clear even though it is not purely literal. From this example it is also demonstrable that there is really no such thing as literal language in the sense that the word is the thing. Quite to the contrary, *all language is metaphorical*, in the sense that we use words, whether spoken or written, to stand for things or concepts in the world inside and outside of the language system itself.[2] Sometimes we use words to refer to specific things, concepts, or people in the world around us, and sometimes we use them to denote things, qualities, and concepts. Some of the things we refer to or denote may be more easily conceived of than others. For example, it may be easier to think of "cow" or "cowness" than it is to think of "hope," "faith," or "love," but this does not change the fact that all language is metaphorical. The natural question that arises is: When we refer to literal and metaphorical language, what are we referring to? The question becomes whether the symbols on the page are to be taken in their usual way in the language vocabulary system—that is, whether they are being used to indicate their generally accepted equivalent—or whether some other, less than usual or perhaps even unique meaning is involved on the basis of how that word is being used in the context of its surrounding words.

This distinction between literal language and metaphorical language may sound like a fairly picky and insignificant differentiation, but I want to stress that it is not. First, it makes us aware of and reinforces one of the points I wish to make throughout these chapters: language is a very complex phenomenon that requires the full attention of those who use it, especially those of us who interpret it. This is especially true for those of us involved in reading and understanding the Bible. Since the Bible is written in language—and ancient languages at that (see below)—we must bring our most well-informed understanding to its interpretation. Second, it makes us suspicious of accepting too much at face value, whether we hear it or read it. An act of interpretation was required when the language was first used and heard or read by those who shared the same language (e.g., when one of Paul's letters was read to one of his churches), and an act of interpretation is required before we can say that we, in any sense, understand what is being communicated, especially as we are reading either a no-longer-living language (ancient Hebrew or Greek, etc.) or a modern translation of that language, several millennia or more removed from the time of writing. These issues pose major interpretive challenges that we

2. There are many works on metaphor. As an introduction, see Turbayne, *Myth of Metaphor*; Lakoff and Johnson, *Metaphors We Live By*.

must address in our hermeneutical efforts. Third, this kind of a basic understanding is a prerequisite to understanding the traditional figures of speech
in any language. These figures of speech are not categorically different from
the ordinary uses of language at all but are merely some of the manifestations
of language in its various forms. Once we acquire an understanding of what
is involved in interpreting language (and everyone has this understanding to
some degree as a user of their first language), then we are a mere step or two
away from appreciating some of the varied intricacies of language.

The Languages of the Bible

The languages of the Bible are three. This in itself is perplexing, because our
modern translations of the Bible into a single language, such as English, mask
the fact that the two testaments were written in languages that are not just
different but completely genetically unrelated and are parts of two distinct
major language groups.[3]

Most of the Old Testament is written in Hebrew, one of a group of North-
west Semitic languages. Aramaic, another language in this group, is the second
language of the Bible and is reserved for two words in Genesis, a single verse in
Jeremiah, and portions of Ezra and Daniel (as well as a few quotations in the
New Testament).[4] There are some very important differences between Aramaic and Hebrew, but there are also many similarities because they are from
the same language family. Aramaic was the most important Semitic language
of Palestine for administrative purposes when the Jews spoke it upon their
return from Babylon after the exile in the sixth century BCE. It continued to
be used well past the New Testament era and probably constituted the first
language of a good portion of the people living in Palestine even during the
first century. We would expect Hebrew to have continued, since it was the
language of the Scriptures of the Jewish people and so closely associated
with important events in their history, but it did not continue to be as widely
used as Aramaic. In fact, a Jewish form of commentary/translation called the
Targum was developed because the average Jew of postexilic times could not
understand Hebrew sufficiently to have their own Hebrew Scriptures read to
them, and thus, they needed the Targums' interpretive translations.

A point of continuing dispute among Old Testament scholars is the relationship of Hebrew to its sister Semitic languages (e.g., Ugaritic, Phoenician,

---

3. There are many introductions to the biblical languages, including in books on exegesis
and interpretation. For example, see Osborne, *Hermeneutical Spiral*, 65–67, used here.
4. See Greenspahn, *Introduction to Aramaic*, 1.

Akkadian, and Arabic) and how that affects our understanding of the Hebrew of the Old Testament, some of which is very difficult because of the presence of words that occur only once in the entire Old Testament.[5] There are two sides to this issue. On the one hand, many scholars see the value of using sister languages to help establish the text of the Old Testament; in other words, other languages are seen as useful for knowing how to spell certain words and determining which word belongs in a given place.[6] On the other hand, there is less agreement on the role the sister languages should play in determining the meaning of a difficult Hebrew word. Scholars such as Mitchell J. Dahood depended heavily on these languages, especially Ugaritic, for understanding the Psalms, on which he wrote three volumes of commentary,[7] whereas many more recent scholars, such as Peter C. Craigie, who also wrote on Psalms, and David Clines, who wrote a three-volume work on Job (a book full of linguistic oddities), argue that it is better to depend first and foremost on the Hebrew text itself before venturing into the rather uncertain waters of cognate languages.[8] Most scholars probably tend toward the latter viewpoint.

Besides the matters of individual words and their meanings, two major language issues should be mentioned regarding Hebrew. The first is that the *text* of the Old Testament in Hebrew that is currently used is called the Masoretic Text (MT), and its earliest complete manuscripts date to around 900–1100 CE. This seems quite late for a document that was finished probably, at the latest, in the third century BCE. It is true that discoveries at Qumran (near the Dead Sea) of Hebrew texts dating to around the second century BCE, such as Isaiah (what is called the Great Isaiah Scroll), have reinforced scholarly faith in the text of the MT, but we are still dependent on a long period of textual transmission. A further complicating factor is that the Hebrew text was written without vowels until the Masoretes, a group of pious scribes in the fifth through tenth centuries CE, inserted vowels to ensure the preservation of their understanding of what the individual words were and how they were to be pronounced. This text was also written with words and sentences run together, another factor that must be considered when interpreting the text of the Old Testament.

The second major language issue to consider is the *verb system* of Hebrew. To set up a comparison, consider how Indo-European languages—among

5. The corpus of ancient Hebrew texts is in fact relatively small, consisting mostly of the Hebrew Bible, some inscriptions, and a handful of other texts.

6. An example would be the considerable number of cognate words in Ugaritic and Hebrew. However, see the cautionary comments of Craigie, "Ugarit and the Bible."

7. See Dahood, *Psalms*.

8. See Clines, *Job*; Craigie, *Psalms 1–50*.

which English is one—often have time-oriented tense systems, which allow users of these languages to speak of past, present, and (often with periphrastic forms) future time by means of their choice of verbs in sentences. In other words, verb forms have an inherent temporal component in many Indo-European languages. The Hebrew verb system, however, probably emphasizes something else: verbal aspect.[9] This means that the Hebrew verb system denotes not essentially the time when a given event occurred but the author's conception of *how* the action occurred.[10] While this may at first seem unclear, and perhaps even inconsequential, it has a significant impact on the ways meanings are made in Hebrew, and so it is with purpose that I introduce this component of Hebrew grammar here. In our translations of the Hebrew text into Indo-European languages, the matter of translation of tense forms depends on many more contextual factors than simply the individual form used in Hebrew.[11]

The third language of importance in the Bible is Greek. The New Testament is written almost entirely in what is best called Hellenistic or koine Greek, the common Greek of the Greco-Roman world of the first century CE. Classical Greek scholars have sometimes been critical of New Testament Greek because it does not conform to the standards they were taught when they learned classical Greek. It is true that in a number of ways Hellenistic Greek does not conform to classical Greek standards, but this is not the same as saying that the Greek of the New Testament is in any sense inferior or bad Greek. The Greek of the classical period consisted of regional dialects, often associated with important city-states. The most important of these was Athens. As a result of its cultural and economic importance, the Attic dialect was widely used in classical literature and even for more widespread administration. When Alexander the Great, who was a Hellenophile, undertook his vengeance on the Persians on behalf of Greece, he used a form of this administrative Attic Greek as the language that unified his group of Greek mercenary soldiers. As a result, during the period of rapid Greek expansion

9. See Arnold and Choi, *Guide to Biblical Hebrew Syntax*, 53–60. There are other proposals regarding the Hebrew verbal system, but the aspect system seems to be the most persuasive, certainly more so than the temporal one.

10. Hebrew has two tense forms: a perfective, which depicts an event as complete, and an imperfective, which depicts an event as incomplete. Moreover, the term *tense form* is rather unfortunate but is retained due to convention; when this term is used in relation to verbal aspect, it ceases to retain its temporal sense, which is appropriate for some other languages, but rather serves as a way to maintain convention in discussing the semantic components of verbs.

11. For example, a perfective verb may be used regularly in either past-time or future-time contexts. And only the context can determine whether a past or future translation should be used.

brought about under the military leadership and conquests of Alexander the Great (around 330 BCE), a form of Greek suited to second-language users became the lingua franca or common language of communication of the eastern Mediterranean world. Some of the elements of New Testament Greek reflect the variety in the Greek language that was used by people across widely divergent social, economic, and educational strata throughout the Greco-Roman period.

The Septuagint is a Greek document from the Hellenistic period that is important for biblical study. When the Jews of Ptolemaic Egypt (the Ptolemies were successors to Alexander the Great) realized that many of their fellow Jews could no longer understand Hebrew, they decided that a translation of the Hebrew Old Testament into the language of the day would be appropriate, and so one was begun in the third century BCE. There are ancient myths about a group of seventy Jewish scholars translating for seventy days to come up with a document that agreed on every point, but these stories have little factual basis.[12] They probably reflect the fact that Jewish scholars undertook to translate their Scriptures into the language of the Jewish people in Egypt (as well as the Diaspora elsewhere). What is certain, however, is that the Septuagint is the largest Greek translation project of the ancient world and, as can be seen from the dates involved, may attest in many cases to a version of the Old Testament much earlier than that found in the Masoretic Text. The books of Jeremiah and Job, and some of the history books, are particularly noteworthy in this regard, as they differ in significant ways from their Hebrew counterparts. Septuagint Greek (in its different varieties) also represents forms of koine or Hellenistic Greek.

The Greek language has its own configuration of systems by which its various elements are organized and work together to create meaning. One of the most widely discussed areas in recent research concerns the Greek verbal system, although there are other areas of importance as well. What I have said about the tense forms of Hebrew also applies to the tense forms in ancient Greek: they indicate verbal aspect. There are three major tense forms in Greek, and each is used to describe an event from a different perspective (i.e., perfective, imperfective, and stative), rather than to emphasize time.[13]

12. See Aristeas, *Letter of Aristeas* 121–27; Justin Martyr, *Dialogue with Trypho*, 68:6–7; Irenaeus, *Against Heresies* 3.21.2. For an introduction to the Septuagint, see Jobes and Silva, *Invitation to the Septuagint*.

13. A helpful way to understand the tense and aspect of Greek verbs is through the multiple angles of viewing a given event, such as a parade:

If I am a television correspondent in the BBC helicopter flying over the parade, I view the parade or process in its immediacy from a vantage outside the action as "perfective," i.e., in its entirety as a single and complete whole. If I am a spectator sitting in

This does not mean that Greek users could not refer to time, but they did not do so primarily using tense forms. Temporal reference is indicated by other factors, such as context. Much more could be said about New Testament Greek, but I will leave the discussion here and trust that interested readers will attempt to gain appropriate linguistic knowledge and that others will at least attempt to incorporate sound linguistic knowledge gained from reliable sources, some of which are mentioned below.

The original languages of the Bible are just one example of the inherent sense of foreignness created by the fact that modern interpreters are separated by so many factors from the original authors. Even if we believe that we are using our best insights to study an ancient text, that text remains in some sense foreign. If someone picks up a Bible, they are picking up an anthology of three different languages, with texts ranging over, at minimum, twelve hundred years in composition, written nearly two millennia ago at the least. The ease with which one can move from Genesis to Revelation in a contemporary English Bible is not so easy in the original languages. Each language has its own idioms and means of expressing particular concepts. For example, Hebrew literalistically says "to turn to" for what we would translate as "to repent." In Greek, for example, passive voice verbs may take direct objects, as in Luke 7:29 where Jesus "was baptized with regard to the baptism of John" (βαπτισθέντες τὸ βάπτισμα Ἰωάννου, *baptisthentes to baptisma Iōannou*).[14] It is amazing how many of these particular idioms have been maintained even through translation. In English perhaps the most notable instance is the occasional use of "thou" as the second-person singular pronoun (Greek distinguishes second-person singular and plural, unlike contemporary English, apart from when one wants to sound like the King James Version). But it also makes us sensitive to distinguishing particularly biblical idioms and other idioms of the languages involved. Not only should one be cautious in using them for mileage in sermons, but we can also appreciate them as elements of a living and dynamic language.

---

the grandstand watching the parade pass in front of me, I view the process immersed within it as "imperfective," i.e., as an event in progress. And if I am the parade manager considering all of the conditions in existence at this parade, including not only all the arrangements that are coming to fruition but all of the accompanying events that allow the parade to operate, I view the process not in its particulars or its immediacy but as "stative," i.e., as a condition or state of affairs in existence. (Porter, *Verbal Aspect*, 91)

For a concise summary of verbal aspect, see Porter, *Idioms*, 20–22. This grammar explains other features of Greek from a linguistic perspective.

14. Scholars propose to explain this in various ways, but many explanations are based on the scholar's understanding of English, where supposedly English passive verbs do not take objects. Without going into detail, one can explain this phenomenon in terms of such verbs in Greek being able to express goals of the verbal process.

Words and Sentences: Problems and Potentials

Another important issue is the way we interpret individual words and how they are related to each other. We cannot cover all the necessary elements of Greek grammar, so I will focus on some of the major issues surrounding words and the organization of these words.

The tendency for interpreters—including both scholars and nonprofessionals—is to give words maximalist meaning, when in fact words tend to carry minimal meaning but gain specific meanings within their grammatical and larger contexts. One of the problems in Bible study today is commitment of what are often called lexical fallacies.[15] One of these is the etymological fallacy. The etymology of a word is its history. At one time it was commonplace among biblical scholars to turn to the etymology of a word as important and decisive in trying to determine its meaning. A classic example is the Greek word ἐκκλησία (*ekklēsia*), commonly translated "church." If *ekklēsia* is broken down into its component Greek parts, it consists of the preposition ἐκ (*ek*), usually translated "out," prefixed to a word meaning "call." The word *ekklēsia* is, in this regard, transparent in its construction. However, some scholars wish to go further and say two things about this word. First, they say that the church represents the "called-out ones." They thereby convert transparency into etymology, in which the history of the word dictates its meaning. Second, every time the word *ekklēsia* or "church" appears, there is a tendency to see in the word everything that one believes about the church, and it is usually a developed view of the church. If we were concerned with the history of the word *ekklēsia*, it may be important that in its earliest uses in Greek literature it had a meaning related to calling out, but this soon came to mean any group of people gathered for a purpose, often political in nature. The *ekklēsia* performed an important function in the governance of the Greek city-state. Therefore, it was a ready-made term to use for that group of people known as the church, a group that met for the purpose of worshiping God. In the New Testament, there are several instances where it is not possible to see any more meaning in the word than a group gathered for a purpose, like Matthew 16:18, where Jesus says that he will build his church. Since this is before the formal beginning of any such "institution" as we know it today, it seems to refer simply to a group of followers called for a purpose.

The second problem already noted above—that of putting every known meaning of a word on every occurrence—is called "illegitimate totality

---

15. See Barr, *Semantics of Biblical Language*, 210–11, 213–14, 218, 222, where descriptions of these kinds of exegetical fallacies can be found.

transfer."[16] This is a very cumbersome phrase even in English, but it illustrates well the problems of lexical maximalism. Because each word in the phrase is important, I will not suggest a new term but instead describe the term with which we have to work. The term *illegitimate totality transfer* refers to the linguistically unsound procedure of transferring to any given word all that is known of its possible range of meanings. This procedure is related to the lexical fallacy of confusing word and concept. Confusing word and concept occurs, for example, when we speak of the concept of *shalom* (which is a Hebrew word) when we mean the concept of peace, or when we use the word *peace* but mean the Hebrew word *shalom*. The word and the concept are different items, even if they are related. And if we unload all our knowledge of the concept of peace on a single lexical item (or word), then illegitimate totality transfer occurs.[17]

Looking again at Matthew 16:18, we can see that one of the reasons this verse has caused considerable trouble for interpreters is that they have wanted to say everything they know about the early church (and sometimes things about the later church). For example, we know that the early church had a certain kind of leadership, with certain standards of behavior. This understanding cannot be made to fit Matthew 16:18, even though there is some intimation of discipline being conveyed. As a result of this error, many scholars have argued that this is evidence of a later editor or writer of Matthew's Gospel putting these words into Jesus's mouth. This may be true, but not for this reason. If it is seen to be an indefensible principle to load every known meaning onto a single word, and if it is recognized that the word *ekklēsia* was a word in current Greek during Jesus's time (and it was), then it is entirely possible that Jesus (who may have known Greek) may have used it to refer to a specific group of his followers, nothing more and nothing less.

If we do not turn to the word's history or to its total theological meaning to determine its meaning, how then is the meaning of an individual word determined? We must begin with the recognition that it is not always easy to determine every exact nuance of a word (lexical item) in any language, especially a dead language like ancient Greek or Hebrew, but there are several potentially productive guidelines. First, the question of meaning must differentiate between reference, denotation, and sense.[18] *Reference* is not a characteristic of a word but something we do with words: we refer to things

16. The specific term is James Barr's. See Barr, *Semantics of Biblical Language*, 218, 222, which uses the example of ἐκκλησία. The result of illegitimate totality transfer is to create miniature word-theologies.
17. See Barr, *Semantics of Biblical Language*, 71, and elsewhere.
18. This distinction is made by Lyons, *Semantics*, 174–229.

by means of words. *Denotation* is the signification that is attached to a word. *Sense* is the relationship that exists among words within a language system. For example, if I am speaking of a cat, I am drawing on the denotation of the word *cat*, even if I don't have a specific cat in mind. The word is still meaningful because the sign is used in English to signify a kind of animal (although such denotation may remain vague or even contradictory if we give different denotations to the word *cat*). If I speak of various kinds of animals, I may use words such as *cat, dog, horse,* or *cow.* These words fall within a domain of meaning that is very broad and includes all kinds of animals. I could speak of pets, in which case I may use words such as *cat, dog, fish, bird,* or *turtle.* This represents a different domain of meaning, even if it overlaps with others. These kinds of domains of meaning, sometimes called *semantic domains* or *semantic fields,* are ways in which individual words are organized within a language. These categories may be variously organized, depending on the context that is appropriate (e.g., differentiating pets from sea creatures from four-legged animals). More is said on semantic-domain theory or semantic-field theory below. Thus, words function in a number of different ways, in relation to the world they attempt to describe (reference and denotation) and in relation to the language system in which they are used.

How is it, then, that we determine the meaning of a word? The tendency is to go to a dictionary (or lexicon) and look up the word to establish what the meaning is. When one looks in a dictionary, one is usually confronted by a list of different meanings. But this is backward, since a dictionary is nothing more than a synthesis of the several different major uses of a given word within a variety of contexts. The word itself is the one common element in all the different definitions or translational glosses that one may encounter in a dictionary or lexicon. There are two schools of thought on whether words have many meanings (polysemy) or a single meaning (monosemy). Most interpreters probably don't think about this issue very much and simply assume that words have many meanings, because they think that they find various meanings in a dictionary or use different glosses depending on different contexts when the word is used. However, I prefer a monosemous perspective, what one scholar has called a "monosemic bias."[19] This bias means that I approach words not as having maximalist meanings (as we discussed above) or even as having multiple meanings (one can see how multiple meanings may feed into maximalist meanings) but as having a minimalist abstract meaning. In other words, the

---

19. Ruhl, *On Monosemy.* See also Porter, *Linguistic Analysis,* 51–53. Two other studies of interest (even if not monosemous in orientation) are Thiselton, "Semantics and New Testament Interpretation"; Silva, *Biblical Words.*

word itself contributes relatively little to the meaning of the sentence, except to denote a relatively vague and abstract meaning, a meaning that may not even be narrowly definable. This meaning is then modulated, narrowed, or focused into a more specific meaning on the basis of context. There definitely are some instances where one word has two distinctly different meanings—such as the English word *cleave*—but instances of this sort are relatively few (and explained as instances of homophones or homographs—that is, two different words that sound or are written the same). A monosemic approach to lexical semantics is better able to account for the stability of meanings of words, the ability to create metaphors (which rely on this abstract meaning without a specifying context), and how context works to shape these meanings.

Context, therefore, is a crucial factor in determining meaning, including lexical meaning. Some go so far as to say that context determines everything in meaning, but that is not evident at all. The context must be shaping something. If every word gets its meaning from the context, then the context has no meaning. The one thing that provides the basis of contextual meaning is the denotation of the lexeme, even if the context shapes it in considerable and major ways.

Context is established in several ways. The first is through syntax, or the function and place of a given word within a larger group of words—usually a sentence. Syntax concerns the arrangement of words in groups of ever-increasing size, from several words that may form a phrase (such as a prepositional phrase), to a clause that consists of several different groups of words (such as the subject), to groups of clauses connected in various ways. Each of these levels of grammar can be profitably examined and is part of the context (or at least one of the contexts) in which words are used. The syntactical relations within a language are complex, but the ways that such groups of words are organized establish meaningful relations between them. Several examples are cited below.

The second way context is established is through paradigmatic choice, or the selection of a word over other words that could occur in the same grammatical construction within the sentence. For example, in Romans 3:21 Paul says, "Now, apart from law, the righteousness of God is manifest, being borne witness to by the law and the prophets" (my translation). One of the most troublesome notions in the New Testament is that of the phrase "the righteousness of God" (δικαιοσύνη θεοῦ, *dikaiosynē theou*).[20] In the context

20. One of the Barrian fallacies mentioned above is sometimes committed in understanding this phrase, when an entire theology of the covenantal God is brought to bear on how this term is rendered. I am trying to show the importance of context over simply illegitimately transferring the totality of one's Reformed theology.

of Romans 3:21, what is "the righteousness of God," or the relationship between "righteousness" and "God"? There are several observations that can be made. The first is that a current situation is being described (now), whether this is a current temporal situation or the current result of Paul's argument. Second, the righteousness of God is contrasted with law. Third, the righteousness of God is the subject of the sentence, and the referent for the participial phrase "being borne witness to by the law and the prophets." Fourth, the phrase "of God" (in Greek this is called a genitive phrase) follows the noun "righteousness" and modifies or qualifies it. So far, these observations are all based on the syntax of the verse. In Romans 3:22 Paul clarifies the relation between these words by saying that the righteousness of God is "through faith of Jesus Christ unto all who believe" (my translation). This seems to point not to a righteousness toward God or a righteousness that constitutes God's character (though several of these interpretations may be true in other contexts) but to a righteousness that God gives, that comes from God and distinguishes this life from the life related to the law not mediated by Jesus Christ. Last, Paul here uses righteousness as his metaphor for salvation as opposed to any other (such as reconciliation); this is a choice Paul made when he could have used other metaphors and words that would have invoked these other metaphors. This is one of the paradigmatic considerations we must make as interpreters. I would argue, therefore, on the basis of syntactic and paradigmatic criteria, that Paul is here emphasizing that being made right with God is God's act, mediated through faith in Jesus Christ. This is quite a different interpretation from seeing righteousness as humanity's right acts toward God, which is a possible (though much less likely) interpretation given the context in Romans 3.

When determining the meaning of a word, it is important to see individual words as being in relationship to each other within the vocabulary of a language, either as synonyms or more likely as antonyms or even hyponyms. In other words, this is the process of determining which word or words mean similar or different things than other words. This process relies on semantic-field theory or semantic-domain theory. To explain: in any given language, to speak of certain ideas or concepts, different words are often used, and they are used in relationship to each other. These relations may be horizontal relations (e.g., cats, dogs, and fish are all on the same level as pets), or they may be hierarchical or vertical relations (e.g., flower, rose, and English rose are in a hierarchical relationship from broadest to narrowest). The way this field of meaning is divided shows the concept's semantic field. An important milestone in biblical lexicography was reached in the publication of Johannes P. Louw and Eugene A. Nida's semantic-field dictionary of New Testament Greek.[21] In this dictionary, rather than a word being listed, followed by its translational equivalents, or words that can be used to translate the given word (as we note above, these are contextual variations on the meaning of the word), each word is defined by showing how it relates to other words within its given semantic field. The Louw-Nida lexicon is very helpful because of its use of semantic-domain theory to categorize the New Testament Greek vocabulary according to 93 different semantic domains, although it does not use monosemy as its overall approach. This is not the place to go into a full-scale treatment of semantic-field theory, but I wish merely to point out that determining the meaning of a lexical item must be done with consideration for the monosemous sense of a word and what words were possible but were not used.

The Issue of Bible Translations

Now that I have clarified several of the more pressing issues regarding the meanings of words, I would like to turn to the final topic under the heading of linguistics: aids to interpretation, especially translations. There is an unfortunately prevalent school of thought among some biblical scholars that meaningful statements about the biblical text can be made only if one has a thorough command of the original languages. While it may be ideal to think that everyone who ever says anything about Scripture will have exhausted all the biblical tools, including the original languages (and know them according to the principles of modern linguistics, rather than through traditional grammar), the simple fact is that this will never be true. However, much can be done without thorough knowledge of the original languages.

Many tools are available for those unfamiliar with the original languages; the first tool, of course, is the Bible itself. Many people take their Bibles for granted, but from what I have already said it should be clear that the text of the Bible is not a thing to be taken lightly. Every one of the major Western languages now has several competent translations available (even if they are not always literarily stellar). These should be used with relatively high confidence, since for the most part they are the product of many years of hard work that is (usually) performed by a team of experts. Nevertheless, several factors should still be kept in mind. The first factor, and this is a vital one,

21. Louw and Nida, *Greek-English Lexicon*. It is unfortunate that many New Testament scholars have not taken advantage of this excellent lexical resource (despite its having been available since 1988).

is that every translation is an interpretation of the biblical text.[22] When a translation is made, the translator (or translators, as is often the case today) must decide on rendering a particular word or a specific grammatical expression. They are not afforded the luxury of a page or two to elucidate their decision—that kind of comment is reserved for commentaries—but a simple equivalent must be found.

Within biblical studies, there are essentially two kinds of translation, called *formal equivalence* and *dynamic equivalence* (or *functional equivalence*) translations.[23] A formal equivalence translation usually tries to preserve the original syntax and word order as much as possible in the translation, within the confines of making sense in the language into which it is translated, and it often uses the same word in this receptor language for every occurrence of the same word in the source language. Perhaps the paragon of literalistic translation, at least in the English-speaking world, is the Authorized Version (KJV), although it does not follow the principle of consistent translation of a given word. Several other translations would also fall into this category (or want to be seen in this category), such as the Revised Standard Version (RSV), the New Revised Standard Version (NRSV), the New American Standard Bible (and its 1995 revision), and the English Standard Version (which is based on the 1971 RSV).[24]

A dynamic equivalence translation, conversely, argues that in order to make the original text perform in the same way in the receptor culture, the syntax and the vocabulary, and even the idioms and analogies, must be adapted. It has been argued, therefore, that it is meaningless in a culture that does not understand the center of human emotion as being the "heart" to talk of God "cleansing the human heart"; instead, the center of emotion in the receptor culture must be used, which in some cases might be the "throat" or the "stomach." The first modern translation to seriously employ the principles of dynamic equivalence theory was the Good News Translation. Later translations that exhibit elements of the dynamic/functional equivalence principles

22. Without minimizing the valuable work done in recent translations, this realization is a liberating one in light of the multitude of translations available. Unless one is reading directly from an original manuscript, written in the original language, one is reading an interpretation of the original text. This realization can deflate the snobbery that exists among those who uphold certain translations to the denigration of others.

23. The pioneer of the dynamic (or functional) approach is a linguist and translation expert of the American Bible Society, Eugene A. Nida. See de Waard and Nida, *From One Language to Another*; Nida, *Toward a Science of Translating*; and Nida and Taber, *Theory and Practice of Translation*. For excellent entries into translation theory, see Munday, *Introducing Translation Studies*; Pym, *Exploring Translation Theories*. For a recent treatment of Bible translations, see Porter, *How We Got the New Testament*, 178–91.

24. See Porter, *How We Got the New Testament*, 178–79.

include the New International Version (NIV, including the TNIV), the New Living Translation (NLT), and the Holman Christian Bible (HCB).[25]

We must remember that the differences in translations are not different *categories* but different places along a *continuum*, with perhaps the wooden translation on one end and a free paraphrase on the other. This means that even the most wooden translation must have dynamic elements to be understood. For example, it is impossible to maintain Greek sentential word order for very long while creating an intelligible rendering into another language such as English. This also means that even dynamic translations also have formal elements, so that they are recognizable as translations of the Bible. To make any sort of fine division among these categories is nearly impossible. To judge a translation, we must judge its potential use. When someone asks if a translation is a good translation, one must ask, "Good for what?" If a translation is a paraphrase, it may be inappropriate to use it for detailed scholarly work in which one wants something that serves as a surrogate for the original, but this does not make it any less of a translation, especially if an ethnic, social, cultural, or specific age group might find its contemporary idiom particularly meaningful. Ideally, therefore, the use of several translations, perhaps representing different approaches to the translator's task, will form the basis of productive Bible study. Those places where translations vary the most probably indicate where the original language poses the greatest degree of potential debate.

Other Aids for Biblical Study

Many other tools are available to help those doing biblical study. If the original languages are known, then the standard lexicons, suitable grammars, and the text in the original language will be essential.[26] Those who have studied those languages will probably already have an idea of some of their possibilities—although one must still be careful to use the best linguistic sources. For those working from a translation, other tools are worth mentioning: commentaries

---

25. See Porter, *How We Got the New Testament*, 183.
26. I have already mentioned the Louw-Nida lexicon above. I use the term *suitable* of grammars because Hebrew studies and Greek New Testament studies are disproportionately well represented. Hebrew has a number of linguistically oriented grammars worth consulting for those who are able, including van der Merwe, Naudé, and Kroeze, *Biblical Hebrew Reference Grammar*. Most of the standard reference grammars for New Testament Greek study reflect the thought of a previous period, such as the ever popular though now antiquated Blass and Debrunner, *Greek Grammar*. Better options include Porter, *Idioms*; Mathewson and Emig, *Intermediate Greek Grammar*. For a recent assessment of some of these historical trends, see Porter, "Where Have All the Greek Grammarians Gone?"

and a Bible dictionary. Commentaries come in all shapes and sizes, although many are increasingly large and unwieldy and even multivolumed. Some are based on the original languages, while others are based on translations. Some are designed for scholars, while others are designed for laypeople. Some emphasize the original languages, geography, and/or history, while others specialize in practical application. It is best for a pastor/teacher to approach the text using the most sophisticated tools he or she can possibly use, since these tools generally provide the greatest depth of understanding or at least possibilities in that regard. Furthermore, it is most helpful (and most appropriate) to draw practical insights out of the text in response to the immediate needs of the congregation or teaching audience, rather than attempt to rehearse someone else's vague and general practical applications as are often found in application-oriented commentaries. Therefore, it is worth exploring the technical commentaries more so than the practical (or devotional) ones for the very reason that the latter may not be as "practical" as others. The task of *hermeneutics* must come before *homiletics*. This is true in this book just as it is in attempting to be hermeneutically responsible in reading and applying the Bible. Last, a good Bible dictionary, in some ways, is like the answer book to the game Trivial Pursuit—it can help provide not only a general grasp of the milieu in which a particular author wrote but also answers to the more *trivial* and annoying questions, like where the city of Kabzeel is located.[27]

In the hermeneutically grounded interpretive process that I am advocating and will introduce more fully in the next chapter, there is a reciprocal relationship between the level of textual analysis and the level of linguistics. By this I mean that attention to the textual level requires attention to linguistics. I hope that I have made that clear in this chapter, even if much regarding the biblical languages remains unsaid. The language being used in any given historical period, whether it is first-century Greek or twenty-first-century English, comprises a linguistic system that provides the parameters of how that language functions through its grammar and word meanings. Reading of the text must be done in light of the linguistic possibilities and probabilities of the language system in which the text is written. In this way, the language itself is the first connection between the world of the text and the world beyond the text. For example, in Romans 5:11, the word often translated as "reconciliation" (καταλλαγή, *katallagē*) is used. This word is part of the linguistic system of Hellenistic Greek and has the sense of bringing conflicting parties together.

---

27. Among many Bible dictionaries, see Freedman, *Anchor Bible Dictionary*. See also Reid, *IVP Dictionary*, the individual volumes from which this volume is compiled, and the equivalent volumes for the Old Testament. The answer to the question is that Kabzeel is located in the south of Judah, near the region of Edom.

Depending on the context in which it is used, the word may emphasize the reconciler (in this case God) putting aside his hostility and becoming at peace with his antagonist or the one who is being reconciled (in this case humanity) being put on friendly terms with the reconciler. Knowledge of these contextually modulated perspectives—through a grasp of the linguistic system of Greek—provides the parameters for at least beginning a discussion of this term. To understand how the abstract sense is expressed in Romans 5:11, we must find good textual evidence within Romans itself. I will discuss the issue of close textual reading in the next couple of chapters, but the discussion will assume an appreciation of the language system appropriate to the text being discussed—that is, the kinds of topics that we have discussed in this chapter.

Study and Practice

This chapter may have introduced some new concepts and ideas. Even those who have studied the biblical languages may have found information they have not been taught. I do not expect everyone who reads this book to become an expert in Greek and/or in Hebrew, and certainly not in Aramaic. However, as interpreters of the Bible, we must recognize that the Bible was originally written in these now dead languages (yes, ancient Greek is now a dead language, in that no one today speaks or uses Greek that is the same as that of the ancient world). I have presented the above information not to overwhelm readers but to provide some introductory insights or, perhaps, needed reminders about these languages. Consider how further knowledge of the biblical languages might play a part in your teaching or preaching. Consider how dependent we are on biblical translations. Compare two or three translations of the same passage. For example, compare translations of Ephesians 1:3–14 and of Psalm 23. Do you notice places where the translational word choices are different? What about the organization of the sentences? These differences among translations often indicate places in the original text that are subject to various interpretations. Even if you are not eager to further your knowledge of the biblical languages, it is important to avoid the lexical fallacies that are made when language is misunderstood and misinterpreted. There is a tendency in biblical studies to maximize the meaning of an individual word, when in fact individual words in context provide minimal information. The tendency is to create interpretations, and even theologies, based on individual words rather than larger stretches of language. Examine two commentaries on Ephesians and two on the Psalms and note where the commentators create lexical fallacies by over-interpreting individual words.

Conclusion

The main goal of this chapter has been to bring some of the major issues in language and linguistics to light as a foundation for interpretation. A secondary goal has been to stimulate interest in those who would want to learn more about the original languages of the Bible. I first studied Greek on my own when I was already a college graduate, and I later took Hebrew while at seminary. Such study was certainly hard work, but the hours I spent in this pursuit have rewarded me many times over. I realize that this may not be possible for everyone. While knowing the biblical languages is invaluable, the hermeneutical approach to biblical interpretation developed in this book, which relies on sound linguistics, can produce distinct results in interpretation and be adaptable to various needs and purposes, regardless of one's level of education in Greek or Hebrew. Although this book is designed for pastors, students, and others interested in reading the Bible well, some of the principles should stimulate further scholarship and conversation among advanced readers in hermeneutics. My goal in the next several chapters is to introduce a method of analysis that puts the primary burden on the interpreter to formulate the most astute and challenging questions of biblical analysis based on sound linguistic knowledge. Does this sound like hard work? Well, it is. But I think many have found responsible biblical interpretation to be one of the most rewarding tasks that one is ever privileged to be involved in.[28]

---

28. Not only is responsible biblical interpretation a rewarding task; it is also a necessary task for today's pastor or teacher (cf. Eph. 4:12–16).

4

Hermeneutics at the Level of Text: Part 1

Introduction

This chapter will specifically introduce the model for interpretation that I have been promising since the outset. Before I do this, I would like to refer to an important area of discussion regarding methodology. I mentioned in the first chapter that there are currently two major approaches to the question of interpretation of a biblical text. To put the situation simplistically, the first sees the question of meaning answered by determining the origin of a text, its history, and its sources (a diachronic approach); the second sees the question of meaning answered by delineating the argument within the narrative world of a given text (a synchronic approach). Those pursuing a diachronic approach have typically addressed the question of a text's meaning by determining its genesis. The tools for this approach include *form criticism*, which labels and identifies isolated forms found in the biblical text to trace their use and development; *source criticism*, which attempts to identify the various sources behind a document; and *redaction criticism*, which seeks to identify how a biblical author uses and changes their sources.[1]

---

1. For some basic guides to these criticisms, see Habel, *Literary Criticism*; McKnight, *What Is Form Criticism?*; Perrin, *What Is Redaction Criticism?*; Porter and Dyer, *Synoptic Problem*; Tucker, *Form Criticism*. See also Allen, *Contemporary Biblical Interpretation*, which recommends use of such criticism for preaching.

These three critical methods are, of course, much more complex, both in theory and in practice, than I am able to present here. However, I do not think any of them offers the best solution to the question of *how* to interpret texts that can be of profit to those concerned with the interpretation and proclamation of God's Word. Therefore, in this chapter I wish to devote attention to the hermeneutical stream that can do more for our needs of interpreting Scripture today. In this chapter, I flesh out this synchronic model and then apply it to the New Testament book of Philemon.

Interpreting the Text in Its World

In this section, I will begin to present an approach to interpretation that starts with the text itself. It may be important later to consider some of the other, larger questions (which may involve source and redaction criticism), but the first priority should be careful linguistic analysis of a given text. The linguistic level of analysis will be assumed when we speak of the level of the text, because a text does not exist without language. A text may conveniently be defined as a stretch of language that can stand on its own, not only as a unit of structure but as a unit of meaning.[2] It is important and fundamental to realize that we access a text through its use of language, but the text itself is a unit of meaning put into the form of language. Therefore, I would advocate a close analysis of whole and entire texts. Of course, individual parts of a text have their own meaning, but we only understand the meaning of a text if we understand the whole of the text.

Every text consists of a *beginning*, a *middle*, and an *end*.[3] This may sound self-evident, and to a large degree this configuration is not something that distinguishes a text per se. Nonetheless, it is a notable feature that is often neglected. To say that a text has a beginning, a middle, and an end is to say that it begins or leads the reader into its world. The text then develops its argument—no matter how abstruse or difficult it may seem on a first reading—and then it concludes and lets the reader return to his or her own world. Any given idea, event, dialogue, statement, or character must be evaluated in terms of the plot—the progression of events—or argument of this complete "story." I use the term *story* consciously—not to imply anything related to fiction or to a text's inherent truth-value but to stress the fact that any given text is involved

2. There is a lot of scholarly discussion about how to define a text or a discourse. These terms are often used interchangeably.

3. This idea of plot structure goes back to Aristotle's *Poetics*. The notion of beginning, middle, and end is found in Aristotle, *Poetics* 1450b27. See Butcher, *Poetics of Aristotle*, 31. On plot in Aristotle, see House, *Aristotle's Poetics*, 43–67.

in storytelling. This story may be a narrative about people and events (such as a Gospel or a historical book of the Old Testament), but it may also be a set of ideas organized in such a way as to be convincing, persuasive, instructive, descriptive, or a combination of these (such as a letter). In other words, a text engaged in the act of storytelling carries the reader through a series of ideas, events, emotions, feelings, or images. This may be something as mundane as a bill of sale, which includes the place of purchase, the amount, and the figures charged, or it may be a short poem, or even such a monumental and multifaceted book as Fyodor Dostoevsky's *Crime and Punishment*, T. S. Eliot's *The Waste Land*, or Marcel Proust's *Remembrance of Things Past*.[4]

This approach can be applied to any written text, and it is designed to get at what any given text is going on about, or what it *means*. An important distinction to make—whether a text is exemplary (such as a Gospel) or didactic (such as a letter)—is between the *narrative world* and the *referential world*.[5] The narrative world is created and exists within the confines of the text, while the referential world is the world that the story may refer to, the outside world or "real" world. One of the first questions that may be raised is what this method does to the truth claims or historicity of Scripture. I believe that this question jumps ahead of where we are at this point in the discussion. The question of historicity certainly has a bearing on interpretation, but it seems premature to evaluate historicity before we know what the individual work is about and what it has to say. It is not always appropriate to ask the question of the truth-value or historicity of an event *before* we appreciate what exactly is going on or being said in the fundamental documents of our faith. The question of historicity is another sort of question than the question of meaning. Both are important questions, but we must begin in the right place in order even to hope to get to a reasonable conclusion.

Once we have established that the Bible, and each individual book within it, is an individual piece of literature to be interpreted, we must ask ourselves how exactly we arrive at determining *meaning*—in this case, the meaning of

4. I select these three texts because each has an interesting textual (diachronic) history, even if we read each one synchronically. As a case in point, we know that the draft manuscript of T. S. Eliot's *The Waste Land* was heavily edited by Ezra Pound and then later published in this edited form. The diachronic history of this monumental poem describing the twentieth-century condition provides much food for thought (regarding not just Eliot's creative brilliance but the highly perceptive editing and rewriting of Pound), but it was Eliot who was the greater poet and won the Nobel Prize. See V. Eliot, *T. S. Eliot*.

5. This distinction, often referred to as the distinction between story and discourse (although there are many other ways of formulating it), goes back to the Russian Formalists of the early part of the twentieth century and has continued in the field of narratology. For an accessible introduction, see Chatman, *Story and Discourse*. Cf. Alter, *Art of Biblical Narrative*; Dinkler, *Literary Theory*; Porter, "Literary Approaches."

the text. We may assume that a text is the author's meaningful expression, but we only have direct access to that meaning—at least for ancient texts—through the language that the author uses. We must interpret the various patterns of language that are used to convey meaning. I prefer to use the phrase "meaningful language patterns" to describe what we find in a text. This recognizes that everything in a written work appears for some reason and exists in relation to every other item in a purposeful way. By *purpose*, I mean that a text is not a series of accidental and random words and that the quest for meaning is, to a large extent, an attempt to make meaningful connections between the individual items in a text so as to decode the meaning found in these expressions of language.

When I discuss meaning, therefore, I am discussing what some of these meaningful patterns may be. I construe the situation in this way to avoid several hazardous pitfalls in interpretation, the most obvious being an over-reliance on the concept of authorial intention. It is commonplace to hear biblical interpreters say that they are seeking to determine what the intention of the original author was. However, I question whether something called "authorial intention"—that is, a specific and determinative intention regarding the purpose or meaning of a written text—can be determined to an extent that is sufficient for interpretation. Even if such an intention does exist, it is questionable whether it is a useful category for interpreting a text, especially an ancient text. Instead, using whichever interpretive model they choose, a scholar will usually look for the meaningful patterns of a work. These meaningful patterns must arise from the work itself. This applies to analysis of the grand structures as well as to the individual statements, which must be interpreted within the context of the larger work.

What features, then, do we look for in a text, including a text of the Bible? A few important features are also commonly discussed in other written literature. These include *plot*, or the unfolding of the action; *setting*, where the location of the story occurs; *point of view*, the vantage point from which the text is conveyed by the authorial voice;[6] *characters*, those people who are mentioned or appear in the story; and related elements such as *dialogue*, where important and sometimes less important ideas are thrown around by the characters; *statements*, where important observations are made by the narrator or teller of the tale and sometimes by the characters; and *structure* or *form*, which is concerned with how a text is organized. These features that are often used in literary analysis are useful for the text-oriented approach

6. This understudied category in biblical studies has recently been developed in Yamasaki, *Perspective Criticism*. In some narratological circles, the term *focalization* has displaced *point of view*. See Bal, *Narratology*, 145–65.

I model below on the text of Philemon. This is because even the letters in the New Testament have an internal logic that we can construe in terms of a narrative world that is distinct from the referential world in which the letter was originally composed. This will become clearer by examining the sample analysis below.

Even though I discounted the value of knowing authorial intention above, admittedly, when we read texts, we know they are created by authors, but these are authors who are always in some way obscured by the persona they put forward in the text. It is one thing to assert that a historical figure stands behind a text, which is self-evident in the idea of textuality (authors create texts; texts, even the Bible, do not come from nowhere), but it is a completely different thing to say that we can necessarily know anything else about the author, such as their specific personality, likes and dislikes, or even their literary pretensions or knowledge that would be determinative for interpretation.

If the author explicitly states some information that seems to indicate his or her purpose, this needs to be considered along with all the other meaningful patterns at hand. Authors of some texts stand more to the front (as does Paul in one of his letters)[7] than do the authors of some other texts (Gospel authors stand in the background, because the Gospels are formally anonymous).[8] When we read, however, regardless of how present or overt the author may be, we are left with a sense that an author is lurking in the background and has a role to play in the meanings we find in the text. The person that we recreate from reading the text is the *implied author*, the author that a particular text implies or indicates or that we can reconstruct. When we read a given text, we also get the impression that the text was addressed to a person or a group of people. This is the *implied audience*. In this sense, every text has at least two characters—an implied author and a projected audience. In many cases, we do not know the original audience and do not entertain any reasonable hope of recreating it. Even if we could, this still would not answer the question of what sort of audience is implied by the text. Every author seems to write with an audience in mind, even if this audience is nothing more than a convenient authorial projection. In summary, within the confines of the text,

---

7. I must acknowledge that there are many interpreters who believe that Paul did not write all the letters attributed to him. I don't accept this view. See Porter, *Apostle Paul*, 156–69, and discussion of the individual disputed letters. However, for those who do believe this, the author who stands to the front of the work is then the represented Paul (pseudepigraphal Paul), and the actual author stands further to the back.

8. Some wish to argue that the authorship of the Gospels would have been known by its original readers through a variety of means, thus giving greater credibility to the traditionally ascribed authors. See Gathercole, "Alleged Anonymity." The authors may have been known, but the Gospels are, nevertheless, formally anonymous, unlike other works, such as Paul's Letters.

it is best to speak of the implied author as the person standing behind the work who seems to arise from the meaningful patterns of the text. And we can speak of the implied audience as the audience that seems to be addressed by the meaningful patterns in the text, whether or not we can actually equate either the audience or the author with some known geographical locale or historic personage.

The practical consequences of this kind of analysis are potentially quite staggering—but in a positive sense. As a matter of fact, we know precious little about most of the authors of the Bible, with the exception, perhaps, of Paul. For example, all four Gospels and Acts are formally anonymous. They are attributed to several authors, but these attributions, even if they may be accurate, arise from later tradition and are not a part of the original documents themselves. And so, we should reconsider whether it is necessary to know the original author and what he (or she?) was like. The same is true for much of the Old Testament. The Pentateuch, for example, has traditionally been attributed to Moses, but this is a result of tradition and is not stated directly in the text. Many of the prophetic and wisdom books are attributed to specific authors, but much of what we know about them comes from the texts themselves. There can be certain benefits of knowing this information, but when it comes to the practice of interpretation, this information is often not available, especially for ancient texts, and it is usually not necessary. Or it is at least not necessary to arrive at a sufficient interpretation. We may wish to know more, but we must be cautious that we faithfully represent the meanings of the text. If we can discover more information, it may be of benefit (we would still need to interpret it and see if it is relevant), but we should at least begin without it. The same can be said for the matter of audience in many cases. For example, we think that we know something about the audience of Paul's Corinthian correspondence, but these letters provide a good example of where the writer perhaps did not judge his audience entirely accurately, hence his subsequent troubles that demanded at least two (and probably more) letters to be written to them.[9] Even this is a recreated audience based on the text, which sets the limits for reconstruction and interpretation.

The Evaluation of Interpretations

Before turning to analysis of a text, we must ask a final question: How do we evaluate any given interpretation? This is one of the most crucial questions in interpretation. When I was a student, both undergraduate and graduate,

9. See Porter, *Apostle Paul*, 244–90.

my professors seemed to know almost instinctively what differentiated a good student paper from a bad one, or at least they marked my papers as if they did. When I became a professor, I discovered that determining the worth of a paper was far more complex than I had ever imagined. I realized that *right* and *wrong* or even *good* and *bad* are probably not the proper terms to use, since most had at least some redeeming value, and very few were so well done as to solicit no questions or response (though there are always exceptions!). I determined that the best way to evaluate an essay was to say that, within a given context, the better reading was one that was inclusive, sharable, and effective.[10] What does all this mean for interpretation?

Before I turn to these three terms—*inclusive, sharable,* and *effective*—I wish to emphasize the word *context*. The word *context* is one that is bandied about in hermeneutical and interpretive circles. Interpreters often speak of the importance of context, by which they usually mean interpreting elements of a text in relationship to other immediate elements in the text or the wider extratextual situation. Such regard for context is important. However, another notion of context is at least as important. A particular interpretation is always done in terms of a given context of interpretation by an interpreter. If I as an English literature teacher asked for a paper on the word choice of a particular poet and then received a paper on her rhythm and rhyme, or even on another poet's word choice, that would not be a proper paper for that context. The same criterion exists for biblical interpretation. Biblical interpretation is done within the context of the need for a particular kind of interpretation. In this book, for instance, I am stressing interpretation for a pastoral context (of preaching and possibly teaching). The kind of interpretation I am stressing may not be suitable for an academic context concerned with some of the more traditional questions of source and origin mentioned briefly above. I am presenting a means for interpretation for those in a context that calls for preaching and teaching of the Bible.

Context, however, is not enough. To evaluate an interpretation, we must also pay attention to three other factors in particular. These factors are important because they help to identify communities of interpreters that endorse similar conclusions when engaging in textual interpretation.[11] First, the interpretation must treat all the relevant data—that is, it must be *inclusive*. If an interpretation leaves out a major or significant element, then the interpretation must be called into question for failing to address all the relevant questions.

10. Armstrong, "Conflict of Interpretations," esp. 346–48.
11. This observation was central to the descriptive reader-response theory of Stanley Fish. See Fish, *Is There a Text?*, 15–16. One need not endorse his reader-based approach to acknowledge that interpreters with similar views tend to form groups or communities of interpretation.

For example, if in interpreting the prologue in John 1:1–18, the interpreter fails to note the important use of the abstract term *the word* (ὁ λόγος, *ho logos*), not *Jesus* or *Christ*, until the animation of "the word became flesh" (ὁ λόγος σὰρξ ἐγένετο, *ho logos sarx egeneto*) in verse 14, their interpretation has failed to address a crucial piece of information that is part of the meaningful patterns in this opening section of John's Gospel. Or to be more obvious, if the interpreter emphasizes only that the use of *logos* represents a Semitic concept (equivalent to a Hebrew word) or that *logos* represents a Greek philosophical concept (equivalent to reason) and hence fails to consider how their interpretation of the use of *logos* addresses the question of Semitic *and* Greek uses of the word, their reading is incomplete and fails to be inclusive.

Second, an interpretation must be *sharable*—in other words, the results cannot be merely one's personal, subjective, and/or incommunicable findings. These findings may be true and sufficient for the individual involved, but they are not an interpretation if they cannot be discussed by others. They may be inspiring and even meaningful to the interpreter, but they must also be sharable and accessible to others. They must be able to be articulated and explained based on the meaningful patterns in the text so that others may see these patterns as well and examine them for themselves, even if they do not agree with everything that has been said. The shareability of these results often identifies interpretive communities on the basis of what they agree or disagree with in a given interpretation.

Third, an interpretation must be *effective*. Another way of looking at this is that the interpretation must be persuasive to others, not just to the interpreter. In other words, an interpretation must say something that evokes a response, preferably a response that accepts at least elements of the interpretation and generates further creative and productive discussion. Few, if any, interpretations should be considered final, decisive, or beyond further review, even if immediately persuasive. Perhaps the response will be in the form of other interpretations that sort out the meaningful patterns in a slightly different way, but sometimes it will be nothing more than an indication of where this interpretation fails to consider all the relevant patterns. An interpretation that merely restates what is already known is not an interpretation worth much further consideration as it adds nothing new to our knowledge of the text.

Interpreting the Book of Philemon

To aid in discussing these concepts more fully, I will now turn to the book of Philemon. Why Philemon? I have selected Philemon because it is a short book that illustrates that much more can be gleaned from a text, even a short one, than one might imagine. Philemon is one of Paul's less read and studied epistles, even though several commentaries have recently been written on this short book.[12] One of the reasons for this relative under-interpretation is that Philemon appears to be so *occasional* in nature. In other words, it was addressed to a specific personal situation, one that many critics have argued does not have terribly significant, widespread application—especially when compared with Romans, Galatians, or the like. In subsequent chapters, I will demonstrate how Philemon, in many ways, not only presents the ideal text for learning the craft of literary interpretation but contains some very important discussion of Christian theological concepts, arguably some of the most important in the New Testament. Rather than thoroughly examining the text at every point, I will focus my analysis so as to encourage further examination of this important, and often undervalued, letter.

The first noticeable characteristic of Philemon is that it is a *letter*. This kind of literature is widespread in the New Testament, not only in the Pauline writings, which are all letters, but elsewhere in the New Testament. There is a reason for this: letters were important texts in the Greco-Roman world in which the New Testament was written. An ongoing debate in biblical scholarship focuses on whether the letters of the New Testament are simply occasional letters of no literary value (even if they are of other value), like many of the letters found in the documentary papyri of Egypt, or whether they follow the conventions of more literary epistolary writing. I believe this is a largely misconceived debate, since it presupposes a fixed definition of what constitutes literature. Attempting to answer questions of this nature is hopeless if the criteria include such things as the "quality" of writing, whatever that may mean, or some preselected topic or audience. I prefer a more functional criterion, based on the culture in which a text is produced. Works of literature are cultural artifacts and have their place based on their cultural function. The same is true of the writings of the New Testament. Works were included in the New Testament for many reasons, and one question that is helpful in determining their status is, Does it work? Does the text not just grab the reader but also do what it does effectively? Paul's Letters certainly qualify as literature in that they are effective. A second debate is about the role of literary *genre*. This too is an important discussion with many ramifications. I will discuss this in some detail in the next chapter. At this point, however, we need simply to recognize that Paul's writing called "Philemon" was a letter,

---

12. In the discussion that follows in this chapter, as well as throughout the rest of this book when discussing Philemon, I draw on an excellent book by Petersen, *Rediscovering Paul*. For basic issues about Philemon, see Porter, *Apostle Paul*, 375–84.

written by Paul to its recipients, using a genre or form of literature widely known in the ancient world.

As a letter, it has a beginning, a middle, and an end. Many scholars have noticed that all of Paul's Letters seem to share a common style: an *opening*, where the author introduces himself (and possibly a co-sender) and his recipients and greets them; an opening *thanksgiving*, where Paul gives thanks for his recipients (noticeably missing—intentionally—from Galatians, where Paul immediately begins a defense of his apostleship, and from 1 Timothy, but for other reasons); the *body* of the letter, divided into several different sections according to his subject matter; a *teaching section*, where he offers instruction to his recipients (this section is missing from some of the Pauline Letters, such as Philemon, but also 2 Timothy); and a *closing*, usually including final greetings.

Philemon purports to be written by Paul and his ministry companion Timothy (several of the Pauline Letters are written by co-senders: 1 and 2 Corinthians, Philippians, Colossians, and 1 and 2 Thessalonians). This letter is addressed to Philemon (v. 2), "our beloved and fellow worker" (τῷ ἀγαπητῷ καὶ συνεργῷ ἡμῶν, *tō agapētō kai synergō hēmōn*); Apphia, his sister; and Archippus, a fellow worker; as well as the church that meets in Philemon's house. What kind of way is this to introduce a letter? Is this letter meant personally for Philemon and the others, who will then share it with the church, or is it to the church, of which Philemon and the others are prominent leaders, since it probably meets in Philemon's house? In any case, we are already introduced to at least three characters in the story besides Paul and Timothy. "Christ Jesus" (v. 1) and "Jesus Christ" (emphasized again in v. 3) are also introduced in the opening. Is this significant? This invocation, no matter how stereotyped in a Christian letter, is quite important, since it not only establishes who is involved in this correspondence but sets the ground rules for the content that follows. Several other terms arise in the opening that may provide material for further reflection, such as "the church based in your house" (τῇ κατ᾽ οἶκόν σου ἐκκλησίᾳ, *tē kat oikon sou ekklēsia*)—a phrase that may provide insight into the early structure of the Christian church and its meeting places.[13]

The plot of the letter continues with an expression of thanks for Philemon's love and faith. Paul is quite clear that he constantly remembers Philemon in his prayers, that he has heard of Philemon's love and faith toward the Lord Jesus and all the saints, and that he has much joy and comfort in knowledge of Philemon's Christian life. Several terms jump out for exploration: *prayer*

13. However, we must also now recognize that early Christian gatherings occurred not only in houses but in a variety of other places.

(προσευχή, *proseuchē*), *love* (ἀγάπη, *agapē*), *faith* (πίστις, *pistis*), *saints* (ἅγιοι, *hagioi*), *knowledge* (ἐπίγνωσις, *epignōsis*), *joy* (χαρά, *chara*), and *comfort* (παράκλησις, *paraklēsis*). Each term is written using the Greek of Paul's time, even if each seems to have Christian connotations here based on the letter's context (not the words themselves). Paul has clearly chosen to focus his attention almost exclusively on Philemon, and he has only good things to say about him.

Philemon 8 changes this mood completely. Therefore, "in Christ" (ἐν Χριστῷ, *en Christō*) Paul claims the authority to command Philemon to do "the fitting thing" (τὸ ἀνῆκον, *to anēkon*).[14] We might wonder what Paul refers to by this "fitting thing," and we might also wonder whether Philemon would have known right away what Paul meant. However, instead of explicitly demanding what he wants, Paul chooses to approach Philemon more strategically, adding (in v. 9) that he is an "old man" (πρεσβύτης, *presbytēs*) and now a "prisoner of Christ Jesus" (δέσμιος Χριστοῦ Ἰησοῦ, *desmios Christou Iēsou*). What are we to make of this? Does Paul say that he could order Philemon to do the fitting thing because he expects him to resist? Why does Paul switch from giving him a simple command to an elaborately hedged request? Or is this not really a request? Why the acknowledgment that he is now an old man and a prisoner? Does this not reduce his authority?

Paul continues by saying that he is asking on behalf of his child Onesimus, whom he begot in prison. This would have been a shocking statement on its own, but Paul adds that Onesimus was "useless" (ἄχρηστος, *achrēstos*) to Philemon but is now "useful" (εὔχρηστος, *euchrēstos*) to Paul and Philemon, and that Paul has sent Onesimus—his very emotional support (his heart)—to Philemon.[15] Paul wanted to keep him so that he might help him

---

14. The spherical use of the Greek preposition ἐν (*en*), translated "in," in connection with "Christ" (Χριστῷ, *Christō*) plays a key grammatical function in understanding the relationship of someone "in Christ." The spherical function of ἐν can be defined as something or someone who "may be located within the sphere of influence, control or domain of another or larger group ('in'), the same way that one object or person may be within the confines of another" (Porter, *Idioms*, 157). While the spherical use is "a direct extension of the locative sense" (157), the special case of ἐν Χριστῷ may suggest a "corporate mystical union between the believer and Christ" (159). A simple explanation of Paul's use of the prepositional phrase ("in Christ" or "with Christ") is that "one is in the sphere of Christ's control" (159). Paul's ability to command Philemon is directly related to his position "in Christ." And yet, love is the basis of his appeal (διὰ τὴν ἀγάπην, *dia tēn agapēn*), where the accusative case suggests the causal use of the preposition διά.

15. The two words, "useless" and "useful," have the same stem, indicating the notion of making use of something. The word with a negative prefix indicates "useless" (ἄχρηστος, *achrēstos*) and a positive prefix indicates "useful" (εὔχρηστος, *euchrēstos*). What is often translated as "heart" (σπλάγχνον, *splanchnon*) is literally the entrails, bowels, or inward parts of the body, which served as the source of emotion in the ancient world. Cf. BDAG, s.v. "σπλάγχνον."

in prison but says that he was constrained by not wanting to do anything apart from Philemon's knowledge (and probably because he did not want to be harboring a runaway slave, if that is who Onesimus is), so that Philemon's anticipated and suggested good deed would not be based on necessity but on his willingness.

The middle of Paul's letter is quite complex and has led to many different interpretations of what exactly Paul is saying. He has begotten a child in prison, a child who was previously of no use to Philemon but who is now useful, who can be a blessing to both Paul and Philemon. Paul wants to keep this child with him in prison, but he is returning him so that Philemon will do his good deed out of a sense of desire. Knowing that the word for "beget" (γεννάω, gennaō) not only can indicate a physical birth (which is not the sense here, not least because Onesimus would only be an infant!) but can be contextually extended to a spiritual birth, we can start piecing together this puzzle. Paul has helped a man in his spiritual birth, or, rather, Paul is the spiritual father of this new child in Christ, yet this man has a previous obligation to Philemon. Is Paul being cautious for a reason? We need more information.

Paul speculates that perhaps Philemon and Onesimus were separated for a while so that Philemon might have him eternally, no longer as a slave but as a beloved brother. This is the same relationship Paul enjoys with Onesimus. Thus at this late place in the letter (v. 16), Paul finally makes his most important move. Even though Onesimus seems to be a runaway slave who has providentially found his way to Paul, Paul wants Philemon to receive Onesimus on the same relational level as he receives Paul himself: as a brother in Christ! This section (vv. 8–16) falls within the body of the letter (vv. 8–22) and is full of intriguing items for us to observe and seek to understand. The first and most obvious is the subtle pattern of argument. After praising Philemon grandly, Paul asserts his authority but then quickly backs off from it and shifts to a more intimate metaphor of the birthing process. He then makes several moral judgments before making outright reference to the heart of the problem. Second, several significant terms are worth studying in their linguistic and larger context: *beget* (γεννάω, gennaō), *heart* or *emotion* (σπλάγχνον, *splanchnon*), *the gospel* (τὸ εὐαγγέλιον, *to euangelion*), and perhaps most importantly *slave* (δοῦλος, *doulos*). Third, the use of the term *slave* introduces a whole host of sociological questions. Of course, every letter and every piece of literature is a study in sociology, since it is concerned with the textual world of personal relations and the referential world of people, social institutions, and their interactions. A reference to slavery introduces a major question about the entire social makeup of the first-century world and the relationship of this letter to it. From Paul's Letter to Philemon, it may be difficult to reconstruct much about this world, certainly since this may not be a typical case. However, at the very least, it provides a starting point based in the relationships of specific individuals who have textually defined roles to play.[16]

Paul clinches his argument with several brief and terse conditional statements. A conditional statement is one in which the first part poses a presupposition and the second part gives its logical conclusion. Paul says that "*if* you, Philemon, have anything in common with me, *then* receive Onesimus as you would me; and *if* he owes you anything, *then* charge this to my account" (vv. 17–18; my translation). In both cases, Paul takes personal responsibility for Philemon's reception of Onesimus. Philemon is pressured by Paul's denial of his claimed authority (that he could have used) to ask Philemon to receive Onesimus as he would Paul. Then Paul says that if Onesimus has done anything wrong or incurred a financial debt, he will pay it in his stead. And here is the clinching argument: Paul says that he (and he writes this in his own hand) will pay, and, "Oh yes, by the way, don't forget that you owe your very self to me" (v. 19; my translation).[17] Indeed, Paul says, "You owe your life in the Lord to me, brother, so now return this small favor to me" (cf. v. 20). Such a claim can hardly be contradicted. Paul too believes his argument is compelling, saying that he writes in the conviction that Philemon will obey. His confidence extends to requesting that Philemon prepare a room in the hope that he will be able to come. Could this be a subtle, or perhaps not so subtle, way of saying that Paul will check up on Philemon should he be in the area? Paul has indicated that he is himself a prisoner at this time, but does Philemon dare take a chance that this is an idle threat on Paul's part?

I do not think it an understatement to say that Paul's Letter to Philemon hits at a deep personal level on some significant issues. The first is the personal relationship between Paul the apostle (this is not actually stated in

16. The situation of Onesimus is highly unusual, since he is a converted slave of an already Christian master. Nevertheless, slavery in the Roman world was extremely prevalent. Joshel, in reference to the previous estimates of Scheidel, estimates that as many as six million of the sixty million persons living in the Roman Empire were slaves. This estimate can fluctuate depending on geography and chronology. Joshel observes that "by the late first century BCE, in Roman Italy, the heartland of the Empire, slaves numbered 1 to 1.5 million out of a population of 5 to 6 million, or about 20–30 per cent" (Joshel, *Slavery in the Roman World*, 8). And although the "total number of Roman slaves is completely unknown," the six million (empire-wide) estimate is a symbolic yet reliable one (Scheidel, "Progress and Problems," in *Debating Roman Demography*, 61). Without minimizing the unique nature of this letter, the sociological situation of Onesimus was very common.

17. Verse 18 is reminiscent of many letters from the Hellenistic world in which the author would take the pen from the scribe and put his own hand to the letter as a form of authentication.

the letter but is inferred from v. 8) and a man of some importance in one of the congregations with which he has had contact and to which he feels an obligation.[18] How are they to compare their spiritual relationship, in which Philemon is obviously indebted for his spiritual existence to Paul, with a social and financial relationship, which is of this world? Second, questions regarding social institutions, such as slavery, are raised. The typical view of the New Testament is that it does not call into question social problems such as slavery (or limitations on the role of women). This is not the place to discuss these wider issues, but we can see in Paul's argument here that Paul is laying the groundwork for the dissolution of slavery without calling for a slave revolt—at least within the church—when Christian masters treat their Christian slaves as brothers or sisters in Christ, with all the redemptive implications that that implies. Third, crucial theological questions come to mind at this point—and rightly they should—but these will be discussed later. For now, it is important to set out the issues raised directly in the text itself. The fourth issue is the order of argument and the sequence of events referred to. Literary works, including biblical texts such as this one, often relate the events in a different order than they occurred.

The difference between the events in the narrative world of Philemon and the events within the referential world may be plotted as shown in table 1:

Table 1: Sequence of Events

Verse	Narrative World	Event #	Referential World
verses 4–7	I hear of your love and faith.	5	Paul hears of Philemon's faith.
verse 9	I am now a prisoner.	2	Paul is imprisoned.
verse 10	I have become Onesimus's father.	4	Paul converts Onesimus.
verse 12	I am sending him back to you.	6	Paul sends Onesimus back to Philemon.
verse 15	Onesimus is parted from Philemon.	3	Onesimus runs away from Philemon.
verses 17–19a	Receive him, charge it to my account, and I will repay it.	7	Philemon receives Onesimus back.
verse 19b	You owe me.	1	Paul converts Philemon.
verses 20–21	I am awaiting your response.	8	Paul awaits Philemon's response.
verse 22	I hope to visit you.	9	Paul visits Philemon.

Note: This chart is taken from Petersen, *Rediscovering Paul*, 69, with supplements from 70, 71, with some modifications. The referential event numbers indicate the order of events within the referential world and do not necessarily correlate with the sequence of events in the narrative world.

18. Acts does not say this, but there is a chance that Paul even visited Colossae on his second missionary journey while he was ministering in Ephesus.

The sequence of events in the narrative world of the Letter to Philemon is quite different from the sequence of events in the referential world. What difference does this make? How vital to the telling of the story is it that Paul consciously alters this arrangement? How much of the alteration is required by the conventions of letter writing or other conventions he is using? How does this help us learn about significant concepts at play in the letter? I would suggest that this chart makes apparent several things about the relationship between literature and life.

First, literature is not a copy of life, nor is it a perfect mirror. Let us assume—and I think there are good reasons for this assumption—that Philemon is a letter that accurately reflects a historical situation. This situation involves Paul, Philemon, Onesimus, their relationships, Onesimus's conversion, Philemon's being a Christian, and so on. Paul feels free to select items from that referential world, order them, arrange them, balance them, even delete some of them, and then relate them to communicate with Philemon. Paul does this to create the argument he wants Philemon to hear. That he does this has interesting consequences for interpreting other biblical texts and reflects an ongoing debate among historians about the nature of history writing. The upshot of that debate is the recognition that history is not an uninterpreted record of the past but an interpreted and narrated construct that attempts to capture and describe what happened.

Second, the comparison of the two worlds of discourse shows that Paul feels free to make what he thinks are his best arguments. He makes the arguments on his own terms, using the facts as he sees them and knows them. As we see from the letter itself, he also wants Philemon to accept his arguments.

Third, note that the last three events in the narrative world and events 7–9 in the referential world are hypothetical in both worlds. Paul postulates them as facts for the sake of formulating and guiding the sequence his letter puts forward. We should be aware that we have no idea from the letter itself whether the last three events of the narrative world and events 7–9 of the referential world ever occurred or whether they occurred in any way close to how Paul envisioned them. An unstated assumption is that the letter did in fact make it to Philemon and that it was successful, because it is preserved in our canonical New Testament. But the text itself does not say this.

Fourth, the significant turning points in the plot of the letter indicate important concepts dealt with in the letter, such as the nature of human relationships, slavery, Christian love and obligation, and Christian mutuality. If we were to dig even further into the letter, other concepts would also appear.

Finally, Paul closes the letter (vv. 23–25) with greetings to several coworkers, finishing with the verbless clause, a benediction, "the grace of the Lord

Jesus Christ [be] with your spirit" (ἡ χάρις τοῦ κυρίου Ἰησοῦ Χριστοῦ μετὰ τοῦ πνεύματος ὑμῶν, *hē charis tou kyriou Iēsou Christou meta tou pneumatos hymōn*) (v. 25; my translation). Paul thus rounds off his letter with somewhat similar language to that with which he began, providing a complete and meaningful closure.

Much of what I have mentioned during this interpretive description of Philemon may seem rather commonplace. In fact, my analysis may resemble the kind of thing any reasonably intelligent reader would have gathered if he or she had taken the time to read the book straight through, paying attention to some matters of detail, and enhanced by some knowledge of Greek and some other matters of context. This would be correct. I wished to do nothing more than show that it is essential in understanding a literary text, especially a text of the Bible, to concentrate on the level of text itself, since it is my strong conviction that anything else that the text may mean or do grows out of an appreciation of the intricacies and nuances of the text. These are the meaningful patterns that I referred to above. Too often in biblical studies, scholars are anxious to make a quantum leap to the "weightier" matters of sources, history, or theology, without fully appreciating that much of the value and effectiveness of a text is in the way it presents its argument.

Study and Practice

As a personal exercise to practice the principles discussed in this chapter, I suggest reading through and considering the following three passages of Scripture: Romans 5:12–21, Acts 17:16–34, and Psalm 23. Perform on these texts the same kind of textual analysis I have modeled. Read through each passage a couple of times—possibly in different translations, to make yourself aware of points of tension (if you are not able to read the original biblical languages)—before formulating a list of items from each passage that present themselves as interesting for or in need of further investigation. These items may be people, places, concepts, questions about tricky grammar and phrasing—whatever observations seem important or call for more work. So, for example, on Acts 17, one might note the Areopagus (v. 19) as a place that one would need to know more about to understand the passage. One might make a similar note about the statue to the "unknown God." Then, make a list of observations at the level of text, including plot, characters, and the other concepts outlined in this chapter. Finally, attempt to create an outline of events in the narrative world, possibly even contrasting it with events in the referential world.

Conclusion

Much, much more can be said about interpretation at the level of text. That is why I continue discussion of the level of text in the next chapter. However, at this point enough has been laid out to show the fundamental starting point of the hermeneutics of interpretation. Interpretation must begin with attention to the text. Traditional criticism of the Bible begins with questions of source, form, or redaction criticism. These are important for what they are, but they are often not what one needs when attempting to understand the meaning of a text. I suggest that we must first attend to the level of text and observe and describe the meaningful patterns within the text. I have attempted to draw occasional parallels between interpretation of the Bible and interpretation of literature. This is not because I believe that the Bible is simply another literary text but because the same kind of ability that is developed in critically reading a work of literature can be applied to the text of the Bible. The level of text is a necessary starting point for intelligent reading of the Bible because it identifies the major literary features of the text, from questions of genre to basic questions about what constitutes a text (its plot, characters, setting, and so forth) to observations about the argument of the text as it is presented, often in contrast to the world outside the text. These all constitute meaningful patterns that form the basis of an informed and useful reading of the text. Some of these further levels of reading will be explored in subsequent chapters.

5

Hermeneutics at the Level of Text: Part 2

Introduction

In the previous chapter, we began our investigation of hermeneutics at the level of text. Part 1 was concerned with some basic questions about how texts function. I brought up the question of genre and will continue to discuss it in this chapter because it is an important topic that requires further examination. However, I also discussed some of the basics of reading a literary text. Even if we do not think of the texts of the Bible as "literary texts" in the same way that we think of Charles Dickens's novels or Robert Frost's poetry as literary texts, we can learn some basic ways of reading such texts that help us understand the Bible. The Bible is a literary text—and has been studied as such for many years, inside and outside of literature departments—and so must be examined as at least a literary text, whatever else we think of it. Therefore, some of the important ways that we approach other literature will help us become better interpreters of the Bible as well. This chapter continues the discussion of reading the Bible at the level of text.

The Question of Literary Genre

Before continuing the discussion of Philemon and subsequent levels of interpretive reading, I would like to address one topic that is often of concern to interpreters: *literary genre*. It might seem perplexing that I have not introduced this topic much earlier, since genre is important for understanding how a text functions. In fact, several introductory books on hermeneutics frame their entire discussion in terms of answering the question of genre.[1] By the end of this discussion, the reason for this delay will become clear. Let me begin with a disclaimer: I am not going to define specifically what a genre is until I am further into this chapter. This is because the interpretive issues involving genre are, to a large extent, tied up with what *genre* means. I am going to concentrate on the issue of the genre of the Gospels since this is a highly contested question (the Letters of the New Testament are much more straightforward in that regard at least). There have been many different proposals as to the genre of the Gospels: ancient biography, tragedy, myth, history, novel, romance, or Old Testament heroic tales, among others. Others have proposed that they are uniquely Gospels.[2] Those familiar with the debate will know that none of the answers being offered is completely satisfactory and none has satisfied all scholars.

Throughout the history of genre study there have been essentially two major approaches to genre: *prescriptive* and *descriptive*.[3] To summarize them very briefly, the prescriptive approach argues from specific generic categories to individual works, while the descriptive approach argues from the individual works to establishing generic categories.

The Prescriptive Approach to Literary Genre

Taking an essentially prescriptive approach, the literary critic E. D. Hirsch has argued forcefully for what he calls "intrinsic genres" on the basis of the fact that a speaker or writer is able to put one word after another only if his or her choices are governed by what he calls a "controlling conception." This idea of a controlling conception also applies to the reader, who understands the sentences of a work based on his or her conception of the underlying intrinsic genre.[4] In several ways this is an appealing proposal since it makes interpretation rather easy. All an interpreter must do is grasp which controlling concept is at play, and then they can immediately move on to interpreting the work.

---

1. See Klein, Blomberg, and Hubbard, *Introduction to Biblical Interpretation*, 417–567; Corley, Lemke, and Lovejoy, *Biblical Hermeneutics*, 243–354; Fee and Stuart, *How to Read the Bible for All Its Worth*.
2. The list of categories used to talk about the Gospels is apparently nearly endless. See Burridge, *What Are the Gospels?*
3. For a more detailed examination of specific issues at hand in contemporary discussions of genre, see Bawarshi and Reiff, *Genre*, 11–104; Frow, *Genre*.
4. Hirsch, *Validity in Interpretation*, 78–89.

However, there are several problems with this method and, by extension, with most prescriptive approaches to genre: (1) this approach makes the intrinsic genre dictatorial—that is, the governing interpretive category—for both text and reader, as well as for meaning itself;[5] (2) it draws a false dichotomy or opposition between interpretation on the basis of expectation and complete anarchy of interpretation as its alternative, when it is entirely possible to conceive of other, intermediary positions; (3) it devalues the individual text in the process of identifying its intrinsic genre; and (4) as a result, the prescriptive approach distances the interpretive process from its object of interpretation, the text.

While the prescriptive approach does make us aware that the human mind often thinks by using categories, whether these categories have any sort of fundamental and/or independent significance, as this approach seems to imply (at least in places), is questionable. In other words, we should consider whether genres are better described as categories that are defined for the occasion of interpretation at hand and then applied to written works. After all, few scholars wish to employ purely prescriptive terms, which are based on the genres in use at the time of a work's writing, since a reconstruction of these genres cannot be determined with any degree of certainty in many instances and results in admittedly odd sets of categories. Moreover, these categories are often highly idiosyncratic, and they result in a treatment artificially limited by the hypothetical and reconstructed understanding of a previous era. We can do better than that in discussion of genre.

The Descriptive Approach to Literary Genre

In practice, while many scholars would probably recognize that there is value in being aware of the genres used in the past, most find the prescriptive approach unworkable because of historical distance, the limited number of categories to choose from, and a sense that deduction—that is, application of principles to a specific case—assumes too much. Many scholars therefore believe that they must employ a descriptive method, working from individual texts to generalizing statements, thereby treating genres as *descriptive*

5. Wimsatt provides an extension of this critique: "Hirsch thinks he can keep the 'genre' apart from each work but close enough so that he can operate a rule that correct interpretation depends on knowing the genre. I doubt that he can. I think that in all broader (and usual) senses of the term 'genre' we discover the genre of a work by being able to read it, and not vice versa" (*Day of the Leopards*, 191–92). As an example of Hirsch's error in determining genre in advance, Wimsatt describes a small slab of stone apparently commemorating the death of an animal obtained in a lottery and giving no date of birth; the purpose of this inscription could be known only after careful reading of the text.

patternings of literature rather than regulative norms. The term that is sometimes used in such genre studies is *constellation*, meaning that a genre represents a constellation of literary properties, including both content (which
includes function) and form.[6] Proponents of the descriptive method contend
that genres do not remain fixed but that categories shift on the basis of the
works requiring description and classification.[7] As one important treatment
of the topic has said, "Theory of genres is a principle of order; it classifies
literature . . . not by time or place (period or national language) but by specifically literary types of organization or structure,"[8] to which we should
probably add meaning and function. The poet and literary scholar T. S. Eliot
helps account for the apparent continuity in literature from both the writer's
and reader's viewpoint by arguing that literature is a matter of historical
tradition: "No poet, no artist of an art, has his complete meaning alone."
When an artist writes a new work, the "whole existing order must be, ever
so slightly, altered."[9] This artistic orientation accounts for both conformity
and change within the old and new.

The Specificity of the Term **Genre**

What does the term *genre* cover? For illustrative purposes, let's consider
form criticism of the Gospels, a technique I mentioned in the previous chapter.
Certain form critics have made concerted efforts to define the genre of the
Gospels, but they have begun with certain presuppositions about the set forms
used by the biblical writers and the relation of these formal units not only to
the creative process of writing itself but also to the final written product. The
first distinction to make, therefore, is to define *forms* as particular, discrete
literary units distinguished based on their structural (or formal) characteristics (though undoubtedly their content and function will come into play).
This is not sufficient, however, even for discussing these individual forms, as
the forms themselves are based on content, such as stories about miracles or
sayings of Jesus.

Although form critics want to speak of the Gospels as compilations of
various forms, redaction criticism (also mentioned in the previous chapter)
has shown that each Gospel (and hence each genre) is more than the sum

6. For a good introduction to genre within biblical studies, see J. Brown, "Genre Criticism."
7. In other words, an absolute set of genre categories does not exist. The genre categories
we use vary based on the works needing description. If we have a particular set of texts that
we wish to place together, we'll find a genre label for them.
8. Wellek and Warren, *Theory of Literature*, 235.
9. T. S. Eliot, "Tradition and the Individual Talent."

of its individual formal units. As one critic states, *form* refers to "the small individual units representing the material out of which the literary work is composed," while *genre* is "a category for classifying literary works as a whole."[10] The notion of a text as a whole implies not just structure but meaning and, with it, function. This is the definition I would like to endorse for the present.

Now we must also ask, What is the nature of a genre per se? The history of genre discussion, the methods of generic classification, the distinction of *genre* from *form*, and the criticism of previous attempts—all of these factors seem to indicate that, certainly for the Gospels but also for other texts, a genre must consist of both an overall structure (related to its individual forms in the case of the Gospels) and a functional content based on its meaningful patterns. A well-known truism of literary criticism is that form cannot be spoken of apart from content, but this also points to the difficulty of defining *form*. If genre study is going to be used as a tool to enhance understanding of the Gospels or any other biblical text, its terms must be defined and its procedures carefully spelled out so that the results do indeed prove helpful. For example, the Greek philosopher Aristotle's basic genres may prove helpful in labeling the Gospels as more tragic than comic (or is it the reverse, since the hero comes back to life?), but interpreters may well find it necessary to be more precise. If so, we need criteria that allow us to distinguish clearly between the tragic heroes of classical drama and the Jesus of the Gospels.

Seven Criteria for Determining the Genre of Biblical Books

This discussion leads us to ask, How might one go about analyzing the genre of biblical texts, such as the Gospels, or any other text? Seven criteria must be considered in discussion of genre. There may be other criteria, but these should provide sufficient orientation to be useful for interpretation of texts in this and subsequent chapters.

1. The text must be recognized as an object worthy of examination. This is not to say that other written documents may not be examined and their genres even determined, but we often associate genre with texts of significance—that is, ones with features that merit further examination and interpretation. These features are often related to content but may also relate to structure and social function, as well as aesthetic considerations.

10. J. Baird, "Genre Analysis," 386–88.

2. The text must be examined and interpreted according to the method discussed in chapter 4; that is, we must gain as full an appreciation as possible for the meaningful patterns within the given text.

3. A concentration on sources and directions of dependence, which were mentioned in the previous chapter, may be interesting but is of little value for questions of meaning as we are concerned with in this book.[11]

4. Genre is best seen as a descriptive category that determines the specific level of discussion for a grouping of literary works with similar formal and functional properties.

5. It seems almost certain that the question of genre can never be dogmatically decided to everyone's satisfaction, but that is because it is a functional and descriptive means of classification, not an absolute one.

6. Each historical period must weigh and evaluate the work done by previous generations, define its concept of genre and its specific genres, and then put forward its own account of the discussion.

7. Interpreters must be prepared for the possibility of arriving at very different conclusions, not only among themselves but individually, regarding the genre of individual works of literature. A similar situation is found in zoology, where the "tongue worm," so I am told, may be categorized either as a worm, like the earthworm, or as a mite, like spiders. For the sake of discussion, it must be put in one of these categories, though it conforms in some ways to both and in all ways to neither. The situation will determine how it is classified.

With these ideas in mind, let me return to the Gospels, although we might use other books just as well (most of them not nearly as controversial). It should first be noted that the four Gospels can be characterized as narrative in literary mode. As obvious as this may seem, the Gospels and similar literature may be distinguished from that which is non-narrative, perhaps like some poetry or strictly teaching or expository material, and certainly a letter (even if a letter has narrative features, as discussed in chap. 4). The importance of this difference is found in the reader's expectations for narrative versus nonnarrative writing. In narrative, a reader might expect to find a certain kind of progression, based on some motivation (like time or character),

11. The area of intertextuality must be mentioned here. By this, I mean not simply the use of the Old Testament in the New Testament (the way that the term is usually, and unfortunately mistakenly, defined in New Testament studies) but the complex way in which all language is a pastiche of other language, so that there are intertextual uses always at play within literature. This topic merits a much more detailed and extended discussion at another time and place.

from a recognizable beginning point to an end, by way of the story or narrative sequence.[12] Each of the Gospel narratives has such a configuration of beginning, middle, and end. All three of these elements warrant the analysis they are receiving in recent scholarly literature, although much more work remains to be done. I will deal with a few of these topics by way of example.

Though they have much in common, when the narratives of the Gospels are examined, we note that their beginnings differ. Matthew's Gospel begins with a genealogy (Matt. 1:1–17), which is a significant difference from the other Gospels, while Luke opens with a short, distinctive literary prologue (Luke 1:1–4) with details about his audience, sources, predecessors, and general approach. Both Gospels then move on to birth narratives of Jesus, although even here each is distinct. Luke prefaces his version with an account of John the Baptist's birth (Luke 1:5–25) and includes, among other things, two hymns or songs (1:46–55; 1:67–79), while Matthew, alluding to the story of Moses, uses specific Old Testament quotations to signify their fulfillment in the infancy narrative of Jesus (Matt. 1:23; 2:6; 2:15; 2:18). Mark and John are also significantly different. Mark begins with a brief prologue that relates Jesus's ministry to John the Baptist and the fulfillment of Old Testament prophecy (Mark 1:1–3). Thus, Mark cannot be considered an account of the entire span of Jesus's life, although this does not necessarily mean it cannot be considered biographical. John goes back even further in his account, relating the events surrounding Jesus's life to the *logos* (John 1:1–18). As I intimated in the previous chapter, much could be said about the *logos* and how the *logos* is ultimately manifested in flesh in John's Gospel. Most commentaries say something about this dimension.[13] John's description leads smoothly, albeit ambiguously, into his description of John the Baptist, and, like Mark, he begins relating Jesus's life at the beginning of his ministry.

The second distinctive feature to note is that the Gospels are about people, characters who have human traits. I have formulated this in a particularly vague way, but for now let me describe the major actors in these narratives as being humanlike. Some are more fully developed characters than others, to the point that we believe that we know them as they are presented, while others are flatter and without the same dimensions, yet still retain their humanlike depiction. These humanlike features of the Gospel characters provide

---

12. This is similar to the criteria for discourse types used in the text-linguistic analysis of Dawson (*Text-Linguistics*, 98). Dawson uses the variables of Agent Orientation, Continuous Temporal Succession, and Projection to create criteria for the narrative, procedural, behavioral, and expository text-types and their subcategories.

13. See Beasley-Murray, *John*, 6–10; R. Brown, *Gospel according to John I–XII*, 519–24; Carson, *Gospel according to John*, 114–17; Keener, *Gospel of John*, 1:339–63.

numerous points of discussion. I will concentrate here on Jesus. The Gospels all focus on Jesus as their main character, while also containing recognizably different depictions of Jesus. Luke might be characterized as depicting a Jesus of the common person, one who is concerned about the affairs of the dispossessed, including women, the poor, and others, while Matthew seems determined to emphasize that Jesus was the royal king and son of David. Mark shows Jesus, the suffering servant, to be the divine messenger on earth who is conscious of his purpose and the time of his revelation, while John imbues Jesus with a particularly spectacular, other-worldly sense of being the incarnate one who can perform marvelous miracles and make grand prayers (John 17) and pronouncements. These accounts are recognizably simplified, since the individual Gospel accounts also overlap a good deal, but my purpose is to show that Jesus is a protagonist of notable and, in some ways, different characteristics in each Gospel version.

A third feature is the tone of each narrative. Tone can be defined as the attitude conveyed by the implied author or narrator toward the subject matter. The Gospels, though they differ in other ways, seem to be of one attitude toward Jesus. They share a similar tone, at least toward Jesus: it is one of awe and respect. The Gospels do not convey an overall sense of irony or sarcasm, though there are incidents in the narratives where irony or sarcasm is used. Many of Jesus's parables, such as the parable of the good Samaritan or the dishonest steward, seem to rely on the ancient literary convention of irony, which captures and brings to the fore the discrepancy between what the audience expects and what actually happens. The Gospel authors apparently agree in treating the life and ministry of Jesus with the fullest possible seriousness without losing sight of the human dimension of his work. This tension between respect and humanity may be seen as a motivating factor for the Gospel authors in their characterization of Jesus, with implications for how they depict other characters as well.

A fourth feature concerns plot and ending. Apart from the introduction to the body of the Gospel (Mark 1:1–3:6) and the extended and prophetic passion story with which it concludes (13:1–16:8), Mark can be divided into four major sections: (1) an introduction of Jesus by way of the teacher-figure's thought and action (3:7–5:43); (2) a demonstration of the complexity of the teacher's thought when confronted by opposition (6:1–8:26); (3) an attempt at teaching his system of thought to his disciples (8:27–10:45); and (4) a discussion of issues of public concern as a prelude to the death of the teacher (10:46–12:44). Though the balance is different among the Gospels, which have not applied the same scheme as Mark's Gospel, this way of dividing the major sections at least helps prompt us to think about the nature of the Gospel action and its central figure in each of the works. Other schemes have been proposed for Luke, often taking into account what has been characterized as his "travel" or central section (Luke 9:51–18:34) as promoting a rise in tension until Jesus's death in Jerusalem. There are various proposals regarding whether this central section follows a scriptural or other thematic organization, but the main movement involves Jesus heading toward Jerusalem. Concerning Matthew, the schemes emphasize the Gospel's form and function, and they revolve around either a five-discourse proposal, possibly reminiscent of the five books of the Pentateuch (Matt. 5–7; 10; 13; 18; 23–25),[14] or a threefold division of episodes in the life of Jesus (1:1–4:16; 4:17–16:20; 16:21–28:20).[15]

Three of the Gospels (Matthew, Luke, and John) conclude in a way that might be expected or at least hoped for in a narrative with a happy ending, because the risen Jesus is involved in the closing events. Nevertheless, the three Gospel accounts have important differences that are worth noting because they influence the overall shape and understanding of the Gospel.

In John, after Jesus's crucifixion and death, Mary Magdalene finds his tomb empty. This Gospel relates, in a scene of gripping emotion, that she is the first person to see the risen Lord. Jesus appears to her, and she mistakes him for the gardener, until he reveals himself to her (John 20:11–18). Jesus then performs a series of miracles and appears on the beach in the early morning to deliver a final teaching to his disciples. Nothing is said of Jesus's departure from earth; instead the Gospel ends with a sense of confusion on Peter's part, before the narrator mercifully intervenes and re-elevates the narrative to its customary high plane, telling the reader in an enigmatic closing section that the disciple who asked Jesus about his betrayer and who sorts out Jesus's statements about Peter's fate is the one who bears witness to many things. In fact, he bears witness to so many things that if they were all written down, the world could not contain it (John 21:25). This concluding statement has often been interpreted as ironic, since no one says or does enough things to fill too many books for the world to hold. Perhaps a further irony, however, is the fact that more books have been written about Jesus

14. This five-part structure for Matthew was proposed by Bacon, *Studies in Matthew*, esp. 165–249. This proposal is based on the presence of a "sayings" formula that Bacon believed to be modeled after the five books of the Pentateuch, with the implication being that Jesus was a prophet, teacher, and leader like Moses, and was especially concerned with righteousness. See Senior, *What Are They Saying about Matthew?*, 26–28, which reviews this proposal among others (25–37).

15. See Kingsbury, *Matthew*, 25, for a three-part proposal consisting of "the person of Jesus Messiah" (Matt. 1:1–4:16), "the proclamation of Jesus Messiah" (4:17–16:20), and "the suffering, death, and resurrection of Jesus Messiah" (16:21–28:20). See Senior, *What Are They Saying about Matthew?*, 31–34, for an assessment of it.

than about any other figure in history, and certainly more than any single library can hold.

Luke and Matthew, by contrast, relate Jesus's death and resurrection in relatively straightforward terms, each contributing an element unique to their Gospels. Matthew contributes what is called the "great commission" at Jesus's ascension, in keeping perhaps with the royalty motif that Matthew develops (Matt. 28:16–20). In Luke, Jesus appears to two disciples who are walking toward Emmaus and hints at a coming wider ministry (Luke 24:49) before he departs at Bethany.

Mark's disputed ending has caused the most controversy of any of the Gospel endings.[16] There has been widespread and continuing debate over whether its current ending was the original or whether the original ending (and some say the beginning) was lost or even suppressed. Much of this debate confuses historical with literary and interpretive questions. But in this book we are concerned with how to interpret the Gospels, not how to attempt to reconstruct another text. Mark 16:8 abruptly ends on a note of shock and disbelief not only for the characters in the story (three women who appear at the tomb, only to be told of the resurrection by a young man there) but for the reader as well, who is left wondering whether it could really be true that Jesus was alive again (that is what the young man said!) and where Jesus was, what he would look like, what he would be doing, and so on. All these things must have gone through the women's minds too. In a provocative reversal, instead of obeying the young man's command to tell the disciples that Jesus will meet them in Galilee, the women flee, saying nothing to anyone, because they are afraid. I rather suspect that the Gospel ended at Mark 16:8, which explains the various other endings. Mark has the most dramatic ending, with the different (later) alternative endings probably attesting to efforts by subsequent conscientious readers to soften the shock and bring the account into harmony with the other Gospels.[17]

Where does this analysis lead? I have tried to distinguish in a very preliminary way several of the literary criteria on which the genre of the Gospels might be decided. Others certainly will use different criteria, although these—mode of discourse, character, tone, and plot—seem to be fundamental to understanding the Gospels. It seems that future interpretation can begin from the assumption that the Gospels exemplify the major features of good storytelling, like plot and character. In analyzing each feature, I have tried to

16. See the interesting discussion in Croy, *Mutilation of Mark's Gospel*.
17. See Black, *Perspectives*, for various views on the endings. The textual evidence is discussed in Parker, *Living Text*, 124–47.

show how knowledge of each enables comparison and contrast with others in order to distinguish points of continuity and divergence, all of which may potentially enter into genre analysis. From there, other questions of meaning will naturally follow.

Further Characterizations of Jesus in the Four Gospels

I would like to show one potential path of exploration, drawing on all four of the Gospels. This approach is based on study of characterization. Study of characterization has become an important area of New Testament study in recent years, and much can be learned about not just the character but an entire text based on how characters are presented and developed.[18] I concentrate here on the characterization of the major character or protagonist, Jesus.

On the basis of more specific examination, an argument can be made for Matthew's Gospel as a structured, stylized biography.[19] He proceeds from a "royal birth" to Jesus's "coronation" by John the Baptist, to a teaching ministry of distinction (Sermon on the Mount, etc.), and ends with a death/resurrection that leads to final enthronement above, while Jesus's followers are left with final orders for world conquest.

The Gospel of Mark, however, may arguably be better understood as redemptive tragedy, with Mark's abbreviated narrative beginning in the middle of the action and his maintaining traces of the classical Aristotelian unities of time, place, and action.[20] Only concerned with the short period of Jesus's "ministry," Mark stresses Jesus's healings, on the one hand, and his admonitions to silence, on the other. From early on (Mark 2:20) an underlying motif is Jesus's inevitable death, unavoidable and yet purposeful. Perhaps there is a sense of dramatic irony in the conclusion, which forces the reader to believe the signs of Jesus's resurrection, even though Jesus himself is not seen as risen.

Luke's Gospel sets an agenda (Luke 1:1–4) that lets the reader know of his intent to present a history, or at least a history-like account, on the basis of reliable sources that the author claims to have used.[21] This history of a special

18. Many of these volumes take approaches similar to the one found in this volume. See, e.g., Bennema, *Encountering Jesus*; Dicken and Snyder, *Characters and Characterization*; Hunt, Tolmie, and Zimmermann, *Character Studies*. On character in literature, see Bloom, *Shakespeare*.

19. For Matthew as biography, see Burridge, *What Are the Gospels?*; Shuler, *Genre for the Gospels*; Talbert, *What Is a Gospel?*

20. For Mark as Greek tragedy, see Bilezikian, *Liberated Gospel*; Jay, *The Tragic in Mark*; A. Wright, *Of Conflict and Concealment*.

21. For Luke as history, see Aune, *New Testament in Its Literary Environment*, 77; Green and McKeever, *Luke-Acts*; Pitts, *History*; Sterling, *Historiography*.

man begins inconspicuously with shepherds and recounts incidents like his unfortunate reception in his hometown, his extensive travels that all point toward Jerusalem, his acquaintance with the common people, and finally his common death between two thieves. His first resurrection appearances are to two of his followers as they are walking away from Jerusalem and toward the nearby town of Emmaus.

Finally, in the Gospel of John, the story about a god is presented.[22] This story begins in a realm far beyond our own but descends to focus on a single individual who is at first reluctant to show his powers (John 2:4) but who explodes with righteous anger at injustice (2:16) and goes on to do the spectacular, like raising people from the dead and healing them, even from far-off distances. The Jesus of John's Gospel claims equality with God, speaks of himself in unusual metaphors, and, after his resurrection, is even proclaimed to be God by one of his followers.

This discussion of the four Gospels is meant to be more suggestive than definitive, and I have refrained from putting forward firm conclusions, though subsequent analysis must probe various issues in greater depth. Perhaps outlines of this sort could form the backdrop for interpretation of individual passages and form the overall outline for a series of Bible studies or sermons. The question of the genre of the Gospels, therefore, is an important one, but it must be put in its proper perspective as one that is descriptive of the text, without necessarily prejudging the text. Once that is done, it too becomes a productive and beneficial tool for biblical interpretation.

Interpretation of the Parables

We will now shift our focus from the literary description of the genre *of* the Gospels to the use of genres *in* the Gospels. Some biblical interpreters would want to distinguish between the genre of an entire text, such as a Gospel, and the genre (or some would prefer the term *literary text-type* or even *form*, as in form criticism) of a portion of a text. There is merit to this distinction because it enables us to differentiate between the parts and the whole of a literary text. However, in this introduction to hermeneutics and interpretation, at least at this point, I will not be concerned to make such a distinction. Instead, I will use the term *genre* to refer to both the whole, such as a Gospel or an epistle, and the various parts, such as a sermon, a miracle story, or a parable.

22. For John as myth, see Dumm, *Mystical Portrait*; Kanagaraj, *"Mysticism" in the Gospel of John*.

Jesus and the Parables

Within the Gospels themselves is a particular kind of literature that has sparked endless scholarly discussion. Some scholars, in fact, claim that Jesus—apart from any spiritual or religious qualities he may have had—was a master storyteller, and the form of story he told was called the parable. Based on what I have discussed in previous chapters, we have sufficient means to analyze a given parable and appreciate its literary structure and meaning. In this section, therefore, I wish to examine several schools of thought often offered as methods for interpreting the parables, and then I will set down several pertinent reminders about ways to read the parables that will help in biblical interpretation. These ways of reading the parables are also useful for reading other embedded stories or accounts that might be found in other larger texts. The individual stories of the several judges in the book of Judges come to mind.

Two schools of thought have been most instrumental in the history of parable interpretation. The first is the allegorical method of the church fathers, who were some of the earliest interpreters of the Bible.[23] For example, Augustine (354–430) interpreted the parable of the good Samaritan, and one scholar has summarized his interpretation this way: "The man is Adam, Jerusalem the heavenly city, Jericho the moon (the symbol of mortality); the thieves are the devil and his angels, who strip the man of immortality by persuading him to sin and so leave him (spiritually) half dead; the priest and Levite represent the Old Testament, the Samaritan Christ, the beast his flesh which he assumed at the incarnation; the inn is the church and the innkeeper the apostle Paul."[24] Before we laugh too loudly, we should note that such a method of interpretation held sway in the church for nearly fifteen hundred years, and vestiges of it are not gone yet, as a few scholars have recently tried to revive allegory, even if in a more controlled way.[25] What exactly is wrong with Augustine's interpretation? First, it has little to do with the text itself. Certainly, many of the theological thoughts may be correct—the devil does try to kill the spiritual life of humans, and Christ redeems humanity through

23. For the church fathers' allegorical method of parabolic interpretation, see Kissinger, *Parables*, 1–33; Snodgrass, "From Allegorizing to Allegorizing," esp. 3–5; Stein, *Introduction to the Parables*, 42–44. See also Thiselton, *Hermeneutics: An Introduction*, 35–59, esp. 50–52.

24. Augustine, *Quaestiones evangeliorum* 2.19, summarized in Dodd, *Parables*, 1–2, and quoted above from Caird, *Language and Imagery*, 165.

25. For example, Blomberg, *Interpreting the Parables*. A major problem with such interpretation is not that some of the parables do not have God as their central figure but that there is a compulsion to find a specific number of correlates, so that the literary art of the parable becomes a puzzle of limited pieces in which odd-sized pieces are pushed into awkward places.

his life on earth—but there are no textual indicators that this is what the parable of the good Samaritan means, either in the context of the parable within the Gospel (which involves the question of who is one's neighbor) or within the parable itself. Second, this interpretation provides no standard for refutation or verification. The interpretive equations seem to be made because of a controlling theology and are, in fact, reminiscent of the kinds of equations one could make in almost any story, if one were so inclined. Third, this interpretation, like most allegorical interpretations, provides no incentive for exploring more productive readings of the text. Once this interpretation is put forward, all discussion is brought to a complete halt, since all the variables for the equation have been solved.

Since the early twentieth century, much more work has been done on the question of understanding the parables.[26] I cannot hope to discuss all the approaches, but a couple important developments stand out and merit mention. The major school of thought I will treat argues that the parables are indications of the original teaching of Jesus and hence should be used to re-create the thought-world of the earliest days of Christianity.[27] This position is right in appreciating the authenticity and integrity of Jesus's parables. C. H. Dodd was also probably on the right track in appreciating the complexities of the parables when he said that any parable arrests the "hearer by its vividness or strangeness" and leaves the "mind in sufficient doubt about its precise application to tease it into active thought."[28] However, as Anthony Thiselton notes, Dodd still had difficulty integrating the ending of the parable of the unjust steward (Luke 16:1–13), as found in vv. 8b–12, with its list of morals.[29] Dodd ended up taking a purely analytical approach to the parables, in which the surprise of discovery is replaced by the need for cognitive analysis, not necessarily of the story but of its sources, original function, and individual components. It may tell us something about origin and even something about history and interpretation, but it leaves the question of meaning to one side.

There have been several more important recent attempts in parable research to appreciate the reader's side of the experience of reading the parables. To spend time delving into each of the variations in these reader-oriented views would take us too far afield, but it has become evident in recent scholar-

26. Adolf Jülicher, a nineteenth-century German scholar, reacted against allegorical interpretation of the parables and helped to set parable interpretation on more defensible footing. His major work, *Die Gleichnisreden*, has not been translated. For prominent scholars after Jülicher, see Kissinger, *Parables*, 77–230; Blomberg, *Interpreting the Parables*, 82–194.

27. See, e.g., Dodd, *Parables*, 96.

28. Dodd, *Parables*, 5.

29. Thiselton, "Reader-Response Hermeneutics," 97–98.

ship that several factors must be considered whenever parable analysis is performed. First, one must be aware of who the characters are. It is of no consequence to hear Jesus say that the tax collector went away to his home forgiven and the Pharisee did not (Luke 18:9–14), unless one appreciates the radical role reversal that this represents. In Palestine of the first century, the Pharisee was the model of piety and spirituality, while the tax collector was one of the outcasts, despised because he worked for the enemy, the Roman government. How can it be, one might ask, that a tax collector, of all people, could be forgiven? The Pharisee said all the right things, exceeded the requirements of piety by his tithing and fasting, and prayed beautifully, while the tax collector recognized that he had nothing to commend himself before God and so kept his head bowed in humility.[30]

Second, we must be ready to be evaluated by the text, to have our preconceptions challenged, and to change our understanding of human nature and of ourselves. For example, in the parable of the good Samaritan (Luke 10:25–37), if the goal were merely to point out to a Jewish audience the exemplary model of neighborly behavior, it would have been far better to have made the attacked man the Samaritan and the one who stopped to help a Jew. But such is not the case. It was the Samaritan who proved himself to be the good neighbor. If we know on the basis of textual data that the Samaritan was a total outcast, considered a social inferior, and looked on suspiciously especially by the Jews, then we are shocked to see that he is the good neighbor. But what of the Jew who hears? Is he ever able to understand the implication, or is this parable a constant and recurring source of amazement? The fact that the inquirer who comes to Jesus is never able to use the word *Samaritan* when he speaks with Jesus, even when Jesus asks him who has been a neighbor (10:36), may point to the story being beyond his ability to grasp. The logical question, of course, is whether it is beyond our ability or—better—our desire to grasp the implications. Here is where preaching confronts interpretation, in making the parable a challenge to the preacher and the congregation.

The Parable of the Prodigal Son

To conclude this discussion, I will treat one parable very briefly: Luke 15:11–32, the parable of the prodigal son.[31] This parable is a favorite of

30. Once again (as mentioned in chap. 1), Thiselton unpacks the issues involved so as to understand the rhetorical punch this parable would have delivered to a jaded audience. See Thiselton, *Two Horizons*, 12–15.

31. For those wishing to survey the variety of interpretations, see Scott, *Hear Then the Parable*, 99–125; Hultgren, *Parables*, 70–91; Snodgrass, *Stories*, 117–43.

many and is referred to so often that we are very familiar with its details. However, in applying the interpretive model I have been discussing, with the nuances just mentioned, we can increase our appreciation of the story and perhaps grasp the significance of some of the details in new and instructive ways. Luke says that all the tax collectors and the sinners were coming to Jesus to listen to him (Luke 15:1). When the Pharisees and the scribes were grumbling about his associating with sinners, he told them three parables: the lost sheep, the lost coin, and the prodigal son. The third begins with a certain man who has two sons. One asks for his father to give him his portion of the wealth, after which the man leaves for a distant country, where he squanders his estate with immoral living. This parable begins at a place with which we are all too familiar, in a family with dynamics we certainly can understand. Parables have a way of beginning with the known and familiar world, the world of first-century Palestine to be sure, but often a world involving characters and people who also find a place in our contemporary world.

A span of time seems to pass, during which the son spends his fortune, so that when a famine occurs, he is destitute. But the parable does not dwell on this temporal element, and it certainly does not lecture us on it. This content is meant to show the contrast between wealth and poverty, independence and dependence. In fact, the son is in such poverty that he is reduced to feeding pigs for others. This parable is laden with situational and dramatic irony related to the themes of poverty and riches, status and humility, purity and impurity, and race and religion. One day the son comes to his senses and realizes that if he were to work for his own father, he would be better off than he is feeding someone else's pigs. He decides to return to his father and deliberately plans what he will say to him: "Father, I have sinned against heaven and before you; I am no longer worthy to be called your son; make me as one of your paid workers" (Luke 15:18–19; my translation). This is the longest dialogue so far recorded in the parable, and the son speaks it only to himself. With these words in mind, he sets off for home.

Luke 15:20 is one of the crucial verses in the parable. We have been given no insight into the father and the older brother (who has so far not been mentioned but who, we will learn, has been on the margins from the start). What we do know, however, is that while the younger son is still a long way off, his father sees him, feels compassion, and runs to him to embrace him and kiss him. Now we might wonder, "What was the father doing that he would see the son? Did he check the road every day? Did he not have something better to do than to check every day for his son's return, or was this just a fortuitous glance? If he were watching for his son every day, would this not indicate that the father was more than simply compassionate?" These are pressing questions. They are provocative and suggestive, even though they do not yield easy answers. However, does it really matter to know that a man of some wealth in first-century Palestine was not like a rich man today who does not get his hands dirty? Or that rich men of the time supposedly would not run? I do not think so. But the story is not yet over.

The son, true to his resolve, immediately says to the father the words he has so carefully planned: "Father, I have sinned against heaven and before you; I am no longer worthy to be called your son" (Luke 15:21; my translation). But he never gets to the next line. The father turns to his slaves (note that the father is wealthy enough to be escorted wherever he goes) and says, "Quickly bring out the best robe and put it on him, and put a ring on his hand and sandals on his feet; and bring the fattened calf, kill it, and let us eat and celebrate; for this son of mine was dead and has come to life again; he was lost and has been found" (vv. 22–24 NASB95). This makes for quite a welcome—the best robe for a dirty, smelly son, the fattened calf for a man who would eat almost anything, and a ring showing welcome and a place of belonging.

But this is intriguing: Did the father not hear what the son said? Is it that he did not hear or that he did not want or need to hear? There is a wealth of difference between these two. Of course, the further situational irony is that once more the son has repeated the lines essentially to himself. And we know the rest of the story: the older son gets angry with the lavishness of his father's reception of the younger son, and the father must console him with the blunt and uncompromising remarks that "we had to celebrate and rejoice, for this brother of yours was dead and has become alive, and was lost and has been found" (Luke 15:32 NASB95 alt.).

What are we to make of this parable? To reduce it to such a bland statement as "God rejoices if one sinner returns to him" is not simply to state the obvious but to miss the impact of the parable. *This parable is meant not to teach through proposition alone but also to be experienced through emotion.*[32] How many words would it take to capture the feeling of joy that the father experiences on seeing his son, whom he had no idea would return, coming down the road? How many words would capture the sense of humility that the son felt, being reduced to wanting to be his own father's hired worker? And how could we adequately capture the older brother's jealousy and disappointment? Yes, the father does have some of the qualities of God, but then does not any good father? An allegorical interpretation would have a difficult and, I would dare say, impossible time plotting the relationship between the

32. See also Funk, *Language*; Fuchs, "New Testament."

two brothers and their relation to the father, as well as other features.[33] Does not the younger son remind us of ourselves? All too often, I am afraid. But are we not like the older brother as well?

I do not want to give the impression that any attempt to reduce the parable to a few short words is illegitimate, since in the suggestive questions I have just posed I have tried to propose several possible ways to construct a suitable understanding and to create proclamatory material. A sermon on the parables seems to me to be best presented by using a narrative technique, rather than by trying to find the traditional three points. Of course, a sermon compels the use of other words, so the parable must be expounded to some degree, but we must never believe that because we can say something intelligible about a biblical passage, such as a parable, we have fully or exhaustively described its meaning. I would caution against using overly rigid categories to try to draw attention to significant parallels in our own lives. To attempt to reduce the parable to summative words alone is to attempt to capture the parable in some timeless, lifeless state, to have a rough approximation of only a part of the parable's meaning, and to risk missing the parable entirely. I have been through this parable numerous times, and yet every time I reread it—even though I know the outcome—I am struck again and again by the power of its language.

Study and Practice

Select one of the Gospels and read it without pre-deciding its literary genre. Instead, describe the features of the text and attempt to formulate your own estimation of it. Examine the plot, the setting, the characters, and the characters' motivations. Then select one or two other Gospels and perform the same exercise, comparing your results. Once you have positioned your first Gospel in relation to the others, select one specific section of that same Gospel and see how your description of the genre helps or hinders your understanding of that passage. Now read a psalm in light of the rest of the psalms, and go through a similar exercise. How does the entire psalter shape your understanding of the single psalm, and how does that psalm influence your view of the psalter?

We have also discussed the letters in the New Testament as a genre. Read a number of different letters—perhaps one of Paul's and several by Peter or Jude or James—and see if you can describe more precise ways of distinguishing the letters. Are you able to see common features of the construction of the

33. This does not stop some from trying. See Blomberg, *Interpreting the Parables*, 198–211, who draws on a form of synonymous parallelism to arrive at his interpretation.

New Testament letters, and how do these features help you interpret individual passages? Select a parable from one of the Gospels and read through it. Create a sketch of the parable's plot and characters as we did in chapter 4. At the same time, pay attention to who the characters are, especially their distinctive characteristics. Also, be ready to be evaluated by the text, to have your preconceptions challenged, and to have your understanding of the parable change as you experience it through the model outlined in this book.

Conclusion

This chapter concludes our discussion of hermeneutics at the level of text. We have devoted two chapters to some of the important elements in reading and interpreting a text, using New Testament texts as our primary examples (the same principles and procedures apply to the Old Testament as well). We, of course, have not been able to discuss all the possible topics related to how to understand texts, and even for the subjects that we have introduced, we have not been able to go into as much detail as we would like. However, the goal of these two chapters has been to provide a means of approaching a literary text, such as a Gospel or a letter by Paul, and to be able to examine it as a text before we examine it as anything else.

In subsequent chapters we will turn to some of the other considerations, including biblical theology, systematic theology, and preaching. However, before we are able to responsibly participate in the hermeneutical enterprise, we must first be able to read a biblical text and understand it as a text before we understand it as anything else. This provides a necessary and invaluable foundation for whatever we then wish to do with the text. But the text must be the first place we engage in the hermeneutical task of interpretation. We can then eventually proceed to theology and proclamation. If we do not learn to read the text before we introduce other perspectives, then we circumvent the process of responsible hermeneutics and interpretation.

6

Hermeneutics at the Level of Biblical Theology

Introduction

Contemporary biblical studies often focuses on theology. By this, I mean that there is often a compelling interest in reading all the texts of the Bible as theological documents. Certainly, theological understanding of the Bible is an important part of the hermeneutical task as I am defining it in this book. However, to read the Bible theologically often means for some interpreters—for too many, I believe—that the questions to be asked of the text, first and last, are theological questions. There are areas within theological studies that are rightly devoted to theology, such as systematic or dogmatic theology. Some, however, wish to remake the study of the Bible into an almost exclusively theological enterprise in which the results of studying the biblical text are subordinated to theological concerns. These concerns are variously defined in terms of trinitarian readings, premodern interpretation, or the major creeds of the fourth century. This is not the place to argue against such perspectives, although I believe that they can often result in avoiding the hermeneutical process by foisting predetermined meanings on the text. I have discussed the shortcomings of theological interpretations of Scripture elsewhere and will not discuss them here.[1] I wish instead to emphasize that

1. Porter, "What Exactly Is Theological Interpretation of Scripture?"

theological understanding is part of the hermeneutical process, but it must occupy its legitimate hermeneutical place.

In the model that I am developing here, linguistics and then the text occupy the first two levels of understanding (and they are closely intwined), before theological levels are reached. This chapter is the first of two chapters devoted to theological levels of interpretation. This chapter is concerned with biblical theology, and the next is concerned with systematic theology. The two are intertwined around a number of topics, but biblical theology must take precedence over systematic theology, as will be made clear in this and the next chapter.[2]

The Unity and Diversity of Scripture

The unity and diversity of the biblical message is an important topic that involves not just historical questions but the traditional areas of both biblical and systematic theology. I will begin by clarifying the terms *unity* and *diversity*.[3] These apparently straightforward terms become highly problematic once one attempts to use them to talk about the Bible. Those who want to emphasize the unity of Scripture are concerned with identifying and elucidating the common thread, or possibly threads, that run throughout the entire body of texts that make up the biblical canon. Many different unifying principles have been proposed as that common thread, one of the most important among them being Christ and his redemptive or salvific purposes.[4] Many others have been suggested as well. This is not the place to debate one over the other, because our purpose is not to appreciate such a single notion but to understand how the concepts of unity and diversity function in biblical and systematic theology.

It is not difficult, however, to appreciate the degree of complexity in any attempt to determine a common theological notion, if even a broad one, that might unite the entire Bible, or even one of its testaments. First, finding a common thread requires the rather bold assumption that many different

2. For a useful history of biblical theology for each testament, see Hasel, *New Testament Theology*, and Hasel, *Old Testament Theology*.
3. The discussion of unity and diversity was brought to the fore in New Testament studies in Dunn, *Unity and Diversity*.
4. See Hayes and Prussner, *Old Testament Theology*, 257–60, for a brief survey of the considerable diversity of proposals that have been put forward for a "center" of the Old Testament alone. The question of the theological relationship between the two testaments raises further issues that are significant and should be addressed, though we won't be able to discuss them in this book.

writers, in different places, at different times, and even in different languages, were all concerned with the same topic of discussion. Most people who want to argue emphatically for the unity of Scripture may not go so far as to claim that all the different biblical writers are attempting to elucidate the same basic point, but they may claim that the biblical authors, in essence, hold to at least a complementary (and noncontradictory) perspective on this topic. If we recognize the role that canon formation plays within the church, then such unity—because it was not necessarily determined by the individual authors but determined by the process that led to the canon being recognized—is a concept that can be more readily accepted as possible. This concept can become a working hypothesis for doing biblical theology.

Second, once the quest for the single message is deemed possible, the considerable task of determining this common thread still looms before the interpreter. The very range and number of proposals attest to the serious difficulty in assessing all the data available. Beyond a very few simple assumptions (for example, about God's existence),[5] there is not much that seems to specifically unify the biblical message. This applies to the Old and New Testaments taken as a whole, but it is also true of the individual testaments as well, although the New Testament probably appears as a more unified book than the Old Testament because of its focus on Jesus Christ.

In this chapter, I will focus on the diversity of Scripture at the level of biblical theology. I will primarily use the New Testament, recognizing that the Old Testament is even more complex and requires suitable caution. This is an intricate and complex topic. I am not arguing against the unity of Scripture, since even within this chapter I will make some statements about it, but I believe that the diversity must be appreciated—especially between the testaments—in order to fully grasp the range of teaching within the Bible.[6] We have a tendency to want to homogenize what is, in fact, a great amount of diversity that provokes further thought as it offers insights into God and his people. Even then, however, the appropriate level of discussion, regardless of considering the Bible as a whole or its smaller parts, is difficult to establish precisely.

What do I mean by the "diversity" of Scripture? By this, I do not necessarily mean that Scripture has contradictions (often confused with diversity).

---

5. Even this is called into question in a book like Esther, which never mentions God by name. Moreover, the assumption of a strict monotheism is not clear throughout, as some parts of the Old Testament seem to assume the existence of other gods (e.g., Pss. 82:1; 95:3; 135:5). The impact of the possibilities of multi-theism in ancient Israel is explored in Porter, *Jesus as the Divine Son.*

6. Cf. Blomberg, "Unity and Diversity."

By "diversity," I mean genuine differences of thought and expression that complement rather than contradict. Let me give some examples. Do I mean that the Gospels are primarily concerned with elucidating the teaching and life of Jesus, while the Pauline Epistles are concerned with addressing problems in the early church? Yes, I do. But I mean more than this. For example, each of the Gospel writers has a different perspective on the person of Jesus, his role in the world, his mission, and the nature of his followers. Some scholars have even argued that these are contradictory pictures, but that does not necessarily follow from appreciating genuine diversity. Some scholars have argued that Matthew is the Gospel about the new Moses or Jewish leader (note the discussion in chap. 5 of the theory of the five discourses in Matthew's Gospel), that Mark is about Jesus as the Son of Man whose identity may be hidden from others, and that Luke is about Jesus as the liberator-savior of the downtrodden, including the gentiles. The same might be said of Paul's letters, which seemingly reflect diversity from letter to letter. For example, the Letter to the Romans is a very different book from the Letter to Philemon. We no doubt will want to synthesize the theological findings of our interpretation, but we must begin by appreciating diversity.

Now that we have briefly previewed some of the complexities involved in biblical theology, the rest of this chapter will explain the idea of biblical theology as an attempt to understand the significance of the diversity of Scripture, summarize different methodological approaches to biblical theology, present a biblical-theological analysis of Paul's character and view of slavery in Philemon with reference to the broader Pauline corpus, and conclude with some thoughts on the nature of biblical theology.

The Significance of the Diversity of Scripture

An all-too-common tendency in contemporary discussion of the Bible is to attempt to harmonize and unify its message, without coming to terms with the diversity that is also present. Finding unity in Scripture offers a useful goal in the larger scope of hermeneutical understanding, but one can appreciate the unity only if one has recognized the diversity that underlies it. My goal in introducing the diversity of Scripture is threefold. First, I want to demonstrate the value of appreciating the individual characteristics of the different writers of the Bible. In many cases, interpreters have been too quick to overlook important—and perhaps idiosyncratic—aspects of a particular writer's teaching in an attempt to establish the unity of Scripture. How many times, for example, has Hebrews 6:4–6 and its discussion of those who have fallen away been neglected by interpreters wishing to establish a consistent biblical theology or doctrine of the security of believers?[7] I have been trying to emphasize throughout this book that interpretation is both the most difficult and the easiest thing that any reader can do. Appreciating the diversity of Scripture is made more difficult than it needs to be by many interpreters who neglect the level of text itself in their efforts to move immediately to the level of theology (or, worse, simply to begin with theology and then move to imposition of theology on the text), whether biblical or systematic. However, appreciating the individual traits and characteristics of each biblical writer—and even his individual works—is a requirement for producing a convincing interpretation that extends beyond the individual work to make important theological generalizations and applications.

Second, appreciating the diversity of Scripture is foundational for constructing any biblical theology. Before an appreciation of the unity of Scripture can be gained, the interpreter must have a firm grasp of what he or she believes the individual writers and/or books are saying about a particular topic. These chapters have had this as a central interest throughout, although we must keep in mind the importance of moving to synthesis.

Third, biblical theology—like all levels of interpretation discussed in the preceding and following chapters—is a useful construct for making meaningful generalizing statements about a corpus of material. In other words, biblical theology attempts to appreciate the diversity of individual texts, while placing them within a context of larger spheres of coherence of the biblical witness. Here I am making an assumption about the idea of coherence, although I do not wish to give it an overly narrow meaning. As I emphasized regarding interpretation at the level of text, there is no substitute for the text itself; any attempt to interpret is an endeavor to compel the text to conform to the interpreter's categories, and such is also the case with the level of biblical theology. For example, when I read Philippians 2:6–11 after studying this passage as text, I may want to discuss it in terms of Christology. This is an interpretive decision and a very important one, one that others have taken before me. The further use of the findings regarding Philippians 2:6–11 in relation to the whole of Paul's Letter to the Philippians is an additional interpretive decision, and using these findings to form an entire Pauline or even New Testament

---

7. See Bateman, *Four Views*. This volume well illustrates the kinds of contrastive views that are present for just this one passage. This passage is not alone among passages that appear to present diverse teachings on central subjects within the New Testament. The statements of the contributors to this volume show that there needs to be a relationship between discussion of the text and discussion of theology. I contend that attention to the level of text is the necessary starting point for such discussion, as this book attempts to illustrate.

Christology is yet another interpretive decision. I am not saying that these decisions are incorrect—they may be the most persuasive ones that can be made; I only mean that they are, in fact, interpretive decisions and must be recognized and treated as such.

Some Approaches to Biblical Theology

From what I have said, we recognize that textual analysis forms the basis for biblical theology. By "biblical theology," I refer not to the creation of comprehensive volumes of biblical theology but to biblically based theological treatments. If biblical theology is an attempt to make larger generalizations about individual books (such as Genesis, one of the Gospels, or even Philemon) or even a corpus of material (such as the historical books of the Old Testament, the Psalter, the Wisdom literature, or the Pauline Epistles), then these kinds of statements must be made based on some set body of data, and that body of data is composed of the findings of textual analysis. I have demonstrated that the findings at this level are themselves open to much discussion and debate and that the plausibility and persuasiveness of findings at this level are arrived at only through a complex process. This is even more the case for biblical theology. Once the body of material to be treated has been established, various methods are regularly applied to "do" biblical theology. To discuss each of these would take us too far afield, but I will name a few of these approaches so that when they are encountered in the course of study and interpretation they might be recognized and appreciated for both their strengths and their limitations.

I identify here five approaches to biblical theology that are often found in individual testamental theologies, whether of the Old or the New Testament. Others might recognize other approaches, but these five seem to encapsulate the major trends within the discipline over the last hundred and fifty years or so.[8]

1. *Rationalist*: This method of biblical theology uses the critical framework that developed in Enlightenment thinking, when emphasis was placed on rationalism, among other dominant ideas. As a result, biblical theologies

---

8. I have undertaken a more thorough critique of the nature of New Testament theology and its major paradigms and have attempted to propose a new way forward in Porter, *New Testament Theology*. I use the categories developed in that volume as the basis of my discussion here. For further discussion of taxonomies of biblical theology, especially for the Old Testament, see Barr, *Concept of Biblical Theology*, esp. 27–51.

that follow the rationalist approach often have characteristics of systematic theologies because they tend to use the categories of systematic or
dogmatic theology to organize their material in a rationalistic system
of thought. An example of such a category might be God's sovereignty
or soteriology or the like, or even more general topics such as God or
the Holy Spirit.[9]

2. *History of religion*: The history of religion movement developed in
   the mid- to late nineteenth century and continued into the twentieth
   century as a product of comparative-historical thought. This approach
   to the study of Christianity treated Christianity as one religion among
   the religions of the world, even if it was also seen to represent the pinnacle of religious thought. Ideas common to religion, such as redeemer
   myths, were important for the history of religion. From this approach
   arises much of the discussion about how Jesus became Lord—that is,
   how man became God within the Judaism of the first century.[10]

3. *Salvation history*: The salvation-historical approach to theology has
   much in common with the history of religion approach as they are both
   comparative-historical in nature. The salvation-historical approach emphasizes the historical unfolding and development of God's revelation
   and hence the history of salvation of humanity across the testaments,
   culminating in the work of Jesus Christ.[11]

4. *Postmodern*: A relatively small number of postmodern theologies have
   recently been published. Moving beyond the modernist paradigm that
   has tended to dominate biblical studies, such theologies often emphasize
   the social conditioning of the biblical authors and the dialogical rather
   than monological nature of theological discussion.[12]

For the sake of completeness regarding biblical theology, we may also add
a fifth category. This approach has become quite popular in some circles,
especially more evangelical ones.

5. *Canonical*: This method, which has received much attention lately, argues essentially that the biblical canon provides the parameters for all
   interpretation of the Bible. There are differing canonical approaches, but

9. See Guthrie, *New Testament Theology*, which tends to follow the categories of systematic
theology.
10. See Bultmann, *Theology of the New Testament*.
11. See Kümmel, *Theology of the New Testament*; Ladd, *Theology of the New Testament*.
12. Esler, *New Testament Theology*; Schnelle, *Theology of the New Testament*.

the most popular one differentiates between historical and theological concerns and argues that, regardless of historical factors, the canon in its contents and organization provides the parameters for theological interpretation.[13]

These five approaches each have something to offer, as long as the presuppositions and limitations of each are realized. Any interpretive act must be evaluated in terms of whether it presents an analysis that includes all the major data, presents results that are sharable, and has the efficacy to produce new and enlightening discoveries. Rare is the case when a given method is able to meet each of these criteria equally well. The level of text provides plenty of data for consideration in light of these standards. In a very real sense, the level of biblical theology requires the first significant and major step outside of text itself (or a particular text) in an attempt to make connections among texts to determine their generalized meaning. Of course, for a pastor or for any Christian who wishes to convey something about the wholeness of his or her faith, this level is of vital importance.

I completed my undergraduate degree and then a master's degree in literature, with a focus on English literature. A common way of studying literature—at least in those days and in the institutions where I studied—was first to read through a set work to get an idea of its meaning; this is the level of textual analysis (including linguistic knowledge), with all that is entailed in that activity. We would then discuss this level in class. But we would also add another level that required summarizing in our own words, not in the words of the text or its author, what the author seemed to be saying in this particular work about a particular larger or more encompassing theme (e.g., the reasons for the fall of the hero).[14] Sometimes this would require comparison with other works by the same author or even comparison with works by other authors. In doing this, we had moved to the next level in our treatment of the text. We are doing a similar thing as we move from the level of text (see chaps. 4 and 5) to the level of biblical theology.

13. Childs, *Biblical Theology of the Old and New Testaments*.

14. In those days, one of the major themes that seemed to recur in our discussions was called the "fortunate fall" into knowledge; it seemed like every writer of English literature (or of literature in English, as it is now sometimes called), with a very few exceptions, was preoccupied with describing this fall into painful and often personally devastating self-awareness and realization—or so it was represented. In today's climate of English (or cultural) studies, it is much more likely that themes regarding class, gender, and ethnicity will be raised. This is not the place to debate the merits of these various themes, but it is appropriate to note that texts have the potential to be viewed in a variety of ways, often highly influenced by factors outside the text. Such potential must be tempered by one's reading of the text. Hence, we use levels of interpretation in this volume as a means of guarding interpretive and hermeneutical integrity.

Biblical-Theological Treatment of Paul as a Character in Philemon

Before jumping into the task of doing biblical theology, we might want to ask ourselves what topics qualify for treatment. Just about everything qualifies! Of course, depending on the purpose and audience of a study, some items might be more relevant than others. I have chosen to continue discussing Philemon, as Philemon is a text that can be reasonably managed within the constraints of this book, while also considering other texts. We might use Philemon as a starting point for larger biblical-theological discussion. To provide a more comprehensive biblical theology, we would need to treat many more texts, especially those that deal with similar ideas. But a single text is more than enough for making biblical-theological observations. For the sake of continuity, I will deal with Philemon. However, we must acknowledge that much more could and should be said about Philemon. I will select a few of the issues that I mentioned earlier when addressing the level of text, and I will discuss how we might understand them in relation to biblical theology.

We need not look far before a suitable first topic presents itself: *Paul*. Paul is not a usual topic of theological discussion. However, the actions, words, and depiction of Paul, even if by himself within his letters, embody a range of important theological ideas that merit further discussion. For example, what kind of portrait of Paul do we see in Philemon? How does this picture of Paul compare with the picture of Paul we get in his other letters? And how does this picture compare with the picture of Paul we find in the book of Acts? These are three different questions, requiring separate—though not necessarily different—responses, even if they are textually and theologically related.

First, let us consider Paul in Philemon. As mentioned before, Paul is quite conscious of his status with regard to Philemon. Paul positions himself in his relationship with Philemon so as to accomplish his ministry purposes. Paul's overriding concern in his letter to Philemon is to fulfill divinely ordained purposes that Paul believes he is called to perform. As a result, he says that he has the authority to order Philemon to perform the task of receiving back Onesimus (Philem. 8), and he, in fact, substantiates this claim with the strong contention that Philemon's own spiritual birth is because of Paul (v. 19), which is a rather persuasive argument, especially given Paul's suggestion that he may be dropping in for a visit. Paul sees himself as a mediator of God's call of Philemon, which places him in a unique relationship with Philemon, enabling him to make spiritual demands on Philemon with practical consequences. In that regard, Paul is the mediator of a vertical relationship between God and Philemon, in which Paul has played an active role as God's agent of grace for Philemon. Paul manages to ensure that these points are well made.

However, Paul seems more concerned to direct his appeal in another direction: the direction of the imprisoned, aged persona of Paul (Philem. 9). "I could have appealed to these rather powerful facts," Paul says (and I am paraphrasing), "but instead I want you to honor my request as another Christian making a request." Though the basis of Paul's appeal is the vertical relationship between God and Philemon, Paul wishes instead to focus on the horizontal relationship that exists between himself and Philemon—a relationship he wishes to extend to Onesimus as well.

This horizontal relationship is seen in the language of fictive kinship throughout the letter. Paul uses a variety of language to describe the horizontal relationships among those in Philemon's assembly of Christ-followers. He uses the language of work and soldiery and slavery (to which we will turn below), but more often he uses the language of kinship, such as "sister" (Philem. 2), "old man" (v. 9), "child" (v. 10), and especially "brother" (vv. 1, 16, 20). Paul transforms an understandable hierarchical relationship into a model of familiarity. Paul seemingly reduces the importance of social status and position within the church and instead addresses Philemon according to their common position as believers in Jesus—brothers—while still making his authoritative role within the church known.

Paul's appeal here focuses on the joint usefulness of the slave Onesimus (Philem. 16–17), so that Onesimus's position can be transformed from hierarchical subservience as a slave to brotherly affection and equality. In other words, by examining Paul, we are able to define a theological model of authority within the church that recognizes both the vertical dimension and the horizontal dimension. The vertical dimension is vital, as it is the one that is spiritually life-giving, as Paul points out to Philemon. However, the horizontal dimension is also vital, as it is the one that is spiritually sustaining within the Christian community, as Paul further demonstrates in attempting to transform the church that meets in Philemon's home from a place of hierarchy to one of brotherly equality before God.

Second, let us consider how Paul acts in relationship to other churches in some of his other letters.[15] In anticipation of what we are going to find, to varying degrees Paul responds to the situations in churches in relationship to these two axes, the one vertical and the other horizontal. To consider the theological dimensions of Paul's character does not require that we refer to every letter he wrote, but these several strands can be sufficiently seen emerging from a select few letters, though to different degrees and in slightly different ways. For example, in Paul's letter to the Galatian churches, he seems to be

15. For basic knowledge regarding Paul's Letters, see Porter, *Apostle Paul*, 185–442.

addressing a church that is having difficulty with accepting his credentials as an apostle because they have deviated from his preaching and turned to a gospel of works.

In the letter, Paul moves directly from the salutation to a defense of his apostleship in light of the Galatians abandoning the gospel and following another one, apparently based on works of the law and not grace. Paul here does not mince words. In Galatians 1:1 he says he is "an apostle not sent from men, nor through the agency of man, but through Jesus Christ, and God the Father, who raised Him from the dead."[16] Then, he expresses surprise that the Galatians have so quickly deserted Christ, asserting strongly that any teaching they have been receiving that is not in agreement with Paul's message is not to be listened to. In fact, those who teach such things are to be accursed (vv. 8–9). How can this be so? Paul says that his message is not from human beings. He goes on to recount his conversion experience and the outgrowth of it, as well as his position of authority, even extending to the rebuke of Cephas (1:11–2:21).

Paul places high value on his role as an authority figure, not on the basis of something he is but on the basis of the role he is fulfilling as God's selected messenger. In other words, Paul's horizontal relationship with the Galatian churches, which has been called into question because the Galatians have been following a gospel of works rather than of grace, is predicated on the vertical relationship that Paul preaches to the gentiles. Failing to understand the gospel and confusing it with human works and actions has practical consequences in that it affects both our relationship with God and our relationship with others in the church. Paul's role as apostle is, at least in that sense, a relationship created by his vertical position, not his horizontal status with other Christians, as important as such relationships might be. This is a significant distinction in that it does not address the question of actual status before God—which Paul seems to regard as one of equality, at least within the church—but it does make practical distinctions on the basis of function.

Another example may help to put these different perspectives into an appropriate focus. In Philippians 3:4, Paul uses a technique that has direct parallels to Philemon, where Paul's appeal to the horizontal plane of his ministry is a reflection of his vertical relationship. Paul says, "Although I myself might have confidence even in the flesh, if anyone else has a mind to put confidence in the flesh, I have far more" (NASB95 alt.). After recounting his prestigious

---

16. This translation is based on the NASB95. I retain the gendered language because it captures well the move from plural to singular to Jesus Christ, whereas some other, more inclusive translations lose this feature.

bloodline, he quickly dismisses this by saying that "whatever things were gain to me, those things I have counted as loss for the sake of Christ" (v. 7 NASB95). One's birth, position, and education are important by the world's standards, and they are not something that can be jettisoned as if they did not exist. They are important, not just because of what they are and how they might serve one in the world, but because they are reflections of who we are in relationship to others. This includes how we relate to those in the church, whereby our horizontal claims, whether theological or otherwise, are to be transformed in light of our vertical position. While the earthly claims may count for something by worldly standards, they make no difference on the larger scale of things that matter for Christ. In his letters, Paul reveals a balanced view of the tension for Christians of being in but not of the world, and he repeatedly addresses the relationship between the two from varying perspectives.

The next step in widening our concentric circles is comparing this presentation of Paul's activist theology with the image presented in Acts. The complex relation of Acts to the Pauline Epistles—whether at the level of chronology, character depiction, traditional theology, or whatever—is beyond discussion here.[17] To draw just one parallel, in several instances in Acts, when Paul visits cities of the Mediterranean and Greco-Roman world as he founds churches, he often uses marvelous rhetoric. People's reactions to Paul's speeches are varied and often unpredictable, but on more than one occasion he is forced to leave the city prematurely, occasionally with an angry mob at his heels. Perhaps one of the worst examples takes place in Lystra (Acts 14:8–23), where Paul and Barnabas are first mistaken for the Greek gods Hermes and Zeus, and the people attempt to worship them as these gods. Later, the people are convinced to stone Paul, who is dragged out of the city and taken for dead. Paul is right not to put confidence in his rhetorical ability, as impressive as it may be on some occasions.

Even in locations where Paul arouses a positive response from the crowd, he often also encounters adversity. The honor of speaking at the Areopagus is countered by the fact that he saw very few become believers. To the contrary, Paul's successes in Acts are often marked by adversity, trouble, persecution, and hardship, to the point where one might well wonder how it is that Paul

17. There is no doubt that one looking for tensions between Acts and the Pauline Letters will be able to find them. However, these are often overdrawn for the sake of emphasizing contrast. Most scholars, whether they see greater or less harmony between Acts and the Pauline Letters, still end up using the Acts chronology as a means of depicting the development of early Christianity and thereby placing Paul's Letters within it. An excellent example of such a work is Bruce, *Paul*.

can continue to proclaim the gospel under such circumstances. When we probe more deeply into Paul's message—the same message that eventually incites various reactions among his auditors—we can appreciate that though his mission in Acts may be to the gentiles (by way of the Jews and the synagogues), his message is grounded in Jesus's death and resurrection, and Paul mediates this to the gentiles with all that he can possibly muster. The book of Acts is, in large part, a chronicle of the "acts" of Paul in his horizontal relationships with others, which are based on a deep and unwavering conviction that grows out of his vertical relationship with the God of Abraham, the God who called him to this purpose.

In doing biblical theology I am not trying to deny the unity of Scripture. To the contrary, I am trying to arrive at a coherent view of the biblical teaching on a given issue by appreciating the diversity that makes it up. I began with an analysis of how Paul is represented in Philemon in order to get an idea of how Paul theologically comports himself. Then, I expanded my sphere of analysis to include other Pauline Epistles that reveal aspects of the same person, even if in varied circumstances. I concluded by including the non-Pauline witness to Paul found in Acts. The biblical-theological examination of Paul provides a broader but clearer picture concerning how Paul understood God and what he understood about God, how he preached this message to others, and how those he came in contact with—through both his writing and his physical encounters—were impacted by his theology.

All these varied ways that Paul acts in relation to the vertical and horizontal dimensions of his faith are slightly different, yet the comparing, contrasting, and synthesizing of these elements through the study of biblical theology help the reader better understand Paul's theology in a way that grounds it in the text. If we were to examine an issue that might touch on the whole of the Bible—such as a biblical-theological view of God's character—our concentric circles could extend further to encompass the entire biblical witness. The level of biblical theology allows us to compare the results of our analysis of a specific text with other texts. This has a great theoretical advantage in that it helps the interpreter grasp the specific data that make up larger theological concepts.

Biblical-Theological Treatment of Paul's View on Slavery in Philemon

When we move further into our analysis of Philemon, several concepts are introduced that warrant extended theological treatment. I have already discussed several of them above, especially those concerning vertical and horizontal theological axes. In this section, I wish to address one theological concept that has continued to plague the Christian church for nearly two millennia: the issue of slavery. Some may think that dealing with the issue of slavery is anachronistic and not a suitable topic for biblical theology. Yet some experts estimate that there are more slaves in the world today than there were during the height of the American slave trade. Even in North America, with its rampant sex trade, the issue of slavery is not just an economic (or moral or judicial) one but a theological one that demands an appropriate theological response.

Part of the problem seems to begin with Paul himself. For example, Paul refers to himself as a prisoner of Christ Jesus (Philem. 1) and refers to Onesimus as a slave (v. 16). What does it mean to be a prisoner of Christ Jesus, or rather, how is that different from being a regular prisoner or a slave? Is Paul's status as a physical or earth-bound prisoner ironic because he is a spiritual prisoner of Christ? Perhaps Onesimus is living proof of this. Paul says that Onesimus was "begotten in my imprisonment" (v. 10 NASB95). How then is Onesimus's bondage related to ideas of slavery in the ancient world? Or more particularly, what was Paul's view of slavery?

Regarding Paul's view of slavery, just about every position possible has been argued for, and many of them in rather heated terms. Some scholars argue that Paul was merely a product of his own time and that he accepted the institution of slavery and made no attempt to argue against it (after all, he accepts for himself the designation of "slave,"[18] for example, in Rom. 1:1; Gal. 1:10; Phil. 1:1; and Titus 1:1, and he applies it to Jesus Christ in Phil. 2:7). The proof of that would be this letter itself, Philemon, in which Paul appears to accept the social institution of slavery and does not condemn it, as well as passages often called the household codes (Eph. 5:22–6:9; Col. 3:18–4:1) and others that seem to assume such an institution (even the liberating Gal. 3:28–29). Another group of scholars argues that Paul was so benighted that he even endorsed slavery (evidenced by his intention not to free Onesimus but only to convince Philemon to allow him to serve Paul), as well as the total oppression of women and other such positions. But some have asserted the opposite—that Paul argues quite clearly for the category "slave" to no longer have a place in Christian sociology or theology. Of course, there are many views in between.[19]

18. The Greek word δοῦλος (*doulos*) has often been translated as "servant." Even though the Greek term was used of some indentured household servants, I believe a better rendering is "slave." This translation better conveys the idea of Paul as one completely subservient to his master. See Porter, *Letter to the Romans*, 42–43.

19. For the history of interpretation concerning Paul's view of slavery, see Byron, "Paul and the Background of Slavery"; Byron, *Recent Research*; Combes, *Metaphor of Slavery*, 13, 29–37; cf. Garnsey, *Ideas of Slavery*, 5.

What can be said about slavery in Philemon? We have already observed that the text itself is speaking about the complex relationship between essentially three characters, though other people and groups are strategically introduced to serve, apparently, as public witnesses and hence to hold Philemon socially accountable for his reactions. In this instance, Paul seems to be arguing for two things. First, he wishes Onesimus to return to Philemon to repay a debt and to reestablish their relationship. Second, he seems to desire Philemon to release Onesimus as a slave (Philem. 16) and to elevate him to the legal status of a peer, a brother, since this is in fact what he is in his spiritual stature.

At the level of biblical theology, two questions must be asked: (1) What is our biblical-theological view of slavery, based first on Philemon and then on the rest of the New Testament? and (2) Could the application of this pattern in the New Testament be more widely generalized? To forecast my conclusion, I believe that Paul was strongly against slavery and created the mechanism for its abolition, if we had only read him correctly and applied his theological arguments appropriately.[20]

Let's begin with Philemon itself. From Philemon, we get a glimpse of the integral role of slavery within Roman society. In fact, the Roman economic system—which was highly stratified, with inequality running throughout—was based on a slave economy. The expansion of the Roman economy was based on the availability of slave labor, and slaves were owned by those all the way up the socioeconomic ladder, from poor tenant farmers to wealthy landowners. Because of the importance of slaves, there were laws that regulated slavery, including the rights of owners and the obligations of others to help enforce these laws. One of the major fears of the Romans was any kind of public insurrection, such as a slave revolt, which the Romans savagely suppressed. It is in this light that we read Philemon, in which Paul recognizes the laws regarding the need to return a slave to its owner but does so within the larger context of his belief in genuine freedom in Christ.

In his letter to Philemon, Paul attempts to reformulate the relationship between Philemon and Onesimus. He wishes to transform it from the kind of stratified hierarchy typical of the Roman world, with the head of the household at the top and the slave at the bottom, into one of (fictive) kinship and egalitarian relations. Paul identifies himself—and all followers of Christ—as those who are subservient (e.g., a prisoner or elsewhere a slave), but they are subservient to God and to Christ, not to each other. Paul uses the metaphor of family to redefine social hierarchy into a much more egalitarian social

20. This entire discussion is directly dependent on Porter, "Reframing Social Justice," esp. 133–34.

construct where Philemon is a friend and fellow worker, even a partner in the faith and a brother; Apphia is a sister; Archippus is a fellow soldier for the cause; and Onesimus, who was once (so far as worldly values are concerned) useless, has now become a useful person as a son of Paul (as is Philemon) and a brother of Philemon. Paul has defined the Christian household in new terms that strongly reorient social relations along the lines of the Roman family with Paul as the head of the family (the paterfamilias), not Philemon.

As the father, Paul "requests" that Philemon return his brother Onesimus to him for God's service. In other words, Paul raises the question of what slavery means within the Christian community if all those who are in Christ, baptized into the faith (Gal. 3:27 followed by vv. 28–29), are now brothers and sisters and are to treat each other on those terms. I agree with F. F. Bruce that Philemon becomes a letter of emancipation of Onesimus and effectively marks what should have been the end of slavery as an institution within the Christian church, even if Paul—no doubt wisely, due to the possibility of Roman response—does not call for an explicit slave revolt. What Paul asks for here is not a slave revolt but an entire Christian revolt in which Christian leaders, such as Philemon, don't rise up in anger but act instead in Christian love toward others in lower social positions, such as Onesimus. Even though we may, as followers of Christ, be his slaves and prisoners on his behalf, when we are in the family of God, we are family—brothers, sisters, sons, and daughters—and are expected to act that way with one another. Paul made slavery an unviable institution in the ancient world. The pressure of Christians to free their slaves—and to tell others why they were doing this—would have necessitated social change because of the resulting disparity and social unrest.[21]

Once we see this pattern in Paul's thinking, we can extend the concentric circle of examination to include others of his letters—and then beyond that to encompass the rest of the New Testament (and eventually even the Old). Two major passages in Paul's Letters refer to family structure, and they are often thought of as reinforcing oppressive and now outmoded values. To the contrary, I think that the same theological attitude that we find in Philemon is found in some of these passages—the household codes mentioned above. These household codes partially reflect the order within the Roman family, as they refer to members of the household, including the father (paterfamilias), the wife, the children, and the slaves or servants.

In both Colossians (3:18–4:1) and Ephesians (5:22–6:9), Paul transforms the convention of the household codes in two ways. First, he extends the family structure by referring to God or Christ as the ultimate father or master in

---

21. Bruce, *Paul*, 401. See also Petersen, *Rediscovering Paul*, 269, 289–90.

heaven and, second, he introduces a reciprocality not found in other ancient household codes. In another context, I have commented on the various dimensions of these codes,[22] but here I concentrate on what is said regarding masters and slaves. In Colossians, Paul instructs slaves to be obedient to their masters, not with external service but with sincerity of heart. They are to fear God, since one works as for the Lord, who is the giver of rewards (Col. 3:22–25). Does this indicate that God in some way approves of a universal pattern of subservience?[23] Not at all.

Paul immediately continues with a short and pithy statement to masters that puts the previous comment in perspective: they are to give justice and fairness to their slaves, knowing that they too have a master in heaven (Col. 4:1). Do justice and fairness include emancipation? I will return to this below. Ephesians 6:8 and 9 add two interesting and provocative statements: whatever good thing anyone does, this he will receive back from the Lord, whether slave or free; and masters are to do the same, knowing that their master (since they are slaves of Christ/God) is in heaven, and there is no partiality with him. In other words, despite the convention of earthly masters, Paul makes clear that there is another master who is not earthly. Earthly obedience is seen in the larger context of heavenly obedience, to which all are called. Masters are told that they are to treat their slaves in the same way that God and Christ will treat them as their slaves—that is, followers—since both have the same master in heaven.

So, Paul seems again to address two levels here: the level of the human institution and the level of spiritual status. In this case, as is usual, the spiritual trumps the earthly. Both masters and their slaves have the same master in heaven. There is only one head of the household, and those in the faith are all his servants, brothers and sisters in common service, and he demands similar behavior of all. The heavenly relationship that calls for treatment of one's slave in the same way that God/Christ treats his slaves has the same effect as Paul's teaching to Philemon—it renders the institution of slavery bankrupt and hollow, without power to oppress or mistreat.

Another statement by Paul may help put this in even better perspective: 1 Corinthians 7:21–24. Paul addresses this statement to slaves in the context of their freedom. Paul essentially says two things in these verses. First, a Christian should be content to remain in the condition in which he or she finds themself when called to Christ. Second, if one is able to become free, he

---

22. See Porter, "Paul, Virtues, Vices, and Household Codes," esp. 381–84.

23. Some would (unfortunately) say yes. See, as just one example, Schemm, "Kevin Giles's *The Trinity.*"

or she should do that. There are some questions about how verse 21 should be translated—either "Are you called a slave? Don't let it bother you. But if you are able to become free, make especial use of the opportunity," or "Are you called a slave? Don't let it bother you. Although you are able to become free, make especial use of your slavery."[24] The translation that recommends freedom is much more grammatically sound.

I will conclude with a brief examination of Galatians 3:28, where Paul states that there is "neither Jew nor Greek, neither slave nor free, neither male and female, for all of you are one in Christ Jesus" (my translation).[25] This statement is made within the context of those who are baptized into Christ having been clothed in Christ. The three binary oppositions that Paul addresses aim right at the heart of the human, and in particular the Roman, societal condition. They address the three major areas of society and their great imbalances: ethnicity, socioeconomics, and gender. The way that Paul frames these three binary oppositions essentially asserts that the opposition on the basis of race does not exist, the opposition on the basis of hierarchical status does not exist, and the opposition on the basis of gender (although not gender itself, as Paul uses "and" rather than "nor" in the third formulation) does not exist. We could discuss each of these in more detail, but I will focus on the second for this discussion.

Just as he states with the first opposition that he negates, Paul says that such a distinction does not functionally apply for those who are "in Christ." Hierarchical distinctions that often result in aggrandizement or servitude—the two poles of the opposition—are rendered null and void by being followers of Christ. Such distinctions, whether one is a slave or one is a free person, are not germane to this newly reconstituted society. Paul has often been criticized by some for failing to advocate for their conception of social equality, in particular for the kind of statement that they would wish him to make. For twenty-first-century Christians—who rightly should deplore slavery and all that it connotes—Paul is often thought not to have made an explicit statement against slavery, in all its forms and manifestations, or at least as they believe he should have stated it. I find that statement rather difficult to accept in light of what I have said above, and especially in light of Galatians 3:28.[26]

24. Virtually all English translations choose the former meaning. Nevertheless, there is considerable debate over the grammar. Albert Harrill argues that the proper translation is: "You were called as a slave. Don't worry about it. But if you can indeed become free, *use instead freedom*" (*Manumission*, 194).
25. See Porter, "Reframing Social Justice," 130–35, where I discuss this passage in more detail.
26. This concern was one of the driving forces behind the creation of William J. Webb's "Redemptive Movement Hermeneutic." For an accessible introduction to the broad contours

Paul was clear in his stance on slavery—for those who had ears to hear him—but also wise in formulating a theology that did not call for a slave revolt and thus threaten the entire Christian enterprise but instead called for a master revolt that would transform all of society from the top down. Nevertheless, having said that, it is still important to see that Paul is much more concerned with the spiritual level. In 1 Corinthians, he presents a paradox to us: the one who was called in the Lord while a slave is the Lord's freedman; likewise, he who was called while free is Christ's slave (1 Cor. 7:22). I think Paul is saying two things: (1) Christian liberty transcends the boundaries of social institutions, and (2) the Christian life demands an allegiance that is more stringent and demanding than anything demanded by human slavery, as difficult as this may be to imagine. As Paul says, "You were bought with a price; do not become slaves of men" (7:23 NASB95). This helps us to know what Paul is speaking of in Philemon when he says that he is a prisoner of Christ Jesus: the physical chains—hard, unyielding, and inescapable—are mere tokens of an infinitely more tenacious bondage to Christ, a bondage that has its roots in Paul's conception of Christ's mission in coming to earth. As Paul says in the great hymn of Philippians 2, Christ humbled himself as a slave—meaning that he took on a posture of complete servitude (v. 7). This may not be everyone's position, but I would submit it as a plausible and defensible reading of Pauline theology on slavery.[27]

Hermeneutics at the Level of Biblical Theology

By way of conclusion, I will make several points about biblical theology. First, the definition and application I have given of the category called biblical theology may be different from what others call biblical theology.[28] I believe it provides a functional method for further ministry of God's Word, and that is our ultimate aim in grappling with issues of biblical interpretation. I began this chapter by mentioning the issue of diversity in the New Testament, and I hope I have shown that biblical theology is best seen as appreciating the diversity of biblical opinion on a given issue, though, of course, it will appreciate

---

of this mode of interpretation and representative responses, see the various essays in Gundry, *Four Views*.

27. For further discussion, see M. Harris, *Slave of Christ*, although he arrives at a different conclusion (57–59).

28. Edward Klink and Darian Lockett offer five categories in recent discussion: historical description, history of redemption, worldview-story, canonical, and theological construction (*Understanding Biblical Theology*). The one closest to what is described here is probably historical description.

unity in ever-widening realms of discussion as has been demonstrated. Second, I have characterized biblical theology as the next level extrapolated from the level of textual analysis, a level in which the descriptive statements of textual analysis are synthesized in relation to ever-increasing and widening spheres within the biblical corpus as a whole. Third, as this characterization implies, the category of biblical theology—in order to be effective, persuasive, and defensible—must examine the text. With textual interpretation informing biblical theology, the interpreter has a greater chance of formulating a unified description of the concept at hand. Fourth, I have attempted to eliminate as far as possible the idea of an interpreter willfully and flagrantly introducing his or her own theological hidden agenda apart from a substantial basis in textual study. Fifth, the level of biblical theology is vital for the pastor seeking to minister to his or her congregation effectively, since it takes the next logical and necessary hermeneutical step from the text itself—in this case, a document created two thousand or more years ago—and mediates its concepts in language that is more than merely self-referring. It makes vital and necessary connections to larger theological contexts and issues.

Study and Practice

In previous chapters, I invited you to study several passages of Scripture at the level of text. At this point, I wish to use these same passages to move to the level of biblical theology. Read through and consider again the three passages of Scripture you have previously worked on: Romans 5:12–21, Acts 17:16–34, and Psalm 23 (see chap. 4). First, examine and identify the major theological topics treated in each passage. Second, formulate a statement of the theology of this particular passage. At this point, I want to encourage you to move outward in concentric circles of examination. This means, first, moving outward to study these theological categories as they are treated in the rest of the book or corpus and then, second, formulating a revised statement on the biblical theology of this concept. For the final stage, examine how these theological categories are treated within larger sections of the Bible itself, such as in the Pauline Letters, in Acts (and even the Gospels as appropriate), or in the Wisdom literature.

Conclusion

Biblical theology is an important level in the hermeneutical process. It occupies an intermediary level between the very important level of the text and the level of systematic theology. The close relationship between biblical and systematic theology, at least the way biblical theology is often conceived of by scholars and others who write on the topic, means that they are often confused. This is usually to the detriment of biblical theology because the major themes and concepts are often forced into categories more appropriate to dogmatic theology. Biblical theology has not always been well served within the field of biblical studies. As the discussion above has attempted to make clear, biblical theology requires that one think between the levels of text and systematization. In other words, biblical theology is closely aligned with and, in fact, highly dependent on close study and reading of various texts of Scripture. But it is also part of a larger effort to create coherence among an array of data gathered from these various readings. As a result, it is often the case that those claiming to do biblical theology stray into and remain in one of the other categories. A robust biblical theology is comfortable with textual study but expands the scope of such study so as to encompass the data that are pertinent to gain a fuller conceptualization of a given biblical theme or topic, without forcing the evidence into inherited or preconceived categories. There is much biblical theology written that is not as self-conscious of its methods as it should be. This does not need to be the case. Biblical theology can be performed in ways that retain textual integrity while providing clearly formulated statements that represent the larger theological concepts within the Bible.

7

Hermeneutics at the Level of Systematic Theology

Introduction

At this point in our hermeneutical journey, we turn to systematic theology. In the previous four chapters, we have discussed the first three of the five levels of our hermeneutical model for interpretation and proclamation of the Bible. The first level is that of language and linguistics, in which we bring an informed knowledge of language to bear upon our understanding. It is closely linked with the second level, that of text, and we discussed a variety of dimensions of what it means to study the Bible, and especially individual parts of the Bible (such as a letter or even a major section within a letter), as a text.

Many readers may already be familiar with the concept of reading at the level of text, although few probably fully appreciate the relationship between the level of text and the next level of biblical theology. The level of text provides the basis for the hermeneutical model of interpretation and understanding that I set forth here. The third level is that of biblical theology. We differentiated biblical theology from systematic theology, two concepts that are easily confused, even in the minds of some scholars. Much biblical theology tends to emphasize its similarities with systematic theology, rather than recognizing how dependent it is on the level of textual understanding.

In the previous chapter, I distinguished between biblical and systematic theology and there treated biblical theology. I now turn to systematic theology as the next level of hermeneutical understanding. Systematic theology is often not treated in discussions of interpretation of the Bible, as it is thought to represent a significantly different field of endeavor within the theological curriculum. However, in this chapter I will show that systematic theology is always present in hermeneutics, and so being aware of what it is and how we should think about it is a vital part of understanding it as a level of interpretation.

Doing Systematic Theology Today

Systematic theology was once called the "queen of the theological sciences."[1] It was thought to encompass the final and consummate synthesis of all the previous analysis in biblical interpretation, in which all the substantial and sometimes not so substantial orthodox beliefs were cogently presented in their appropriate respective categories so as to form a complete and coherent theological system, or set of dogmas (hence the term *dogmatic theology*).[2] It would not be an understatement to say that systematic theology is being done today on radically different terms than were ever conceived of when the above definition was originally formulated. This old definition grew out of a time when it was glibly assumed that doing theology involved little more than defending philosophically derived categories of Christian dogma by various means, including transferring a number of specific biblical quotations, thought to clearly illustrate the particular doctrine that was being explained, into the logically organized framework.[3] Of course, it was recognized that here and there a little pushing and shoving would be required to make everything fit neatly into place, but it would still all fit nonetheless. Nevertheless, dogmatic theology has persisted within theological studies, even though other forms of systematic theology have also been proposed.

1. Michael H. Shank explains that this concept actually predates Christianity, going back to Aristotle, who saw "the science of being" as undergirding both mathematics and natural philosophy ("That the Medieval Christian Church," 23). Thomas Aquinas, who was massively influenced by Aristotle, popularized this principle within Christian thought, although it has fallen on hard times in more recent discussion.

2. This was perhaps most explicitly articulated by Benjamin B. Warfield in his essay "Idea of Systematic Theology," where he used the analogy of the parts of an army for the various theological disciplines (257).

3. In the first chapter of their Old Testament theology, Hayes and Prussner (*Old Testament Theology*, 1–34) list a number of works from the seventeenth century, when biblical and systematic theology were not differentiated, except that biblical theology explicitly provided proof texts for preformed doctrines. As an example, they look at "Collegium Biblicum" by Sebastian Schmidt (1617–96), which listed proof texts for twenty-two different doctrines.

The fortunes of systematic theology have generally followed the same kinds of trends that have been found within Enlightenment and post-Enlightenment thought in biblical studies and related disciplines (similarities with views of biblical authority will be noted).[4] In the eighteenth century the dogmatic approach was called into question because of its dependence especially on ancient, classical philosophical categories, such as Aristotelian categorization that was then continued in Thomas Aquinas's *Summa Theologica*. The result was development of two major forms of systematic theology to compete with dogmatic theology.

The first was liberal theology, which originated in the eighteenth century and embraced the rationalist, naturalist, and empiricist tendencies of the rise of modern science. The nineteenth-century German scholar Friedrich Schleiermacher is often viewed as the father of modern liberal theology.[5] Influenced by romanticism, an application of German idealism, Schleiermacher was concerned with reconceptualizing Christian faith in terms of the values and perspectives of modernism. Others who have followed in the liberal tradition are more recent scholars such as Paul Tillich and David Tracy.[6]

A conservative reaction to theological liberalism was found in the rise of propositional theology, a form of theology that still thrives within especially conservative evangelical circles. Propositional theology, as seen in the writings of such scholars as Charles Hodge and more recently Louis Berkhof and Carl Henry, places a great emphasis on a literalistic approach to the interpretation of Scripture.[7] This form of systematic theology has some similarities to dogmatic theology but with more emphasis on proof texting its assertions and less emphasis on creating an independent philosophical system. Propositional theology believes that the biblical text contains theological propositions that can be ascertained and laid out in systematic form, as if the process from text to systematic theology were a seamless one.

Systematic theology has continued to develop in various ways, so there are a number of different approaches within the contemporary context besides the endurance of some of the approaches above. Even if classical liberalism is seen to have run its course, postliberal theology has emerged as an attempt to retain the values of liberalism while recognizing the postmodern context

---

4. For a survey of the development of systematic theology over the last several centuries, drawn on here in this brief summary, see Porter and Studebaker, "Method in Systematic Theology," 7–19. This chapter provides reference to a greater number of advocates and their major works.

5. Schleiermacher, *Brief Outline*; Schleiermacher, *On Religion*.

6. Tillich, *Systematic Theology*; Tracy, *Blessed Rage*.

7. Berkhof, *Systematic Theology*; Henry, *God, Revelation, and Authority*; Hodge, *Systematic Theology*.

in which theology must function. Postliberalism emphasizes the importance of theology developing a cultural grammar, in which the culture defines the parameters of contemporary life, and one must learn the correct grammar by which to address these issues. Christian doctrine thus becomes a form of cultural grammar that instructs people in how to embody their faith within their religious community. Hans Frei, George Lindbeck, and the Yale Divinity School of narrative theology are exponents of postliberalism.[8]

In a way that is similar to how postliberalism reacted to liberal theology, post-conservative theology has reacted against the propositional approach of conservative theology and developed as a competing form of evangelical theology. While remaining within the evangelical community, postconservatives reject the propositionalism of their forebears yet retain the broad evangelical beliefs regarding Scripture, orthodoxy, and Christian faith and practice. John Franke, Stanley Grenz, and Roger Olson represent the postconservative movement.[9]

A third contemporary movement to mention is radical orthodoxy. Radical orthodoxy is arguably an attempt to appropriate the classical orthodox position by drawing on postmodern thought. Based on some similar developments within Roman Catholic "new theology," with its appeal to the ancient Christian tradition, radical orthodoxy is postmodern in its focus on addressing culture, while doing so by invoking the orthodox Christian tradition. John Milbank and Graham Ward are major advocates of the radical orthodoxy position.[10] There are many variations on these major areas of theology, but the list given here tends to describe the major ways contemporary systematic theology is being done.[11]

As one can see from the brief survey above, there have been several broader intellectual trends within contemporary systematic theology. One of these has been a general flowering of awareness of the intricacies of biblical interpretation and the implications this has for systematic theology, especially with regard to the underlying philosophical issues.[12] In other words, most forms of systematic theology have in common the desire to interpret an ancient text in ways that are relevant for the contemporary Christian church. This may appear to be a simple proposition, but it actually uncovers a variety of

8. Frei, *Eclipse of Biblical Narrative*; Lindbeck, *Nature of Doctrine*. One might also place here Vanhoozer, *Drama of Doctrine*, although Vanhoozer is also postconservative.

9. Grenz and Franke, *Beyond Foundationalism*; Olson, *Reformed*.

10. Milbank, *Theology*; Ward, *Cities of God*.

11. The five evangelical approaches to systematic theology that are treated in Porter and Studebaker, *Evangelical Theological Method*, despite their diversity, fit within the categories above (propositional, postconservative, and postliberal).

12. McLean, *Biblical Interpretation*; Thiselton, *Two Horizons*; Thiselton, *Hermeneutics of Doctrine*.

difficult hermeneutical issues that must be addressed. These are the kinds of hermeneutical questions that we raised and discussed in chapters 1 and 2. These questions entail issues related (1) to ancient texts and how to interpret them and (2) to modern contexts and whether one is able, and if so, how one is able, to see these texts as having meaning and relevance for a contemporary person. Nevertheless, and perhaps at least in part as a backlash against such awareness, there has also been a revival of the kind of theologizing that depends directly on the invocation of the biblical text, as if simply invoking an ancient authoritative text automatically conveys appropriate interpretation and understanding that enables the contemporary reader to respond accordingly. This form of systematic theology has emerged very strongly, especially in highly conservative contexts.

In fact, at the risk of being reductionistic and annoying most of the advocates of the systematic theological positions I noted above, I would contend that what is now called systematic theology at the academic level takes three major forms, none of which conform to the classical definition. These categories reinforce the notion, worth emphasizing here but applicable to interpretation at all levels, that understanding exists primarily within various communities of interpretation.[13]

The major communities of systematic theology that seem to exist today are biblicist, dogmatic, and philosophical. First, in the biblicist community's approach—which in some ways resembles the dogmatic approach, to be discussed next, because of how it often uses the categories of traditional dogmatic theology to organize its textual data (e.g., Christology, soteriology, ecclesiology)—the Bible is not a text as we have discussed it in previous chapters but a repository of individual propositions that may be productively mined for timeless propositions that are then categorized and organized so as to reinforce and defend traditional dogmatic categories. There is a distinct sense that the biblicist approach, as found in propositional theology, engages in a form of apologetics by drawing on the abundance of textual evidence in defense of its categories of thought. A reciprocal relationship exists between the dogmatic categories and the biblical evidence, with the assumption that the individual passages constitute appropriate data in such a formulation of a modern theological conception.

The second approach to systematic theology is dogmatic. In this approach, systematic theology is taught as a defense of traditional doctrine. It often takes a historical approach that traces the development of doctrine along orthodox

---

13. The importance of communities of interpretation for the study of Scripture is recognized in chaps. 2 and 4 above. For systematic theology, the point is repeatedly emphasized in Smith, *Fall of Interpretation*. See also Westphal, *Whose Community?*

lines (and this historical orientation can be either implicit or explicit). For example, one might be interested in the issue of Christology: What does it mean that Jesus Christ is both God and man? Many courses in systematic theology, therefore, would take an all-too-brief look at the biblical evidence and then move immediately into an analysis of the major Christological controversies of the early church, when the church hammered out its belief about Jesus, even though they often did so using language that was very different from what is found in the Bible itself. An ambitious course would then proceed to trace the major themes through to the twenty-first century. This is dogmatic theology.[14]

The third form of systematic theology is perhaps better called philosophical theology. This form of theology is very often conducted in almost complete and even conscious disregard of the biblical and historical evidence. This kind of theology poses the major philosophical questions of the day and analyzes how Christianity, or a form of Christianity, addresses such questions.[15] For example, several theologians are concerned today with what Christian "hope" implies for the twenty-first-century person.[16] They may ground their discussion in some sort of postulation about what it means that God became incarnate, but the biblical evidence is often no more precise than this.

Within this chapter I intend to offer an approach to systematic theology that differs from the approaches outlined above. Many elements of the above methods have great appeal, including the importance of the Bible, the role that tradition plays in our understanding, the necessity of engaging culture (past and present), recognition of the necessity and limits of interpretation, and the need to maintain orthodoxy while being culturally relevant, among many others. While I admit the importance of church tradition in the task of interpretation, I also believe that such tradition has also often distorted interpretation and created a reception history of misguided interpretation. I believe we must, first and foremost, closely adhere to the text itself. Similarly, while I think it is important to respond to the challenges of our day, we cannot

14. For an example of this, perhaps unintentional, see Grenz, *Theology*, 294–325, in a chapter titled "The Deity and Humanity of Jesus," where much of the discussion centers on summarizing the historical development of the debates, despite Grenz's explicit statement that the Bible is the most important source for theological formulation (16–18). This historical, as opposed to biblical, emphasis is also typical of much of Karl Barth's *Church Dogmatics*, although a multitude of biblical passages are invoked along the way.

15. For an example, see Tillich, *Systematic Theology*, 1:60. This posture of beginning from a certain ideological or political commitment can be seen in various contextual theologies, such as Cone, *Black Theology*.

16. Among others, see Grenz, *Reason for Hope*; Meeks, *Origins*; Moltmann and Meeks, *Hope*; Moltmann, *Theology of Hope*.

do so without being deeply involved in understanding Scripture. Therefore, I will propose that systematic theology be understood as a tool for translation that takes the concepts found in the Bible (through the study of biblical theology) and then translates them so that they can be applied to the contexts in which we live and minister today.

Systematic Theology as "Translation"

I wish to take a slightly different approach to defining systematic theology than what we have identified as the major approaches historically and contemporaneously used. I have already discussed biblical interpretation in relation to language and linguistics, biblical interpretation at the level of textual analysis, and biblical interpretation at the level of biblical theology. Systematic theology moves beyond these levels of interpretation and is essentially a "translation" tool,[17] whereby the biblical concepts formulated through analysis in biblical theology are put into a language that is understandable to modern people and that confronts the current ways of thinking and speaking. This may sound very complex, and it is, but if biblical preaching and teaching are to be effective, systematic theology must be done. The German philosopher Gotthold Lessing, one of the major figures in the German Enlightenment, formulated a dilemma called Lessing's ditch. The ditch is what Lessing referred to as the gap between historical contingency and metaphysics, as seen in his statement that "accidental truths of history can never become the proof of necessary truths of reason."[18] There have been a variety of responses to this dilemma, including answering the problem on its own terms by means of counter-claims; answering the objective problem with a subjective response, thereby shifting the terms of debate; and various means by which generalizations are derived from instances. The last is the way most people understand the data that they encounter within the world. They attempt by means of various principles to generalize. Rather than always being universal truths, these principles may be communicable generalizations that provide guidance for understanding.

17. See Hasel, "Relationship between Biblical Theology and Systematic Theology." Gerhard Hasel identifies Krister Stendahl as explicitly articulating systematic theology as an act of "translation from one pattern of thought into another" (116). This concept is specifically rejected by David Kelsey, who instead sees "patterns" in Scripture as having a "functional" value (*Uses of Scripture*).

18. Chadwick, *Lessing's Theological Writings*, 53 (emphasis removed). Lessing clearly follows in the line of the Scottish rationalist David Hume, his contemporary. See Benton, "Modal Gap," for a summary of Lessing's argument and at least one form of response, although not the one adopted here.

I wish to propose here that one means of addressing the problems of systematic theology, as well as some of the practical problems of Lessing's dilemma, is through the notion of theology as "translation."[19] The notion of translation here emphasizes dynamic or functional equivalence and depends on the model proposed by Eugene A. Nida, a linguist and theoretician of Bible translation.[20] The heart of this translation theory is the attempt to create a similar impact in the receptor language as was created in the source language. I wish to argue here that systematic theology does its best work when it takes the biblical material and creates a similar impact—not just emotional but theological, ethical, and cultural, among others—in its contemporary receptors as did the original biblical material. That is the task not just of translation but of systematic theology. To do this, one must draw on some of the principles that Nida developed in his translation theory. The concept of dynamic equivalence is that one must first determine the kernel or the heart of what is being said in the original text. That has been our goal in chapters 4 and 5 (which were concerned with interpretation at the level of text). Translation theory tends to limit itself to dealing with the sentence, but this approach can also be used with larger units of theological meaning. The major issue is differentiating the essential from the ephemeral, the enduring from the contingent, and the relevant from the irrelevant. This is not necessarily an easy task, but it is required if one seeks to identify the kernel of a unit.

After determining the kernel or heart of what is being said in the original text, one must then move from the source to the receptor. One must put this kernel into the equivalent form of expression in the receptor language—that is, it must be put into today's theological language so that it has the same effect on the present reader or receiver as it did on the original audience. There are many potential difficulties in such an approach. These include questions of how we establish the meaning and reception of the original message, how we reduce it to a transferable kernel, the range of possibilities we have for creating an equivalent response, and the like. I do not wish to minimize the significance of these issues, but they are the same issues that must be confronted by every approach to systematic theology. The advantage of the translation

19. In this discussion I further develop ideas originally proposed in Porter, "Hermeneutics?," 121–27, and draw directly on language in that chapter. Cf. Osborne, who uses a similar model for contextualization (*Hermeneutical Spiral*, 431–33).

20. This is not the place to weigh all the issues connected with Eugene Nida's theory of translation (already discussed in chap. 3). However, his major theories are contained in Nida, *Toward a Science of Translating*; Nida and Taber, *Theory and Practice*; de Waard and Nida, *From One Language to Another*. There are many places to find responses to Nida's theories. As one example, see *The Bible Translator* 56, no. 1 (2005), where several essays are devoted to assessing his work.

approach is that, by using the analogy of translation, one engages a model of meaning-transference that we are already familiar with and often engage in. Even if we are not engaging in interlingual translation—from, say, Greek or Hebrew to English—we often engage in intralingual translation. For example, we translate from one sign system to another (remember the traffic lights of chapter 1?) or perform equivalent exercises—such as understanding what our children mean when they cry or what our spouse means when he or she says—or does not say—certain things. Every day we "translate" other sign systems into our own system of understanding. We should apply a similar level of conscious attention to how we read the Bible and how we translate it into contemporary understanding.

When discussing language and linguistics, we have thus far discussed issues related to the languages in which the original documents were written. Ideally, an interpreter engaged with the language of the text need never transfer linguistic categories to modern language, because the interpreter uses categories appropriate to the language under examination. Of course, this is an unattainable ideal, but it does make the interpreter appreciate the problems of the original language so that they formulate their linguistic understanding in terms of the original languages themselves, not some other language— namely, their own.

At the level of textual analysis, I have demonstrated how to trace the development of a given piece of text, plotting its narrative and ideas in terms of the text itself, with its own beginning, middle, and end. In biblical theology, I took the results of textual analysis and tried to compare and contrast similar kinds of texts, all within the biblical documents themselves. Here I noted that biblical theology appreciates the fundamental diversity of thought within the Bible, although it does see the Bible's unity at more general levels. Systematic theology is now the second stage of removal, whereby we *translate* the concepts of biblical theology into the kinds of ideas that a modern person can grasp. Here the unity of the biblical message comes into focus, not by ignoring the diversity of opinion, but by seeing that the Bible as a whole confronts us with a pertinent and timely message.

Philemon and Systematic Theology

We now return to Philemon as an example of how to proceed in systematic theology. I would like to begin with several issues mentioned in the earlier discussion of biblical theology and Philemon, where I concentrated on two particular issues: (1) what it means for Paul to be a prisoner of Christ and

(2) Paul's view of slavery. Until now, I have not been able to say what Paul's treatment of these topics means for a Christian living in the twenty-first century. In fact, most Western Christians alive today have little experiential knowledge of what it means to be a prisoner of anything, and perhaps even less knowledge of slavery, although many Christians know of grave abuses of civil rights in their own and in other countries. Provided that this cultural disconnect exists, can we formulate any meaningful generalizations about what it means to be a prisoner of Christ when we are so removed from the idea and the institution? There is much to consider here.

Paul as Christ's Prisoner from a Systematic Theological Perspective

Perhaps a better way to approach what Paul seems to be saying to us about being a prisoner of Christ is to say what being a prisoner of Christ *excludes*. This requires analyzing not only what Paul says and the social conditions in which he speaks but the presuppositions of this social condition. First, it seems to exclude taking advantage of one's place or station in life, whether in terms of sociological status or Christian status. In fact, the way Paul seems to move between the two tends to erase any firm and fast distinction. Paul does not openly use his position of authority but places himself on the same level as Philemon. Second, being a prisoner or otherwise restricted does not cause Paul to lose heart over an apparent lack of opportunity for service. One might think that if a person is restricted so that they cannot perform a task, then they could hardly be held accountable for failing to perform such a task. Paul continues to work for God despite being imprisoned. Third, being imprisoned does not seem to mean that a person's feelings and rights are denied. This may seem particularly strange to us. It is altogether too easy in our society to equate our rights and status with the particular position we find ourselves in (i.e., in rags or in riches). I am not sure that Paul entertains such a concept.

By determining what being a prisoner of Christ does *not* mean, it is much easier to explain what being a prisoner of Christ involves. Paul recognizes that he is in some way a *victim* of being a devout follower of Christ. In other words, he appears to have counted the cost of following Christ, even if the cost involves being socially and perhaps physically ostracized from his fellow humans, and he has decided that the benefits far outweigh the risks. It appears from the Letter to Philemon as if no regrets have ever entered Paul's mind, but if they did, they left it again long before this letter was written, since he makes no mention that his being in prison should be understood as a negative circumstance. How can this be? Would we not agree that to be in prison is hardly an occasion for joy? Imprisonment in the ancient world took different forms (from severe punishment to the equivalent of house arrest),[21] and Paul's imprisonment may not have been what we might call solitary confinement. Nevertheless, Paul's account makes it seem hard enough. We see that one of the ways that Paul takes advantage of the situation is that he uses the time wisely. Not only is his writing of the Letter to Philemon a strong indication that Paul is making good use of his time, but the letter itself contains much information to suggest that Paul's spirits are riding far above the limitations of his circumstances. This perhaps helps to explain his reference in verse 22 to his coming to Philemon: "I hope that through your prayers I shall be graciously given to you" (my translation).

Being a prisoner of Christ—whether this status is physical or spiritual, and the context of Philemon certainly includes both—leads to two apparent results. These results extend the meaning of being a "prisoner of Christ" and suggest some important, related theological concepts. The first is what it means to live one's life on the basis of Christian hope. Paul recognizes that knowledge of the future is beyond his or anyone else's view and that even for the next day's provision one can only speculate. When he says he hopes to visit Philemon, he is in effect saying that if it were up to him, he would visit; but he knows that God's plan may be different. The tension between human will and God's sovereign will seems to be resolved in the fact that Paul takes the initiative in anticipating the future, and he makes it plain what his preferences are, though he also recognizes that ultimately the events rest securely in God's hands. Much more could be said about this balanced approach to the Christian life, but perhaps I have said enough to make the point that systematic theology allows us to translate the text in a direct and personal way for our own understanding and benefit.[22]

The second result of Paul's attitude concerns prayer. Prayer would constitute a separate subject unto itself in any systematic theological treatment

21. See Harrill, *Slaves in the New Testament.*

22. It is interesting to note how Philemon has been used in different systematic theologies. Grenz, *Theology for the Community of God*, 498, uses v. 6 as an example of intercessory prayer in the chapter "Ministry of the Community." Erickson (*Christian Theology*) only refers to Philemon as an example of an instance where Paul does not specifically mention receiving his message from God (213) and v. 13 as a place where Paul uses the term *gospel* with no immediate qualification (1071). The index of Barth's massive *Church Dogmatics* lists a scant six references to Philemon. For example, he lists v. 10 as an example of Paul talking about having a spiritual son in the context of the broader discussion of Christian community (*Church Dogmatics* III/4: 244). Geisler refers to v. 14 as an instance of the free will of humanity to believe and act in relation to both worldly and spiritual concerns (*Systematic Theology*, 3:129, 278). I hope that I have shown that Philemon, a book apparently widely neglected in systematic theological treatment, has much more to offer than is usually realized. There are no doubt many other passages about which the same may be said.

of Philemon, or practically any book of the New Testament, especially the prayers of Paul.[23] Paul displays a healthy attitude toward prayer in several different ways. One is that he does not focus on using prayer for himself or for his personal needs. Instead, even though he is the one in a dire situation, he looks to the spiritual and physical well-being of others long before he is concerned for himself. In fact, he seems to acknowledge that others are praying for him, and he certainly appreciates it, since he recognizes the potential effectiveness it has. But in his letters, Paul shows that his first priority is the particular church or even the individuals receiving his letter. Prayer as communication with God is meant to be focused not on ourselves but on the needs of others.

Paul's View of Slavery from a Systematic Theological Perspective

Having said something about Paul being a prisoner, I will now turn to Paul's view of slavery. This, of course, is a complex issue, and not one on which I can say anything comprehensive. Such a task would require the study of much more than just Philemon. On the basis of this letter alone, however, we can speak to the significance of this topic in the area of systematic theology.

LIVING IN THE PRESENT WORLD

Paul first examines the world in which Christians live and recognizes the social structures of the day. In other words, he has a very reasonable estimation of the structure of society, its built-in safeguards for behavior, and the potential punishments that come with violation of it.[24] This is perhaps indicated by his prison sentence as well. Would it be going too far to say that Paul's knowledge and appreciation of the intricacies of first-century life go far beyond the understanding that many Christians have of their societies today? In the United States there is a tendency among many Christians, especially those from more evangelical backgrounds, to be largely ignorant and even suspicious of the inner workings of the social structures of American life.

The response to such a situation takes several different forms of expression. One might be called the *heavenly* attitude. In this expression, many Christians realize that the society in which they live is not perfect, so they focus overwhelmingly on the spiritual realm, as if there is virtually no connection between the two. They may pray fervently, and I would not want to

---

23. Heil, *Letters of Paul*; Longenecker, *Studies in Paul*, 28–52; Wiles, *Paul's Intercessory Prayers*.
24. See Rapske, *Paul in Roman Custody*.

deny the effectiveness of prayer, but they seem to be surprised that society is not instantly transformed. Consequently, their focus is often almost entirely on the realm beyond the troubles of this life.[25] As we have seen, this is not an attitude that Paul, or any of the New Testament writers, such as James and Peter, would be able to condone, and we do not see this perspective reflected in their writings in the New Testament.

The second group might be typified as having an *idealist* attitude. These Christians are at least aware of the difficulties of society, but their approach is to mount a sudden Christian blitz of the entire social, and often political, scene, apparently hoping to radically transform all the evil institutions in a very short time.[26] With the turn of every election cycle, there are always certain well-known religious figures who contemplate making incursions into politics. These individuals are usually the figureheads of the idealist approach.[27] Again, Paul and the New Testament writers (I would include Jesus as the most obvious example) would not condone this kind of an approach to life.

If anything, the New Testament seems to advocate a very *realistic* attitude toward the social conventions of the time.[28] Yes, it advocates change—and sometimes quite radical change, such as the elimination of social injustices like slavery through top-down measures that do not incite social destruction—but this change does not come about as a sudden strike that leaves only chaos in its wake.[29] Christians are called to be in but not of the world; in other words, believers are to be truly informed and involved in transforming their culture,

25. For the curious story of how fundamentalism gradually abandoned its early interest in social concerns, see Marsden, *Fundamentalism*, 85–93.

26. This impetus has appeared in a number of contexts, most notably in the early twentieth-century "social gospel" of Walter Rauschenbusch and his ilk. See Evans, *Kingdom*; Rauschenbusch, *Christianity*.

27. For example, the televangelist and self-styled faith healer (and founder of Regent University in Virginia) Pat Robertson ran for president in 1988. Although he ultimately lost, his massive influence behind the scenes did much to pave the way for the resurgence of the "religious right." See Marley, *Pat Robertson*.

28. At the same time, some today see no need for ethical advance beyond what is on the pages of the New Testament. For example, Wayne Grudem states, "In the writings of the NT we have a written record of the revelation that God gave us in Christ and the revelation that Christ gave to his apostles. We are not to look for doctrinal or ethical development beyond the teachings and commands of the NT, for that would be to look for development beyond the supreme revelation of God in his Son" ("Review Article," 308).

29. For example, see James Barr's heavy-handed (yet humorous) critique of Walter Brueggemann's *Theology of the Old Testament* in Barr, *Concept of Biblical Theology*, 561, where he states, "*Advocacy* is of supreme importance (e.g., 63), but what does Brueggemann really advocate? . . . When distributive justice is to be 'concrete, material, revolutionary, subversive and uncompromising' (745), are we to think of Brueggemann as a real bomb-throwing, Kalashnikov-waving revolutionary? Probably not. It's only rhetoric, after all. As in many churchly attempts to pronounce on social matters, there is no consideration of the practical

and in so doing, they are to be as wise as serpents but as innocent as doves (Matt. 10:16).

This role of a Christian must certainly begin with personal redemption, as Paul makes absolutely clear in Philemon (and here many advocates of a primarily social gospel have lost their way from the outset), but it also includes ongoing activity in the society in which he or she lives. Paul knows that Philemon, as the owner of Onesimus, is potentially a very powerful man, one who may even hold the power of life and death, and that Onesimus takes a big risk in returning to him. Paul also realizes the power of the gospel as evidenced through his own life. He stakes his claim on this, offering an example to all of us on how to live our lives.

GOD'S ORDAINED PATTERN OF PERSONAL BEHAVIOR

The second important observation about Paul's view of slavery is that Paul seems to subordinate his knowledge of the limitations and even potential abuses of the social system of his day to his primary goal of fulfilling God's ordained pattern of personal behavior. This may strike us as being particularly moralistic, since Paul appears to be recommending to Onesimus that he return to Philemon. Paul advocates this out of some sense of restoring the situation and correcting the wrongs involved, whether they are simply Onesimus's escape or the apparent stealing of money.

Would it not be better, we might ask, if Paul wrote to Philemon to tell him that Onesimus was staying with him, since slavery is an inhumane and cruel social institution that should be eradicated? Paul certainly seems to think that slavery is an institution to be dismantled from the inside out. However, Paul's priorities seem to run in other directions. This is not to deny his knowledge of the social system when he reminds Philemon in verses 16–17 that he wishes for Philemon to accept Onesimus back, not as a slave but as a brother on an equal plane with Paul himself! Again, Paul shocks us with the currency and immediacy of his position. Here he directly confronts the evil institution itself; without labeling it as such, he simply renders it redundant and obsolete. Paul advocates the complete transformation of the institution of slavery, but he does so individual by individual, with Philemon taking the first step. Paul is a *social realist*. These changes can take time. He is not afraid to confront social ills, but he is also prudent in arguing for transformation by Christians beginning with Christians, rather than calling for the kind of destabilizing insurrection that leaves nothing to salvage.

---

politics involved" (page numbers within the quotation are references to Brueggemann, *Theology of the Old Testament*).

RANK AND STATUS IN CHRIST

The third aspect of Paul's view of slavery in Philemon, regarding rank and status, seems to revolve around both the necessity and the unfortunateness of it. As was also true of the first-century world, hierarchy and status are apparently necessary constructs for behavior in the kind of society we live in today, one in which certain human beings have quite obvious roles to play that are not the same as the roles of others. This is even true within the context of the church, since some are older in the faith than others, and with this maturity comes a responsibility to watch over and guide those with lesser Christian experience (cf. 1 Pet. 5:1–5).

Paul also seems to be saying that in the issue of our status before God, such rank in the world holds very little weight. All human beings are created in the image of God, and they maintain this status, whether fallen or redeemed, whether slave or free. Of course, Galatians 3:27–29, the passage we partially discussed in the previous chapter, immediately comes to mind: "Whosoever is baptized into Christ, you are clothed in Christ. There is neither Jew nor Greek, there is neither slave nor free, there is neither male and female; for you are all one in Christ Jesus. And if you belong to Christ, then you are Abraham's offspring, heirs according to promise" (my translation; cf. Col. 3:11). The practical implications of such a philosophy of one's fellow human are most staggering, especially when we realize that God does not have respect for race or wealth or social status. One's status in Christ, as baptized, means that one is now enfolded within the Christian community. This is a community that does not reinforce (or at least is not meant to reinforce) the structures that typically distinguish members of society, such as ethnicity, social position, or gender—and we could name others as well that have developed from these. Instead, being one in Christ, we are all equal heirs of the promises of God. This is a great pronouncement of the egalitarian ethic of Christianity.

FORGIVENESS AND RECONCILIATION

The fourth issue that emerges in Philemon is forgiveness and personal relationship with God.[30] As I mentioned earlier in the discussion of Paul's logic in his approach to Philemon, Paul uses several pieces of evidence to persuade

---

30. Systematic theological treatments of forgiveness would include Jones, *Embodying Forgiveness*; Volf, *End of Memory*; Volf, *Exclusion and Embrace*. Systematic theologies are full of treatments of what it means to be in right personal relationship with God, although many of them emphasize justification over reconciliation. Some important works on reconciliation are Barth, *Church Dogmatics* IV/1: 2; Gunton, *Theology of Reconciliation*; Kärkkäinen, *Christ and Reconciliation*.

Philemon to welcome back Onesimus. One of these is the simple fact that Paul had led Philemon to Christ. Why would this be so significant? When we think of the person who led us to Christ, do we think of the person as someone we owe our lives to (cf. v. 19)? While some very well may, I think we can talk about these as exceptions to the norm. For Philemon, one of the reasons he would have felt indebted to Paul is that by becoming a follower of Christ, he would have experienced the almost indescribable feeling of relief when he realized that all his sins had been forgiven through Christ's death on the cross and that he was now in close relation to God. Surely this is one of the great theological concepts of the entire New Testament, if not the primary justification for the New Testament itself: to illustrate the great work of God through Christ for humanity, that of forgiveness and entering into personal relationship with God. When Paul asks Philemon to welcome back Onesimus, in essence he is asking Philemon to then, in a small but tangible way, pass a human version of God's forgiveness along to Onesimus (who now is also a believer and has experienced forgiveness by God) and be reconciled to him, whatever it is that has come between them to sever their personal relationship. Philemon can be God's agent and example.

How in the world, one might ask, could Philemon be a grateful recipient of God's forgiveness and not be willing to forgive his fellow human, especially when the circumstances are not so different?[31] God took the initiative in sending his son to die for humankind so that the act of forgiveness might be performed and reconciliation enacted. This was a costly act, as the Gospel accounts and as Paul's further reflection on the event record. What did Philemon lose? A valuable slave? Some money? Perhaps he suffered some embarrassment in the community and among his friends, but what is that in comparison to what he gained? This is where the theological emphasis lies: if we have experienced such a gracious and valuable act of God, should we not be more than willing to take the initiative in forgiving others for their "offenses" against us and in being reconciled to them? God's standard is high, a standard we can only hope to imitate in an imperfect and flawed way, yet, by its very nature, it demands our best efforts.

Christology in Philemon from a Systematic Theological Perspective

A final topic to consider at the level of systematic theology is the role of Christ in Philemon. It is easy to neglect what this text has to say about Christology.[32] One of the major reasons is that Philemon seems to be a letter that

---

31. Compare with the parable of the ungrateful servant in Matt. 19:21–35.
32. Among the few who consider this topic, see Martin, "Christology of the Prison Epistles."

is purely motivated by the situation it addresses, which involves only a select few characters. A second reason is that there are so few actual "teaching" passages in this letter, unlike many other books of the New Testament (this is one of the reasons I chose to use it in this book). One could cite Romans with its distinct sections on the sinfulness of humanity (Rom. 1:18–3:20) and the role of Israel (chaps. 9–11), Galatians with its teaching on the law (Gal. 3:1–22), and the Thessalonian letters with their references to the return of Christ (1 Thess. 4:13–18; 2 Thess. 1:7b–10) to show that theological sections are not lacking in the Pauline writings, to say nothing of the rest of the New Testament. The Gospels abound in clearly instructive materials, though of course these must be interpreted as well. A third reason is that several other themes seem to take the spotlight in Philemon, especially slavery.

However, despite all these reasons, Philemon offers significant insights about Christology at the level of systematic theology. The questions we ask the text are instrumental in determining the answers we receive. Christology forms a foundation on which Paul seems to build much of his thought, and this is what I would like to emphasize. Paul assumes a common ground with Philemon, the Christian experience of God and Christ. Here we return once again to one of the topics that I raised in the first chapter's discussion of paradigms. I note that Christians and non-Christians have fundamentally different paradigms through which they view life itself. It is next to impossible for the two groups to see things eye-to-eye, since their basic assumptions about the world are so radically different. Paul understands this and intentionally engages Philemon according to the assumption that they share the same paradigm—that is, Paul begins his discussion with Philemon with the assumption that they are going to have fundamental interests at heart and that they will be able to conduct their business by appealing to similar criteria for discussing and evaluating their points of view. The fact that Philemon, Onesimus, and Paul are all Christians is fundamental to what facilitates Paul's communication with Philemon. The consequences, if such were not the case, are equally sweeping. For example, it would make no sense to appeal to Philemon on the grounds that they share redemption in Christ if, in fact, one of them were not redeemed. Moreover, what about Paul's position in the church? Paul's recognition of this would be of no positive consequence to one who was not within the church structure; it would result only in confusion.

Do we realize that such is the case for us also? Let me make three points drawn from this exploration of Philemon before I bring this discussion to a close. First, like Paul, I have, or at least I should have, a fundamentally different orientation to life than most of those I come into contact with every day in the non-Christian world. For me—and what I say is, I believe, applicable for all Christians—the ultimate values that guide my conduct are established by God, and it is he who created and controls the world in which I live. While Paul's primary opponents were not atheists (to the contrary, they may have been very religious, but they were following other gods), I, like Paul, experience a certain clash between my Christian beliefs and those of the larger world around me. Against many in my society, I would affirm that life does not end with death, and the mere movement of molecules, though important and a wonder to behold, is not the fundamental essence of the universe.

Second, when I deal with those around me, there is a temptation to try to create a common ground for doing our business, whatever it may be. As a result of trying to find this common ground, the temptation is also present to compromise my standards since, after all, I am in the minority. How can I expect someone else to hold to my particularist and narrow standards when we can probably conduct our business on non-Christian principles? Now, in many cases, no apparent difference in outcome will result, since the particular issue at hand does not impinge on what might be called ultimate values. In others, however, our standards will clash, so that cooperation is exceedingly difficult.

Finally, our ultimate goal should be to introduce those we come into contact with to our value system, to our orientation to life, which involves fundamentally a commitment to Christ. Paul modeled this commitment to mission through the various methods he used to communicate the gospel to Jews and gentiles.

These three points are all drawn from a recognition that the book of Philemon has something to say about and is influenced by Christology. Philemon and Paul share common assumptions concerning the person of Jesus and his saving power in their lives. This unifying aspect of their relationship has significant connotations regarding how we conduct ourselves within the church today and with the world around us. Today we continue to confront the same kind of dilemma that is discussed in the Letter to Philemon, even if the exact circumstances are different. We are called to function as those called by Christ when the dominant structures around us are built on an entirely different foundation and attempt to command our obedience. Paul makes clear that Christ calls us to a different standard of behavior, both within and outside the church. This treatment of the Christological aspects present within Philemon shows how systematic theology functions to take an element of Scripture, like the person of Jesus, and "translate" it into our lives today in a way that remains faithful to the text.

A Call for Practical Relevance

I hope that my approach to what I have called systematic theology has helped to expand the categories for those who were expecting something a bit more traditional. After all, I can imagine some saying that what I have said has been distinctly practical and related to formulating principles and generalizations based on the text, which communicate to our present situation. I make no apologies for this. Since when must theology be purely cerebral and of no practical relevance to our current predicament as Christians living in a non-Christian world? I seriously wonder if part of the problem of the modern church is that we have made theology too abstract and not allowed it to address our daily lives. Christian theological scholarship does the technical side of theology very well and with ever-increasing skill as it learns more and more of the historical background of the fundamental documents of the faith. In the process, many have lost sight of the fact that all this work cannot be done abstractly and that it does have practical relevance. Practical relevance is part and parcel with doing theology at virtually every level.[33]

Study and Practice

Consider again the three passages of Scripture you have already worked on: Romans 5:12–21, Acts 17:16–34, and Psalm 23. This time, however, look at the materials that you gathered when you studied these passages as part of your study of biblical theology. When you undertook that study, you not only considered the text but identified a number of important biblical-theological concepts that were directly suggested by your consideration of the text. In this chapter, you are to use the biblical-theological insights that you have identified and engage in systematic theology. In other words, using the model of "translation," you are going to translate as many of these biblical-theological concepts as possible into systematic-theological concepts. First, identify a

---

33. This practical relevance has played out in different ways. Gordon Lewis and Bruce Demarest, in their book *Integrative Theology*, give thoughts on application as a final step after investigating a given topic historically and biblically. By way of contrast, for Stanley Grenz, truth is found by participating in community, and the most important theological statements are narratives of God's truth having an impact on believing communities. See Grenz, "Participating in What Frees." This is also seen in statements such as this: "The task of systematic theology is to show how the Christian mosaic of beliefs offers a transcendent vision of the glorious eschatological community that God wills for God's own creation and how this vision provides a coherent foundation for life-in-relationship in this penultimate age, life that ought to be visible in the community of Christ as a sign of the age to come" (Grenz and Franke, *Beyond Foundationalism*, 54).

significant number of biblical-theological topics in each passage and how they are directly related to the passage. Second, translate these biblical-theological topics into systematic-theological concepts suitable for your contemporary context. Third, attempt to organize these concepts into a cohesive whole so that you can begin to identify a systematic theology that you can communicate to your present situation and that can guide you in your Christian life.

Conclusion

There are many works of systematic theology that one may consult. Many of those that are the most helpful for contemporary study have been identified in this chapter, especially in the footnotes. However, many of these works do not make clear how one moves from the text of Scripture to the concepts of systematic theology. Some make proposals, but they are often sufficiently arcane or opaque as to hinder this necessary level of hermeneutical understanding. This chapter has introduced the notion of "translation" as a means of transferring the biblical-theological concepts directly grounded in the text of Scripture into concepts current for our present situation. Just as we translate an ancient text (such as the Bible) or even a more recent text (such as a contemporary novel) into our contemporary language so we can access it, the notion of systematic theology as translation provides a means by which to identify the kernels of a concept and then find the direct correlate within the contemporary context. In this chapter, we have discussed some examples of how such systematic theological concepts may be formulated in light of the letter of Paul to Philemon. This text is not used often within systematic theology. The reason for this is that it does not appear to have the kinds of propositional theological statements that are typically thought to be appropriate in a systematic theology. However, with the right hermeneutical stance and approach, even a letter that addressed a particular situation within the ancient world is able to reveal important systematic-theological insights for contemporary Christian readers.

8

Hermeneutics at the Level of Homiletics

Introduction

We have arrived at the final substantial chapter of this volume on hermeneutics. We have covered a generally large topic in a relatively small amount of space. I have chosen to approach this topic by means of various levels of understanding and interpretation, and so we have discussed language and linguistics, the text, biblical theology, and systematic theology. We arrive now at the final level: the level of homiletics. I believe that it is entirely appropriate to have homiletics, a more technical term used to speak of preaching, as the highest level in the hermeneutical hierarchy. Language provides the foundation of our understanding. From there we move to text, which is the focus of our hermeneutical model and underlies the other levels of interpretation. From the text we move to biblical theology, where we begin to think about the Bible not just as a text but as a theological document. We move from there to the level of systematic theology, where we translate theology into the world and situation in which we live.

All human beings are constantly involved in the hermeneutical process. Pastors and other teachers of the Bible are constantly involved in the first four levels—language, text, biblical theology, and systematic theology—but so are other active Christians in the course of their Christian lives. The task of homiletics or preaching does not fall to all Christians in the same way.

We perhaps wish that other Christians took it upon themselves to proclaim God's Word—and all Christians are called to be witnesses to their faith—but the task of homiletics itself is usually reserved for pastors and other, similar Christian teachers. This chapter is addressed to everyone, but it focuses on those who are specifically called to the task of proclamation.[1]

Hermeneutics and Preaching

It may come as a surprise that yet another chapter discussing interpretation is needed after considering the theological levels and the notion of practical relevance discussed in the previous chapter. Actually, there is nothing more in the interpretive process itself that must be addressed in this book. At this stage, the method and categories needed to grasp most of the fundamentals of interpretation have been discussed and modeled through the examples in each chapter. In this chapter, therefore, I will not include new information about what it means to interpret but will instead address how interpretation relates to preaching. Likewise, in the remarks that follow, I will not address technical or presentational questions, except for a brief word about the *physical act* of preaching itself. Plenty of works address the physical elements involved in preaching, and these are worth considering because of how they may help the preacher overcome some obvious limitations that can be corrected (a mirror might help as well, in front of which to practice).[2]

Many volumes on preaching also give undue assurances regarding learning to preach. I am highly skeptical of many, if not most, of these volumes. Preaching is not about finding a single "big idea" (big idea of what? a verse, two verses, a paragraph, a chapter?) or simply taking each individual clause as a proposition and constructing a usable sermonic outline or any number of ideas that have been proposed through the years.[3] Let me state it quite plainly:

1. It is unfortunate that, even today, I must make clear that I am referring to those *men and women* called to the task of proclamation. I believe that the evidence for limiting the roles of women in the church is much less exegetically strong than many assert. However, this issue was more than adequately addressed by Klaas Runia, *Sermon under Attack*, 97–108, where he offers wise words that appear to be overlooked by many.

2. There is a long tradition of books on preaching that deal with technique, including physical presentation. For example, see the classic work of Broadus, *Treatise*, which includes a major section on it; R. White, *Guide to Preaching*, where a full two-thirds of the book is dedicated to technique; Quicke, *360-Degree Preaching*; and, most recently, Carter, Duvall, and Hays, *Preaching God's Word*.

3. Such approaches are found in, e.g., Kaiser, *Toward an Exegetical Theology*; Robinson, *Biblical Preaching*. I do not mean to single these out for especially critical treatment, only to notice that they present approaches that, while they may have merit, do not provide guaranteed results.

I believe that preaching is an art form, the kind of gift that great performers have (even if it is more than this and requires devoted hermeneutical work).[4] For those born with this ability, developing into a preacher is virtually the same as growing up itself, with some of the rough edges shaved off in the process. For those who are not born with the gift (to speak colloquially), preaching may never come as naturally as it does to others. Certain techniques and procedures have proven themselves through the years, and almost anyone who wants to improve his or her skills in communication can learn these.

This book, especially this chapter, is an attempt to aid in this refinement process. This chapter serves as the culmination of the hermeneutical process that was instigated in the first chapter and has proceeded from basic assumptions and ideas to language and textual matters to theological matters and, finally, to homiletics. Though we all want to be successful in our preaching, however that success may be measured, it is crucial to note that "success" in ministry comes only as the result of the work of the Holy Spirit. The Holy Spirit is the essential component in ministry,[5] yet his work seems to be done through the agency of human beings, and that is what I will be discussing in this chapter: how the Holy Spirit uses preaching, or the practice of homiletics, to convey God's message to others through human beings like you and me.

In this chapter, I will confront several more important hermeneutical issues. First, I want to define what preaching and teaching are, since I have found in talking with pastors and in preparing my own sermons and Bible studies that it is quite easy to lose sight of what the goal of preaching is. Second, I want to point out some of the major issues that arise when facing situations in which we are called on to preach and teach. Third, I will try to give some practical guidelines on how the material discussed in these chapters can inform creative approaches to preaching and teaching.

Preaching versus Teaching

Many readers are probably used to the terms *preaching* and *teaching* being used together, connected by the word *and*, and often being treated as if they are roughly equivalent. This is not uncommon, especially in evangelical church

4. Cf. Stout, *Divine Dramatist*, for descriptions of the thespian background and successful preaching of George Whitefield. For further discussion of the nature of performance in preaching, see Childers and Schmit, *Performance in Preaching*.

5. See also Osborne, *Hermeneutical Spiral*, 435–37, where Osborne discusses the empowering of the Holy Spirit in his analysis of homiletics. See also Heisler, *Spirit-Led Preaching*.

circles, which often emphasize a pastor's teaching ministry. I do not wish to call the importance of teaching within the church into question (I will say more about this below). One of the major problems with the contemporary church is that its essential teaching function has been largely abandoned. One of the greatest contributions of the North American church has been its emphasis on and development of the Sunday school movement, where people of all levels, from very young children on up, were given appropriate and even graded instruction in the Bible and their faith. In many churches today, any vestige of what might be called Sunday school has been either abandoned or transformed into something unrecognizable from what it once was. The church has an important and perhaps even unreplaceable teaching role to play, and one might well pray that the church will regain this teaching function at some time in the not-too-distant future before it is too late to think of the church as being able to marshal a pedagogical function. However, in no way am I saying that preaching and teaching are the same thing or that they should be lumped together.

Readers will notice, therefore, that I have not used the term *and* in the heading above regarding preaching and teaching but used the term *versus*. This is for several reasons. The first is that I believe there are major differences between preaching and teaching. There are several dimensions to these differences. One of these is the appropriate context in which they are employed. Sermons and teaching sessions should be designed and used in different contexts. The more sermons I listen to, the more I am convinced that many pastors do not believe there is a serious distinction to be made between the two. The reasons for that may be varied, either because of their lack of understanding of the difference or their feeling compelled to make up for deficiencies elsewhere in the church educational mission so that their sermons become teaching sessions.

Another dimension of this difference is that preaching and teaching serve different practical purposes and, as a result, require different forms of presentation. Perhaps I am unusual in this opinion, but I believe that there is such an important distinction between preaching and teaching that each will require a very different set of applications of hermeneutics to the text, theology, and dissemination. One of them is appropriate to a service of worship, and the other is appropriate to a variety of other occasions—that is, non-worship contexts. Countless pastors and teachers have no doubt experienced some trouble over this distinction when preparing a Bible study for a midweek service as opposed to a Sunday morning sermon.

Before we can go further and make more distinctions between the two, however, we must define another important concept I have introduced, so that we are all clear on what I am saying. This is the concept of *worship*.[6] It would be quite easy to take a look at various depictions and descriptions of worship in the Old and New Testaments. Several important points are made there: worship is to be addressed to God (Exod. 34:14); it is done through the Spirit (Phil. 3:3); it should include the gathering of believers (Acts *passim*); and it includes, at the least, prayer, singing, ministry of the Word, and the ordinances of the Lord's Supper and baptism, all performed in the proper atmosphere (many of the epistles are addressed to churches that seem to have gotten the balance wrong in one or more of these areas).

What I wish to emphasize is the *aesthetic* side of worship. Worship is meant to be an inclusive, total experience that includes genuine communication—or give and take—with God *and* fellow Christians. In our day and age, a pragmatic approach has apparently taken over in many of our churches, an approach that has left services disjointed, fragmented, unfocused, and I suspect pleasing neither to God nor to the people gathered.[7] I choose not to go into specifics here, since I am sure most will be able to identify examples that they have experienced, but I want to make those in leadership aware that as important as the ministry of the Word is in any given service, it is neither the only thing being done, nor is it to be discounted. Instead, it should add to the entire experience of worship.[8]

First Kings 7:13–22 is an interesting and challenging passage.[9] The author records that, when he was building the temple, Solomon sent for Huram, a man skilled in working with bronze, and he fashioned two pillars, which were

6. This important aspect is neglected in the section on homiletics in some of the major evangelical hermeneutics and biblical interpretation books. It is found in some preaching books, such as Broadus, *Treatise*, 510–41. For a historical perspective on Christian worship, see J. White, *Introduction to Christian Worship*.

7. This pragmatism is not simply an unsupported accusation. A significant body of research on the North American megachurch movement bears out some deeply troubling trends. First, one of the popular techniques for church growth was to simply make sure that people only had to interact with others from the same social group, a far cry from the diversity that should make up the kingdom of God—and that originally did make up the early church as it spread throughout the Mediterranean world (see Bishop and Cushing, *Big Sort*). Second, the unabashed trend to "market" a church made many congregations adopt a corporate model and a business mentality. For critique, see Maddox, "'In the Goofy Parking Lot.'"

8. I note here, unfortunately out of necessity, that worship is the entire experience of coming before God, not just the musical portion of such an occasion (apparently a problem as early as Broadus, *Treatise*, 510). As this volume has attempted to make clear, language is important. I cannot help but think that when we use language in loose or even inappropriate ways—such as calling the music in a service "worship," as if the rest is not—we are both being careless and expressing ideas that need to be analyzed and rethought.

9. One of the most challenging and edifying sermons I have ever heard was preached on the pillars in Solomon's temple. I have tried to capture the gist of that sermon here, many years later. See Porter, "Pillars of Worship."

placed in the porch of the nave (v. 21)[10] of the temple in Jerusalem. Solomon's temple must have been an impressive sight. It clearly dominated the entire hill that formed the highest point in Old Jerusalem. It had a large, paved area with increasingly restricted courtyards, concentrically arranged around the temple proper, which included in its center the holy of holies, into which the high priest entered once a year to make atonement for the sins of the people of Israel.

This was a marvelous structure, and it is interesting to consider what the pillars contributed to this great construction. From an architectural standpoint—that is, in considering the architectural integrity of the temple—it might be surprising to find out that these pillars served no identifiable purpose at all.[11] Solomon erected them solely because God told him to. As far as we can tell, they were simply objects of beauty to enhance worship. Now, I am not endorsing the erection of two useless pillars outside every church, but I do wonder whether we always take seriously what worship, in all its grandeur and dignity, means. Certainly, it is more than a few ill-selected choruses, more than several old and boring hymns sung at a plodding pace,[12] more than the same old dull routine every Sunday, and more than merely filling twenty to thirty minutes with vague words on some topic and calling it a sermon. The worship experience is a *religious* service of the highest spiritual meaning,[13] in which believers voluntarily come before God and express their desire to praise him because of who he is, to make joyful noises to him, and to learn from his Word.[14] This should be the most important and glorious hour or two of every week. But for how many is this so?[15] The sermon is designed to be one of the

10. This term could also be translated as "portico" (NIV) or "vestibule" (ESV).
11. Scholars have attempted to speculate on this question but ultimately have been inconclusive. Donald Wiseman briefly summarizes various proposals for the structural and theological significance of the two pillars, though he notes the lack of consensus (*1 and 2 Kings*, 114).
12. Complaints about the dullness of music in church are nothing new. The great early eighteenth-century English hymnwriter Isaac Watts was motivated to write new music because of the lackluster quality of the hymns of his day. He once stated, "To see the dull indifference, the negligent and thoughtless air that sits upon the faces of a whole assembly, while the psalm is upon their lips, might even tempt a charitable observer to suspect the fervency of their inward religion" (quoted in Galli, *131 Christians*, 154). The controversy over Watts's songs in his day shows that the "worship wars" are nothing new.
13. James, *Varieties of Religious Experience*. While he erred in making "feeling" the pinnacle of the meaning of religion, Friedrich Schleiermacher gives a fine account of religious experience in Schleiermacher, *On Religion*.
14. A number of practical guides have been written for the purpose of assisting worship leaders with designing services that are both creative and appropriate for conveying theological truth. See Cherry, *Worship Architect*.
15. I realize that I run the risk of dating this volume when I note that the effects of the COVID-19 crisis will no doubt be seen in the church as we return to "normal." We will probably

major components of a worship service to God and so has a particular, even a unique, place within worship.

I wish I could treat every aspect of this topic in some depth, since these subjects have such great importance. However, I will confine my remarks to the proper approach to preaching as that unique event in which the preacher delivers the Word of God in a challenging and compelling way to the congregation gathered in communal worship. Though preaching can be defined in a number of ways, I wish to deal with the topic of *expository* or explanatory preaching. I will define this kind of preaching as I go along, but from the outset it is important to note that it is distinctly different from teaching. *Teaching*, to my mind, can be part of a kind of spiritual service or devotion, but it is best not to use it in a worship service. Preaching is a spiritual discipline in itself, whereas teaching is a more academic, intellectual, and perhaps even highly practical exercise involving the useful exchange of ideas in a learning process. The preacher must have done appropriate biblical analysis to be able to minister effectively, but to flaunt one's analysis is to detract from its spiritual impact. Conversely, in teaching we might look at the same biblical passage from the other side, with its raw analysis more comfortably exposed and open for discussion and further analysis. This is meant to be not a distinction based only on the New Testament differentiation of teaching and preaching but a recognition that different contexts demand different approaches to sharing God's Word.

Defining the Preaching Situation

The greatest tension encapsulated every time a person stands up to preach is best summarized in the title of a book called *Between Two Worlds*.[16] In it, John Stott, a well-known British clergyman and preacher of an earlier era, summarizes the difficulty of being the vehicle for mediating God's message to contemporary people. The preacher must be the one who bridges the gap between a static text—in the sense that it was written years ago in and to another context or other contexts—and a live congregation seeking a word from God. He offers one way to approach the problem, in many ways one

---

discover something, perhaps some disappointing things, about how people view church, especially whether they perceive it as a worship experience that involves genuine communion with God worth getting up for on Sunday mornings. Effective preaching is one way of addressing some of these issues, although certainly not the only one.

16. Although Stott addresses the twentieth century, the same situation applies in the twenty-first. Readers will note that the issue of two worlds is very similar to the issue of the two horizons mentioned earlier in this book.

that is similar to the one I am offering here, beginning from the recognition that preaching is an art, not something that can be formulaically prescribed.

The tension that Stott identifies might be formulated another way as well. On the one hand, the preacher must contend with the needs of an individual congregation. Without going into the specifics of how these needs are determined (through personal contact, prayer, etc.), this concern should weigh heavily on every pastor who steps into the pulpit, since one of the primary goals of the ministry of preaching is to minister to the needs of the congregation (those Christians placed in the care of the pastor by God). This requires a constant and sensitive reassessment of the issues that are at the heart of the congregation's concern and that have relevance for their maturing Christian life.[17]

On the other hand, the minister who preaches from God's Word must feel an obligation to deliver *God's Word* to the congregation so that it is comprehensible, understandable, and relevant to their current situation.[18] A sermon is not meant to be simply a history lesson or a repetition of the biblical story. I remember hearing far too many sermons that were recapitulations of the content of a text rather than exposition on the meaning of a text. Anyone who has spent time with the preceding chapters of this book should be able to speak to some of the aspects of what is involved in the interpretive process. One of the most important things discussed has been the quest for meaning. Even if a person possesses the relevant and effective tools to answer the question of what a passage means, they must also be faithful to this message when delivering it to a congregation. Not all preachers are able to bridge this gap.

Preachers use various methods in their preaching ministries. Some preachers preach large series of sermons on a particular book. There is some virtue

---

17. Douglas Stuart also asserts, "A sermon is a presentation designed to apply the word of God to the lives of people. Without application, a talk is not a sermon; it may be a lecture, a lesson, or the like, but it is not a sermon" (*Old Testament Exegesis*, 80).

18. Some thoughts from Karl Barth, *Church Dogmatics* I/1, on the nature of the proclamation of the Word of God are appropriate here. Barth helpfully reminds us that all proclamation of the Word of God is only an act of service, of pointing to God's previous speaking of his word (52). This act of pronouncing God's Word has the character of "the repetition of His promise" (58), an "announcement" (59), going beyond the mere reading of Scripture to making "the promise given to the Church intelligible in his own words to the men [*sic*] of his own time" (59). In Barth's larger theology of the Word of God, its form as preached is one of the three aspects of its event, along with its written and revealed forms. This background is necessary for comprehending such assertions as, "The Word of God is the commission upon whose givenness proclamation must rest if it is to be real proclamation" (89), and perhaps most of all, "Real proclamation, therefore, is the Word of God preached, and . . the Word of God preached means human talk about God which by God's own judgment, that cannot be anticipated and never passes under our control, is true with reference both to the proclaimed object and also to the proclaiming subject, so that it is talk which has to be listened to and which rightly demands obedience" (93).

in preaching through entire books of the Bible, both theological and practical. From a theological standpoint, some books in the Bible may speak directly to the needs of the congregation. A church that is struggling with finding its identity and perhaps, as a result, having problems with a variety of ethical and moral issues might well benefit directly from a series on 1 Corinthians. From a practical standpoint, preaching through a book of the Bible lets everyone know—including the pastor on a Saturday night—what the text of the next sermon is going to be. Since there is much to be gained from preaching through entire books, I suggest that one begin by proceeding roughly chapter by chapter, rather than verse by verse. If the preacher focuses on units that are too small, they run the distinct risk of losing sight of the overall context of the book and its larger theological connections and thus end up being out of touch with the needs of their congregation by the time the series ends.

I once had the experience of sitting in on a small group Bible study led by a pastor who was determined to teach through the entire book of Isaiah, an endeavor that would take more than a year, even at the rate of a chapter per week. To my astonishment, they were working through only a few verses at a time, which had the unfortunate side effect of losing the larger context of the book as a whole in the discussion of individual words within verses. I imagine that that group is still working through Isaiah, years later. I was also part of a church where the pastor preached through Ecclesiastes over the course of more than a year. I still know people who are talking about that sermon series, but not always with fond memories. Conversely, one can point to the rare exceptions, such as Martyn Lloyd-Jones, who preached through Romans from 1955 to 1968 and is (still) regarded as one of the greatest preachers of all time—but this is one of those instances where the exception proves the rule.

Many other pastors choose to preach more topically or even to use specific texts as pretexts for addressing the needs of their congregation. I appreciate the fact that the pastor is trying to find specific biblical texts that address the congregation's situation. However, as we have discussed throughout this book, finding this kind of direct correlation in very many specific verses is usually not possible or reasonable. The pastor may end up preaching his or her own predilections rather than being guided by the text. What are such pastors then offering their congregation that an advice column or simple humanistic kindness could not give?

Each of these extreme options is to be avoided. In the first, sensitivity to pastoral concerns is sacrificed for planning and looking ahead, while in the second, a vital and life-inspiring link to God's Word is sacrificed to the modern buzzword *relevance*. A preaching ministry that is faithful to the Word of God is the essential backbone of the church and is an indispensable component of revival.[19] Having said this, I would not want to pretend to be able to give a definitive answer to how this conflict is resolved, except through constant and prayer-filled reassessment from both sides.

It seems obvious when someone preaches a mediocre or even bad sermon, and it is usually easy to point out specifically what went wrong. I have heard a range of sermons over the course of my career, as well as delivered a good many of them myself (not all of them exceptionally brilliant, I must admit), some of which have left me incredibly confused, if not angry (those of others, not my own). To give an example, I once sat through a sermon where the preacher used the film he had seen two nights before as the text for his sermon. The result was more of a film review, the kind of thing I could have read in the daily paper, if I had not seen the same film already. Incidentally, I had seen the film, and I thought the preacher greatly misrepresented it, since he was obviously (at least to me) wanting to make specific points, whether he had good basis for them or not.

On another occasion a different preacher gave what he no doubt thought was an inspiring Christmas message by retelling the story of Scrooge from the English author Charles Dickens's *A Christmas Carol*, except his version was slightly altered. In this story, Scrooge, renamed Mr. Smith, abused his wife and children, did not work at any gainful employment, and was very mean, as we might expect, before Christmas. Then, on Christmas Day, this pathetic individual would dress up in a tattered old Santa Claus outfit and go down the corridors of a giant housing block wishing all the residents of the building a merry Christmas. The next day he was back to his same old self. This happened every year with regularity. Nothing ever changed. The minister seemed to think that there was something special in the transformation—if only momentary—of this man. As he said, "You have to believe in Mr. Smith."[20] I am still trying to figure out that sermon, but I am convinced that not only do I not have to believe in Mr. Smith, but if I do believe in Mr. Smith, there is something wrong with my understanding of the importance of Christmas.

Preaching can go wrong in many ways, even if we have the best intentions. We may think that preaching through all fifty chapters of Genesis will be an edificatory blessing to our people, but it may prove to be more of a chore for both them and us. Or we may think that preaching on the hot topics of the day, as ascertained through social media, is the way to connect well with

19. On the topic of revival, see Lloyd-Jones, *Revival*; Murray, *Revival*.

20. As strange as this example may seem, I have heard more than one version of this sermon in different venues. It is perplexing to think that one particular preacher thought that this was a suitable sermon—but it is even more perplexing to think that on another occasion someone else thought similarly!

our congregation, only to find that it is more of a shallow avoidance of the heart of the difficulties. There are better ways to both address the problem of contemporary and relevant preaching and be faithful to the Word of God.

Practical Approaches to Preaching

Among the more realistic options for the evangelical who is trying to bridge the gap between the two horizons, or, to use Stott's metaphor, the two worlds, several different sermon types may be appealing. The late twentieth century and early twenty-first century have been full of homiletical innovation, all with the goal of theological and cultural connection between the original text and context and our contemporary world.[21] Some of these new forms of sermonizing are driven by contemporary cultural trends, and others are driven by the availability of new media.[22] There may well be a place for some of these approaches, but often they represent outward frames into which content is placed rather than substantive inward reconceptualizations. If I had more space, I would welcome the chance to offer a more detailed response to the variety of homiletical means available to the contemporary preacher. However, in light of the hermeneutical model I am propounding here, let me suggest that the *expository* sermon, or biblical explanatory sermon,[23] is the one that commends itself best, both in terms of the concerns of the preceding chapters and also in terms of the concerns of the biblically centered pastor, even in a contemporary church.

This endorsement of the expository sermon may come as a surprise to some, who may have been expecting something far less traditional and more culturally relevant. I have used a variety of sermonic forms over the course of my own preaching, including not only expositional sermons but topical or thematic sermons, narrative sermons, and various forms of storytelling,

21. Other types of preaching include topical, narrative, first-person, evangelistic, and enactment, among many others. For discussion of different styles of sermons, along with their application to different settings and theological contexts, see Allen, *Patterns of Preaching*. On the role of the Bible in various approaches to preaching within theological traditions, see McKim, *Bible in Theology and Preaching*.

22. As a result, there is a lot of thought about the future of the sermon in the contemporary, postmodern, and, some would definitely say, post-Christian world. Some of that concern may grow out of anxiety that good preaching is becoming, at least in some circles, a dying art. On the topic, see Johnston, *Preaching to a Postmodern World*; Stevenson, *Future of Preaching*.

23. See Carson, "Accept No Substitutes." For other references to expository preaching, see Chapell, *Christ-Centered Preaching*; Liefeld, *New Testament Exposition*, esp. 5 but also throughout (still one of my preferred books on this topic and a constant companion as I have written this chapter); and Robinson, *Biblical Preaching*.

among others. However, at the heart of each sermon, even if it is presented in a format designed to appeal to a particular audience, is the same preparation that I do for an expository sermon, because I want the text and its resultant theology, both biblical and systematic, to form the substance of the sermon and the message that I apply to my hearers. Besides its basis in the text of Scripture (the necessary starting point and grounding of every sermon), the expository sermon should include several components. These include a text-based structure, hermeneutical integrity, a cohesive structure, and clear movement and direction. I will consider each of these in turn.

Characteristics of an Expository Sermon

I recognize that there are many different discussions of expository preaching, but few of them suggest the four characteristics I am outlining here. That is not a problem. A lot of what is often discussed regarding expository sermons I have already treated in one form or another in previous chapters when I have discussed the levels of the language, text, biblical theology, and systematic theology. I concentrate here on characteristics unique to the sermon.[24]

THE TEXT-BASED APPROACH

The hermeneutical model that I have been developing in this volume focuses on the text. The text of Scripture—taking all of Scripture as the maximal context but focused on a particular text for the sermon—comprises the basic content of the expository sermon that results from this hermeneutical approach.[25] The sermon should address *one* basic text of Scripture. The obvious application of the method I have been developing—one that is highly text-based—need not be specified in great length, but it would be difficult to overstate the importance of this feature. It is quite easy to make true and potentially helpful spiritual-sounding statements, but I am convinced that Christianity should be text-based. This is not only for the benefit of preachers, in that it gives them something concrete to delve into and to use to direct their comments, but for the sake of their parishioners. Worshipers come to church for a variety of reasons, many to find out what God's Word has to say

24. These four characteristics are derived from Liefeld, *New Testament Exposition*, 6–7. He also includes application, which I treat below.

25. There are many books written about preaching, and many are even about expository preaching, but fewer are written by biblical scholars. Some of those worth mentioning are Beasley-Murray, *Preaching the Gospel*; Hunter, *Preaching the New Testament*; von Rad, *Biblical Interpretations*; and, arguably the best of the group, Liefeld, *New Testament Exposition*. See also Griffiths, *Preaching*.

to them in their particular life circumstances. I believe that the preacher who does not give that person something from God's Word—the only concrete, specific message we have from God—has betrayed their sacred obligation.

I remember a sermon that had three main points (as many do, although this is much more of a convenience than a necessity): human beings are spiritually dead, God is sovereign, and human beings have responsibility. While these statements are each potentially important theological truths, the minister said he was using Ezekiel 37:3—a passage about the dry bones—to demonstrate how God has communicated these truths. There are several major problems with this example. The first is that this is simply not a passage of adequate exegetical bulk to sustain the three points suggested. A passage needs to be of enough significance to bear the weight of the sermon. A second problem is that, regardless of its length, this passage cannot sustain those three points without a lot of homiletical legerdemain. A third is that, based on the pattern by which the preacher extrapolated these points, I am convinced that he could have made the same points from virtually every passage of the Bible. But for some unknown reason, he chose this one. In other words, his sermon failed to deal with a text of Scripture on its own terms; the sermon was not text-based.

HERMENEUTICAL INTEGRITY

The sermon should have hermeneutical integrity.[26] This means that a sermon embodies the kinds of hermeneutical principles that we have been speaking about in this volume. This encompasses a recognition of what is involved in the complex notion of understanding, especially of understanding a written text. In order to understand, we must do the following before we engage in homiletics:

address the two horizons of text and reader;

recognize the foreignness of the text, as reflected in its language and in other respects; and

acknowledge the importance of further levels of understanding, beginning with the text and then moving to the level of biblical theology and then systematic theology.

26. There has been increasing recognition of the relationship between hermeneutics and homiletics, although I am not sure that all of us are speaking about the same thing when we speak of hermeneutics. See, e.g., Gibson and Kim, *Homiletics and Hermeneutics*. Some attempts to address some of the same issues as this volume, but with a focus on preaching, are Bartlett, *Between the Bible and the Church*; Kuruvilla, *Privilege the Text!*

All the various dimensions that we have been discussing are part of what it means to maintain hermeneutical integrity. Again, this should not be surprising in light of what I have been saying. Not only does this mean that the preacher uses all the best methods of interpretation on a text—this is a given that should not be up for debate, even if the specific methods are subject to critique—but this also means that the preacher needs to explain the passage while maintaining the same kinds of balance and concerns as are found in the text.

This is merely sound literary perception in appreciating the structure, balance, and tenor of a given work. But on the other hand, it is also theologically sound, since it communicates the biblical message in the same kinds of proportions as it is given. A recurring problem in some contemporary preaching—whether one uses expository preaching or any other mode—is the violation of hermeneutical integrity. This occurs in a variety of ways. One of the most common is the tendency to read every text, and hence preach every sermon, as if it were a reflection of the major points of one's systematic theology. As I indicated in chapter 7, there is a right and legitimate place for systematic theology as a translation of the theology of the text into contemporary thought. However, the reciprocal process is not warranted—that of then reading the major points of one's theology back into the text, as if Moses or David or Paul or one of the Gospel authors were reading a page or two out of one's favorite systematic theology book. And yet, we know how frequently such "illegitimate theological transfer" occurs.[27] This violates hermeneutical integrity, even if it is done in the best interests of professing one's theology.

COHESION

The expository sermon should have cohesion. *Cohesion* is a term borrowed from linguistics that I am using here to mean that the sermon hangs together. This goes beyond the sermon simply having an outline and arguing for three or four main points. Cohesion is much more involved and indicates that there is an intricate and interwoven pattern of ideas that creates the sermon's unified message. A potential difficulty with expository sermons is that preachers are so keen to base their sermon on the text that they end up repeating the text (the other problem of simply preaching their theology is no better). Preachers should not be content merely to repeat the text of Scripture. It is right to base one's sermon on the text, but the sermon must move beyond the text so as to become its own text that conveys meaning. The shortcoming of being

27. I create this term based on the lexical fallacy that Barr originated (*Semantics of Biblical Language*, 218).

content to stop with the original text and not create a new text is a common flaw of those who attempt to be textually based in their preaching. However, in this approach, the sermon amounts to little more than a list of the findings of the preacher's analysis.

In teaching, as opposed to preaching, the cohesion of the teaching material is not as important as the cohesion of a sermon since the teaching exercise may involve textual exploration as a part of the pedagogical process. The sermon, however, calls for a larger overall framework that includes not only analyzing the text but also building on that analysis to arrive at application.

To clarify what I do not mean by cohesive structure, consider the following example: I once heard a sermon on Paul's missionary journeys, and the pastor's three points were Paul's three journeys. This certainly has a kind of cohesion, but it is not the kind of which I am speaking. This merely shows one's exegesis (and, admittedly, not much of that), whereas a cohesive sermon understands how a passage is constructed and emphasizes that there is reason and purpose to this structure. Much better would have been to explore the book of Acts more fully, to examine the nature of each of the Pauline missionary journeys, and to use this detailed study as a means of beginning to understand Paul and his missionary strategy as he moved to various parts of the Mediterranean world.

MOVEMENT AND DIRECTION

The sermon should have movement and direction. By *movement* and *direction*, I do not simply mean that the text moves from one word to another or that it, as some perhaps might say, unfolds as the reader reads it. Textual understanding is undeniably linear in at least one of its dimensions, but it is not only linear. It also has, on the basis of how one understands it, its own internal propulsion so that it moves beyond being simply a linear succession of words to become words that are meaningfully related to each other in ways that compel the reader in response. Not only does a text such as Scripture have this characteristic (it does, and this should be recognized), but the sermon should have it as well.

The sermon should be concerned with adequately explaining a single text of Scripture (however this is constituted, which may vary depending on the circumstances) and should have its own cohesive structure. But the preacher must, in some way, show that the passage itself has persuasive power and must convey this to the congregation through a sermon that itself has movement and direction. A successful expository sermon will usually capture the force of its text by means of its own compulsion.

Several scholars recommend the use of what is called *principlizing* at this point. This presupposes that they have done all the work covered in the previous chapters and that, when it comes time to put the material into sermon form, they arrange the text according to various principles that not only summarize the analysis they are emphasizing but include the heart of the application as well. More often than not, these "principles" form the outline of an expository sermon. We no doubt must create generalizations as we move through the levels I have been discussing. I am not convinced that principlizing is the only, or even the best, way of doing this. Principlizing tends to equate the individual principles with individual clauses or sentences of Scripture, when we must be aware that moving from text to theology involves levels of generalization. That is why in one's textual study one must capture the movement and direction of the text as well as simply its words, and a sermon must do so as well.

A Sermonic Example: Romans 5:1-11

At this point, it will be helpful to include an example that ties several of these ideas together. I wish to provide a brief example of how to approach a passage and move from text to theology to homiletics. Preaching books often provide examples, some of them well-developed and full of ideas. These may be of some value. However, we must be careful in how much we draw on such examples, because, as I have emphasized at several points in this chapter, preaching is not an abstract task but a personal theological activity in which the pastor addresses his or her own congregation to deliver God's Word to that particular group. Several years ago, I undertook to read a number of Charles Spurgeon's sermons, based on his fame and renown as a great preacher. I found the sermons generally flat and lifeless, until I realized that these were Spurgeon's sermons for his people, not words addressed to me. So, in the example that follows, I am only able to offer comments as a means of suggesting and encouraging good preaching. Individual preachers and teachers will have to discern and address their own words to their own congregations.

Romans 5:1–11 provides an ideal passage for examining the challenges of preaching.[28] First, it forms a suitable unit for preaching (and possibly teaching) a specific text of Scripture. Scholars have debated how this passage fits into the argument of the book of Romans. Some have contended that it is best seen as part of the discussion of what constitutes righteousness in Romans

---

28. I note that Liefeld, *New Testament Exposition*, esp. 50–55 and 127–32 (see also 6), uses Rom. 5:1–11 as an example among several.

1–4, while others argue that it introduces the chapters on holiness (chaps. 5–8). I made a lengthy investigation of this passage and was impressed by the fact that it seems to come at a transition point for the entire book. More than that, I believe that the topic of this section—reconciliation—forms the climax of the argument of the body of Paul's Letter to the Romans.[29] It summarizes the argument of Romans 1–4—which moves from human sinfulness to justification, by which humanity's legal problem with God is solved—and it moves beyond this argument to transition into the next section of the letter, which deals with life in the Spirit. More specifically, it pushes Paul's argument from justification through to sanctification by means of reconciliation—that is, God providing a means to reestablish peace with humanity through the death of Jesus Christ. As a result, the passage forms an appropriate unit for preaching and teaching.

Second, all of the above-mentioned criteria for a sermon can be fulfilled by using this passage, whether a preacher wants to stress the human situation in relation to God, the work of God or Christ toward humanity, or the potential peaceful human relationship to God. We can observe that this text has hermeneutical integrity and cohesion as it purposefully unfolds. In Romans 5:1, Paul begins by recapitulating his argument: "Therefore, having been justified by faith . . ." (my translation). He then makes an interesting progression in verses 2–5; no matter how its various elements are construed, they all seem to revolve around Christian hope. In verses 6–8, Paul makes a comparison of one choosing to die on behalf of a righteous or good person, showing how difficult it is to conceive of such an act but emphasizing that even when we were *evil*, Christ died for us. Finally, in verses 9–11, Paul says that we are reconciled to God. In other words, there is no longer enmity between God and humanity because of the work of the Lord Jesus Christ.[30] Of course, much more could be unpacked in this passage, but clearly a sermon could be constructed that would fulfill all the criteria specified above.

Now, let's consider how a preacher might use this passage in a sermon. After stressing the sinfulness of humanity and the fact that justification only addresses the legal situation before a righteous God, the preacher could point out that humanity remains antagonistic to God, with hostility between the two parties. These ideas could be further developed into a number of suitable concepts. Or, after stressing that justification is the starting point in our relationship with God, the preacher could suggest three points of engagement that

29. See Porter, "Newer Perspective on Paul," 366–92, which is later used as the basis of my argument in Porter, *Letter to the Romans*, 112–23. Cf. Lee, *Paul's Gospel in Romans*.
30. See Porter, *Apostle Paul*, 320.

could follow: reconciliation, also called peace with God (this notion of peace with God would, of course, need elucidation), is the basis of the Christian hope; reconciliation occurs through the work of Christ; and reconciliation allows for the life of salvation or sanctification. If making the third point, the preacher might want to stress that humanity's hope comes from faith, that humanity is inadequate to enact a relationship with God, and that humanity is no longer an enemy of God after being reconciled. Of course, these are not preaching points, but they try to capture the cohesion and movement of the passage from different perspectives.

Application

The expository sermon must have application. By *application*, I do not mean reducing the passage to a spiritual "thought for the day," just one step above a greeting card; I mean that the pastor must show that the message from God is relevant to the situation of his or her congregation. Here we arrive back at the problem I introduced earlier in this chapter. Whether a preacher selects a given passage to address the individual needs of a congregation, or whether the preacher's message grows out of the passage, there must be a point of contact. The person in the pew—and hopefully the pastor—must say, "Yes, I understand what this passage is about," and then say, "Yes, I see what this passage is saying to me." The passage must confront the person where they are, not so much to reinforce what they already know, though this is at times very important, but to call for reassessment and reanalysis of their life. In this sense, the Bible is our adversary. It is impossible for me to make practical applications from Romans 5:1–11, since I do not have a specific congregation in mind, but several generalizations seem obvious: (1) Reconciliation comes through faith in the work of God through Christ, and this is a necessary stage in any further relationship with God. (2) Christian hope can only grow out of such a relationship and is what propels us through the times of trial and tribulation. (3) God's example of sending his son can serve as a model for our treatment of other people, though we can only be imperfect in its imitation. (4) We are reconciled to God—at peace with him, a status that carries rights and responsibilities in relation to him and to other people.

I will now briefly address what it means to make application in a sermon. Specific application is often difficult to achieve—it requires much sensitivity, the pastor having their finger on the pulse of their congregation, as it were—but I believe it can be more easily grasped when seen as part of an overall framework of application. It may be true that each passage can be made applicable to the lives of individual believers, but I wish to address the question of what some of the larger uses of application are.[31]

DIRECTION FOR THE CHURCH

The first goal of application is to give *direction for the church*. The church today is the direct descendant of the original church founded by Jesus Christ.[32] Just as in the days of the apostles, the church today needs direction. God is no longer revealing himself by giving supplementary written words. I believe that he used the written words of Christ's early followers because of the unique circumstances of launching a movement that has never had an equal in the history of the world. We are part of that great heritage. We turn to the foundational documents of the church—God's inspired communication—for continued guidance today as they contain the full counsel of God for his people. The expository sermon therefore has the task of communicating what God's Word has to say to present church circumstances.

SPECIFIC HUMAN NEEDS

Second, the expository sermon makes application to *specific human needs*. A great error of modern society, I believe, is to think that our present circumstances are unique and that no other time in history, and no other people in history, has ever confronted such horrendous prospects. I do not wish to minimize that we currently live in a day of turmoil and strife, but I wonder if there was ever a time when this was not the case. If anything, Scripture teaches us that humanity's failure to achieve peace and harmony dates back to Adam and Eve and their progeny. The biblical documents, it must be remembered, were inspired by God but were written by people who were in every recognizable way the same kinds of human beings as we are today. Like any piece of literature, the biblical documents were written in specific circumstances; in other words, they address an audience of some sort. If the Bible means anything, it addresses itself not only to the peripheral issues of today but also to the specific human needs of all ages—humanity's sinfulness, its need for salvation, and the need for continual transformation in a fallen world. It is the rare biblical passage of substance that does not

---

31. See Liefeld, *New Testament Exposition*, 13–15, for these points, although not in this order.

32. The Baptist theologian James William McClendon elevated this principle into a hermeneutical axiom. He states, "In a motto, the church now is the primitive church and the church on judgment day; the obedience and liberty of the followers of Jesus of Nazareth is *our* liberty, *our* obedience, till time's end" (*Ethics*, 30).

address at least one of these issues. Once it addresses one of these issues, it is amazing how it seems to address virtually all the problems of modern humanity.

AN EVANGELISTIC EFFECT

Third, the expository sermon has the very useful practical application of having an *evangelistic effect*.[33] If the pastor has done his or her textual study properly and has been faithfully attentive to the leading of the Holy Spirit, then the expository sermon will be evangelistic. In other words, it will confront the unbelieving listener with the fact that he or she is an outsider and stands beyond the boundaries of the community of faith. The New Testament was written to and for a certain kind of community—we call them Christians today. When the message of God's Word is communicated to his people, it is alarmingly evident to the outsider that he or she does not belong to this group of people. There is the classic joke about a non-Christian who once complained that he got nothing out of reading Paul's Letters. A Christian friend replied, "No wonder. What do you expect when you read someone else's mail?" In the same way, when the unbeliever hears the Word of God preached, the message is clearly directed toward another group of people. The same message, however, goes beyond any spiritual exclusivity in beckoning and calling those outside the family into a relationship with Christ. The expository sermon can be a useful tool in this process.[34]

Putting It All Together

How does one go about putting all that one has learned about hermeneutics into the practice of preaching? Below I have included a summary of the model I developed in this book and the necessary steps for using it to develop sermons.

1. An analysis of a biblical text should begin with a thorough reading that appreciates all the literary features of the text and understands it as much as possible in terms of the language of the day in which it was written. This may require reference to monographs and commentaries and use of other aids to ensure that one's understanding has not jumped

---

33. For evangelistic preaching, see Gresham and Keeran, *Evangelistic Preaching*.
34. On this topic, see Carson, "Challenge from Pluralism"; Carson, "Challenge from the Preaching of the Gospel."

to the contemporary scene too quickly but has appreciated each of the two horizons.

2. The next stage should be an examination of the flow of the story or argument of the passage from start to finish within its larger context. Usually the larger context entails the entire book and perhaps involves appreciating the genre of the book in relation to others that are similar or dissimilar. At this point, you should be able to select the significant events or statements on which the passage turns, and these are the items that ought to be stressed in the sermon.

3. The next stage is to determine the major biblical-theological topics treated in the particular passage, with some understanding of how these theological categories are treated both in the rest of the book and in larger sections of the Bible.

4. Next, select a significant number of systematic-theological topics and explain how they are directly related to the passage. As I have emphasized, this forms the basis of the application, since systematic theology is the translation of theological ideas into the language of today.[35] Making direct application, then, is seeing how God wants to use these ideas to minister to the specific needs of particular congregations.

5. The final stage is to reduce everything learned about the passage, along with the application, to a sermon outline on the basis of the specific points that can be preached.

Study and Practice

There are a number of different ways to practice developing sermons that are informed by this book's hermeneutical model. You may begin by developing sermons from the few passages already considered in this book. (But you will soon need to move on to other texts as well.) First, make practical applications from Romans 5:1–11 with reference to a specific congregation you know. Next, choose a text that you have already worked on in the previous chapters. Using the principles and generalizations that you wrote in chapter 7, make practical applications from the passage with a specific congregation you know in mind. Last, choose a new passage and start the whole process again as summarized in the "Putting It All Together" section above.

35. As mentioned in the above discussion of making application to specific human needs, examining the parallel situation between the original context and the modern context will also help a preacher discover some points of similarity within the two horizons in his or her process of contextualization.

Conclusion

While more can be said on the subject of homiletics, and consequently on the entire field of biblical interpretation, I have sought to demonstrate the importance of hermeneutics as it relates to homiletics. Of course, I have not exhausted the topic, even in this specific endeavor, but I have addressed several major issues. Hermeneutics, especially for pastors, can be a complex and even confusing field. Being well aware of this, I have aimed to present a model for preaching that considers a wide range of hermeneutical sensibilities and is, at the same time, not overwhelming to the pastor. I would urge those who make use of this book not to give up if their first attempts to implement the ideas I have surveyed do not go well. Be persistent. Biblical interpretation is not easy; it is not for the timid. Continue to expand your knowledge by practicing the approach, discussing it with others, and reading related resources. Be encouraged—biblical interpretation has great rewards not only personally but for the entire people of God.

Bibliography

Allen, Ronald J. *Contemporary Biblical Interpretation for Preaching*. Valley Forge, PA: Judson, 1984.

———, ed. *Patterns of Preaching: A Sermon Sampler*. St. Louis: Chalice, 1998.

Alter, Robert. *The Art of Biblical Narrative*. London: Allen & Unwin, 1981.

Aristeas. *The Letter of Aristeas*. Edited by R. H. Charles. Oxford: Clarendon, 1963.

Armstrong, Paul B. "The Conflict of Interpretations and the Limits of Pluralism." *Publications of the Modern Language Association* 98 (1983): 341–52.

Arnold, Bill T., and John H. Choi. *A Guide to Biblical Hebrew Syntax*. Cambridge: Cambridge University Press, 2003.

Aune, David E. *The New Testament in Its Literary Environment*. Library of Early Christianity 8. Philadelphia: Westminster, 1987.

Bacon, Benjamin W. *Studies in Matthew*. New York: Holt, 1930.

Baird, J. Arthur. "Genre Analysis as a Method of Historical Criticism." In *Society of Biblical Literature Proceedings 1972*, edited by Lane C. McGaughy, 2:385–411. Missoula, MT: Scholars Press, 1972.

Baird, William. *History of New Testament Research*. 3 vols. Minneapolis: Fortress, 1992–2013.

Bal, Mieke. *Narratology: Introduction to the Theory of Narrative*. 3rd ed. Toronto: University of Toronto Press, 2009.

Barker, William S., and W. Robert Godfrey, eds. *Theonomy: A Reformed Critique*. Grand Rapids: Zondervan, 1990.

Barr, James. *The Concept of Biblical Theology: An Old Testament Perspective*. Minneapolis: Fortress, 1999.

———. *The Scope and Authority of the Bible*. Philadelphia: Westminster, 1980.

———. *The Semantics of Biblical Language*. Oxford: Oxford University Press, 1961.

Barth, Karl. *Church Dogmatics*. 5 vols. Edited by Geoffrey W. Bromiley and Thomas F. Torrance. Translated by G. W. Bromiley et al. Reprint, Peabody, MA: Hendrickson, 2010.

Bartlett, David L. *Between the Bible and the Church: New Methods for Biblical Preaching*. Nashville: Abingdon, 1999.

Bateman, Herbert W., IV, ed. *Four Views on the Warning Passages in Hebrews*. Grand Rapids: Kregel Academic, 2007.

Baur, F. C. *Paul the Apostle of Jesus Christ: His Life and Works, His Epistles and Teachings*. 2 vols. Reprint, Grand Rapids: Baker Academic, 2011.

Bawarshi, Anis S., and Mary Jo Reiff. *Genre: An Introduction to History, Theory, Research, and Pedagogy*. West Lafayette, IN: Parlor, 2010.

Beasley-Murray, G. R. *John*. 2nd ed. WBC 36. Nashville: Nelson, 1999.

———. *Preaching the Gospel from the Gospels*. Peabody, MA: Hendrickson, 1996.

Beckwith, R. T. "The Canon of Scripture." In *New Dictionary of Biblical Theology: Exploring the Unity and Diversity of Scripture*, edited by T. Desmond Alexander et al., 27–34. Downers Grove, IL: IVP Academic, 2000.

Bennema, Cornelis. *Encountering Jesus: Character Studies in the Gospel of John*. 2nd ed. Minneapolis: Fortress, 2014.

Benton, Matthew E. "The Modal Gap: The Objective Problem of Lessing's Ditch(es) and Kierkegaard's Subjective Reply." *Religious Studies* 42 (2006): 27–44.

Berkhof, Louis. *Systematic Theology*. Grand Rapids: Eerdmans, 1939.

Bilezikian, Gilbert G. *The Liberated Gospel: A Comparison of the Gospel of Mark and Greek Tragedy*. Grand Rapids: Baker, 1977.

Bishop, Bill, and Robert G. Cushing. *The Big Sort: Why the Clustering of Like-Minded America Is Tearing Us Apart*. Boston: Mariner, 2009.

Black, David Alan, ed. *Perspectives on the Ending of Mark: 4 Views*. Nashville: B&H Academic, 2008.

Blass, Friedrich, and Albert Debrunner. *A Greek Grammar of the New Testament and Other Early Christian Literature*. Translated by Robert W. Funk. Chicago: University of Chicago Press, 1961.

Blomberg, Craig L. "The Historical-Critical/Grammatical View." In Porter and Stovell, *Biblical Hermeneutics*, 27–47.

———. *Interpreting the Parables*. 2nd ed. Downers Grove, IL: InterVarsity, 2012.

———. "The Unity and Diversity of Scripture." In *New Dictionary of Biblical Theology*, edited by T. Desmond Alexander and Brian S. Rosner, 64–72. Downers Grove, IL: InterVarsity, 2000.

Bloom, Harold. *Shakespeare: The Invention of the Human*. New York: Riverhead Books, 1998.

Bray, Gerald. *Biblical Interpretation: Past and Present*. Downers Grove, IL: InterVarsity, 1996.

Broadus, John A. *A Treatise on the Preparation and Delivery of Sermons*. Revised by Edwin Charles Dargan. New York: Doran, 1926. Originally published in 1870; 2nd ed., 1898.

Brown, Jeannine K. "Genre Criticism and the Bible." In *Words and the Word: Explorations in Biblical Interpretation and Literary Theory*, edited by David G. Firth and Jamie A. Grant, 111–50. Downers Grove, IL: InterVarsity, 2008.

Brown, Raymond E. *The Gospel according to John I–XII*. AB 29. Garden City, NY: Doubleday, 1966.

Bruce, F. F. *The Canon of Scripture*. Glasgow: Chapter House, 1988.

———. "The History of New Testament Study." In *New Testament Interpretation: Essays on Principles and Methods*, edited by I. Howard Marshall, 21–59. Grand Rapids: Eerdmans, 1977.

———. *Paul: Apostle of the Heart Set Free*. Grand Rapids: Eerdmans, 1980.

Brueggemann, Walter. *Theology of the Old Testament: Testimony, Dispute, Advocacy*. Minneapolis: Fortress, 1997.

Bultmann, Rudolf. *The History of the Synoptic Tradition*. Translated by John Marsh. Oxford: Blackwell, 1968.

———. "Is Exegesis without Presuppositions Possible?" In *Existence and Faith: Shorter Writings of Rudolf Bultmann*, translated by Schubert M. Ogden, 289–96. London: Hodder & Stoughton, 1961.

———. *Theology of the New Testament*. 2 vols. Translated by Kendrick Grobel. New York: Scribner, 1951–55.

Burridge, Richard A. *What Are the Gospels? A Comparison with Graeco-Roman Biography*. 2nd ed. Grand Rapids: Eerdmans, 2004.

Butcher, S. H. *The Poetics of Aristotle*. 4th ed. London: Macmillan, 1922.

Byron, John. "Paul and the Background of Slavery: The *Status Quaestionis* in New Testament Scholarship." *CBR* 3 (2004): 116–39.

———. *Recent Research on Paul and Slavery*. Sheffield: Sheffield Phoenix, 2008.

Caird, G. B. *The Language and Imagery of the Bible*. Philadelphia: Westminster, 1980.

Calvin, John. *Institutes of the Christian Religion*. 2 vols. Edited by John T. McNeill. Translated by Ford Lewis Battles. Library of Christian Classics 20, 21. Philadelphia: Westminster, 1960.

Carson, D. A. "Accept No Substitutes: 6 Reasons Not to Abandon Expository Preaching." *Leadership* 17 (1996): 87–88.

———. "The Challenge from Pluralism to the Preaching of the Gospel." *CTR* 7 (1993): 99–117.

———. "The Challenge from the Preaching of the Gospel to Pluralism." *CTR* 7 (1994): 15–39.

———, ed. *The Enduring Authority of the Christian Scriptures*. Grand Rapids: Eerdmans, 2016.

———. *The Gospel according to John*. Pillar New Testament Commentary. Grand Rapids: Eerdmans, 1991.

Carter, Terry G., J. Scott Duvall, and J. Daniel Hays. *Preaching God's Word: A Hands-On Approach to Preparing, Developing, and Delivering the Sermon*. Grand Rapids: Zondervan, 2005.

Chadwick, Henry, ed. *Lessing's Theological Writings*. Stanford, CA: Stanford University Press, 1957.

Chandler, Daniel. *Semiotics: The Basics*. London: Routledge, 2002.

Chapell, Bryan. *Christ-Centered Preaching: Redeeming the Expository Sermon*. 3rd ed. Grand Rapids: Baker Academic, 2018.

Chatman, Seymour. *Story and Discourse: Narrative Structure in Fiction and Film*. Ithaca, NY: Cornell University Press, 1978.

Cherry, Constance M. *The Worship Architect: A Blueprint for Designing Culturally Relevant and Biblically Faithful Services*. Grand Rapids: Baker Academic, 2010.

Childers, Jana, and Clayton J. Schmit, eds. *Performance in Preaching: Bringing the Sermon to Life*. Grand Rapids: Baker Academic 2008.

Childs, Brevard S. *Biblical Theology in Crisis*. Philadelphia: Westminster, 1970.

———. *Biblical Theology of the Old and New Testaments: Theological Reflection on the Christian Bible*. Minneapolis: Fortress, 1992.

———. *Introduction to the Old Testament as Scripture*. Philadelphia: Fortress, 1979.

———. *The New Testament as Canon: An Introduction*. Philadelphia: Fortress, 1984.

Clines, David J. A. *Job*. 3 vols. WBC 17, 18A, 18B. Waco: Word; Nashville: Thomas Nelson, 1989–2011.

Combes, I. A. H. *The Metaphor of Slavery in the Writings of the Early Church: From the New Testament to the Beginning of the Fifth Century*. Sheffield: Sheffield Academic, 1998.

Cone, James H. *A Black Theology of Liberation*. Maryknoll, NY: Orbis Books, 1986.

Corley, Bruce C., Steve W. Lemke, and Grant Lovejoy. *Biblical Hermeneutics: A Comprehensive Introduction to Interpreting Scripture*. 2nd ed. Nashville: Broadman & Holman, 2002.

Cowan, Steven B., ed. *Five Views on Apologetics*. Counterpoints: Bible and Theology. Grand Rapids: Zondervan, 2000.

Craigie, Peter C. *Psalms 1–50*. WBC 19. Waco: Word, 1983.

———. "Ugarit and the Bible: Progress and Regress in 50 Years of Literary Study." In *Ugarit in Retrospect: Fifty Years of Ugarit and Ugaritic*, edited by Gordon D. Young, 99–112. Winona Lake, IN: Eisenbrauns, 1981.

Croy, N. Clayton. *The Mutilation of Mark's Gospel*. Nashville: Abingdon, 2003.

Dahood, Mitchell J. *Psalms*. AB 16, 17, 17A. Garden City, NY: Doubleday, 1966–70.

Dawson, David Allan. *Text-Linguistics and Biblical Hebrew*. JSOTSup 177. Sheffield: Sheffield Academic, 1994.

de Waard, Jan, and Eugene A. Nida. *From One Language to Another: Functional Equivalence in Bible Translating*. Nashville: Nelson, 1986.

Dicken, Frank, and Julia Snyder, eds. *Characters and Characterization in Luke-Acts*. LNTS 548. London: Bloomsbury, 2016.

Dinkler, Michal Beth. *Literary Theory and the New Testament*. New Haven: Yale University Press, 2019.

Dodd, C. H. *The Parables of the Kingdom*. Rev. ed. New York: Scribner, 1961.

Dumm, Demetrius. *A Mystical Portrait of Jesus: New Perspectives on John's Gospel*. Collegeville, MN: Liturgical Press, 2001.

Dunn, James D. G. *Unity and Diversity in the New Testament: An Inquiry into the Character of Earliest Christianity*. London: SCM, 1977.

Eco, Umberto. *A Theory of Semiotics*. Bloomington: Indiana University Press, 1979.

Eliot, T. S. "Tradition and the Individual Talent." In *The Sacred Wood: Essays on Poetry and Criticism*, 47–59. London: Methuen, 1960. First published in 1920.

Eliot, Valerie, ed. *T. S. Eliot, The Waste Land: A Facsimile and Transcript of the Original Drafts including the Annotations of Ezra Pound*. New York: Harcourt, Brace, Jovanovich, 1971.

Ellis, E. Earle. *The Old Testament in Early Christianity: Canon and Interpretation in the Light of Modern Research*. Reprint, Eugene, OR: Wipf & Stock, 1991.

———. *Paul's Use of the Old Testament*. Grand Rapids: Baker, 1991.

Erickson, Millard J. *Christian Theology*. Grand Rapids: Baker Academic, 2013.

Esler, Philip F. *New Testament Theology: Communion and Community*. Minneapolis: Fortress, 2005.

Evans, Christopher H. *The Kingdom Is Always but Coming: A Life of Walter Rauschenbusch*. Grand Rapids: Eerdmans, 2004.

Farrar, Frederic W. *History of Interpretation: Eight Lectures*. London: Macmillan, 1886.

Fee, Gordon D., and Douglas K. Stuart. *How to Read the Bible for All Its Worth*. 3rd ed. Grand Rapids: Zondervan, 2003.

Fish, Stanley. *Is There a Text in This Class? The Authority of Interpretive Communities*. Cambridge, MA: Harvard University Press, 1980.

Fishbane, Michael. *Biblical Interpretation in Ancient Israel*. Oxford: Clarendon, 1985.

France, R. T. *The Gospel according to Matthew: An Introduction and Commentary*. NICNT. Grand Rapids: Eerdmans, 2007.

Freedman, David Noel, ed. *The Anchor Bible Dictionary*. 8 vols. New York: Doubleday, 1992.

Frei, Hans. *The Eclipse of Biblical Narrative: A Study in Eighteenth- and Nineteenth-Century Hermeneutics*. New Haven: Yale University Press, 1974.

Frow, John. *Genre*. 2nd ed. New Critical Idiom. London: Routledge, 2015.

Fuchs, Ernst. "The New Testament and the Hermeneutical Problem." In *New Frontiers in Theology*. Vol. 2, *The New Hermeneutics*, edited by James M. Robinson and J. B. Cobb Jr., 1–45. New York: Harper & Row, 1964.

Funk, Robert W. *Language, Hermeneutic, and Word of God: The Problem of Language in the New Testament and Contemporary Theology*. New York: Harper & Row, 1966.

Galileo Galilei. *Galileo's Selected Writings*. Translated by William R. Shea and Mark Davie. Oxford World Classics. Oxford: Oxford University Press, 2012.

Galli, Mark. *131 Christians Everyone Should Know*. Nashville: Broadman & Holman, 2000.

Garnsey, Peter. *Ideas of Slavery from Aristotle to Augustine*. Cambridge: Cambridge University Press, 1996.

Gathercole, Simon. "The Alleged Anonymity of the Synoptic Gospels." *JTS* 69 (2018): 447–76.

Geisler, Norman. *Systematic Theology*. 4 vols. Minneapolis: Bethany, 2004.

Gibson, Scott M., and Matthew D. Kim, eds. *Homiletics and Hermeneutics: Four Views on Preaching Today*. Grand Rapids: Baker Academic, 2018.

Grant, Robert M., and David W. Tracy. *A Short History of the Interpretation of the Bible*. London: SCM, 1984.

Green, Joel B., and Michael C. McKeever. *Luke-Acts and New Testament Historiography*. Grand Rapids: Baker, 1994.

Greenspahn, Frederick E. *An Introduction to Aramaic*. RBS 46. Atlanta: SBL, 2003.

Grenz, Stanley J. "Participating in What Frees: The Concept of Truth in the Postmodern Context." *RE* 100 (2003): 687–93.

———. *Reason for Hope: The Systematic Theology of Wolfhart Pannenberg*. Grand Rapids: Eerdmans, 2005.

———. *Theology for the Community of God*. Grand Rapids: Eerdmans, 1994.

Grenz, Stanley J., and John R. Franke. *Beyond Foundationalism: Shaping Theology in a Postmodern Context*. Louisville: Westminster John Knox, 2001.

Gresham, Charles, and Keith Keeran. *Evangelistic Preaching*. Joplin, MO: College Press, 1991.

Griffiths, Jonathan I. *Preaching in the New Testament: An Exegetical and Biblical-Theological Study*. NSBT. Downers Grove, IL: InterVarsity, 2017.

Grudem, Wayne. "Review Article: Should We Move beyond the New Testament to a Better Ethic?" *JETS* 47 (2004): 299–346.

Gundry, Stanley N., ed. *Four Views on Moving beyond the Bible to Theology*. Counterpoints: Bible and Theology. Grand Rapids: Zondervan, 2009.

Gunton, Colin, ed. *The Theology of Reconciliation*. London: T&T Clark, 2003.

Guthrie, Donald. *New Testament Theology*. Downers Grove, IL: IVP Academic, 2013.

Habel, Norman C. *Literary Criticism of the Old Testament*. GBS. Minneapolis: Fortress, 1971.

Harrill, James Albert. *The Manumission of Slaves in Early Christianity*. HUT 32. Tübingen: Mohr Siebeck, 1995.

———. *Slaves in the New Testament: Literary, Social, and Moral Dimensions*. Minneapolis: Fortress, 2006.

Harris, Horton. *The Tübingen School: A Historical and Theological Investigation of the School of F. C. Baur*. Reprint, Grand Rapids: Baker, 1990.

Harris, Murray J. *Slave of Christ: A New Testament Metaphor for Total Devotion to Christ*. NSBT. Downers Grove, IL: InterVarsity, 1999.

Hasel, Gerhard. *New Testament Theology: Basic Issues in the Current Debate.* Grand Rapids: Eerdmans, 1978.

———. *Old Testament Theology: Basic Issues in the Current Debate.* 3rd ed. Grand Rapids: Eerdmans, 1972.

———. "The Relationship between Biblical Theology and Systematic Theology." *The Trinity Journal* 5 (1984): 113–27.

Hayes, John H., and Frederick Prussner. *Old Testament Theology: Its History and Development.* Atlanta: Westminster John Knox, 1985.

Hays, Richard B. *Echoes of Scripture in the Letters of Paul.* New Haven: Yale University Press, 1989.

Heil, John Paul. *The Letters of Paul as Rituals of Worship.* Eugene, OR: Cascade Books, 2011.

Heisler, Greg. *Spirit-Led Preaching: The Holy Spirit's Role in Sermon Preparation and Delivery.* Nashville: B&H Academic, 2007.

Henry, Carl F. H. *God, Revelation, and Authority.* 6 vols. Waco: Word, 1976–83.

Hill, Andrew E. *Baker's Handbook of Bible Lists.* Grand Rapids: Baker, 2006.

Hill, Andrew E., and John H. Walton. *A Survey of the Old Testament.* 2nd ed. Grand Rapids: Zondervan, 2000.

Hirsch, E. D., Jr. *Validity in Interpretation.* New Haven: Yale University Press, 1967.

Hodge, Charles. *Systematic Theology.* 3 vols. New York: Scribner, 1871.

Hordern, William E. *A Layman's Guide to Protestant Theology.* Rev. ed. New York: Macmillan, 1968.

House, Humphry. *Aristotle's Poetics.* Revised by Colin Hardie. London: Rupert Hard-Davis, 1967.

Hultgren, Arland J. *The Parables of Jesus: A Commentary.* Grand Rapids: Eerdmans, 2000.

Hunt, Steven A., D. Francois Tolmie, and Ruben Zimmermann, eds. *Character Studies in the Fourth Gospel: Narrative Approaches to Seventy Figures in John.* Reprint, Grand Rapids: Eerdmans, 2013.

Hunter, A. M. *Preaching the New Testament.* Grand Rapids: Eerdmans, 1981. First published in 1963.

Irenaeus. *Against Heresies.* Translated by John Keble. Oxford: Nashotah House, 2012.

James, William. *The Varieties of Religious Experience.* London: Longmans, Green, 1902.

Jay, Jeff. *The Tragic in Mark: A Literary-Historical Interpretation.* HUT 66. Tübingen: Mohr Siebeck, 2014.

Jobes, Karen H., and Moisés Silva. *Invitation to the Septuagint.* 2nd ed. Grand Rapids: Baker Academic, 2015.

Johnson, Luke Timothy. *The Writings of the New Testament: An Interpretation.* Minneapolis: Fortress, 1999.

Johnston, Graham. *Preaching to a Postmodern World: A Guide to Reaching Twenty-First-Century Listeners.* Grand Rapids: Baker, 2001.

Jones, L. Gregory. *Embodying Forgiveness: A Theological Analysis*. Grand Rapids: Eerdmans, 1995.

Joshel, Sandra R. *Slavery in the Roman World*. Cambridge: Cambridge University Press, 2010.

Jülicher, Adolf. *Die Gleichnisreden Jesu*. 2 vols. Tübingen: Mohr, 1910.

Justin Martyr. *Dialogue with Trypho, the Jew*. In *Ante-Nicene Fathers*. Vol. 1, *The Apostolic Fathers, Justin Martyr, Irenaeus*, edited by Alexander Roberts and James Donaldson, revised by A. Cleveland Coxe, 194–270. Reprint, Peabody, MA: Hendrickson, 2004.

Kaiser, Walter C., Jr. *Toward an Exegetical Theology: Biblical Exegesis for Preaching and Teaching*. Grand Rapids: Baker, 1981.

Kaiser, Walter C., Jr., Darrell L. Bock, and Peter Enns. *Three Views on the New Testament Use of the Old Testament*. Edited by Kenneth Berding and Jonathan Lunde. Grand Rapids: Zondervan, 2008.

Kanagaraj, Jey J. *"Mysticism" in the Gospel of John: An Inquiry into Its Background*. Sheffield: Sheffield Academic, 1998.

Kärkkäinen, Veli-Matti. *Christ and Reconciliation*. Grand Rapids: Eerdmans, 2013.

Käsemann, Ernst. "Unity and Multiplicity in the New Testament Doctrine of the Church." In *New Testament Questions of Today*, translated by W. J. Montague, 252–59. London: SCM, 1969.

Keener, Craig S. *The Gospel of John: A Commentary*. 2 vols. Peabody, MA: Hendrickson, 2003.

Kelsey, David. *The Uses of Scripture in Recent Theology*. Philadelphia: Fortress, 1975.

Kingsbury, Jack Dean. *Matthew: Structure, Christology, Kingdom*. Philadelphia: Fortress, 1975.

Kissinger, Warren S. *The Parables of Jesus: A History of Interpretation and Bibliography*. Metuchen, NJ: Scarecrow, 1979.

Klein, William L., Craig L. Blomberg, and Robert L. Hubbard. *Introduction to Biblical Interpretation*. 3rd ed. Grand Rapids: Zondervan, 2017.

Klink, Edward W., III, and Darian R. Lockett. *Understanding Biblical Theology: A Comparison of Theory and Practice*. Grand Rapids: Zondervan, 2012.

Kruger, Michael J. *Canon Revisited: Establishing the Origins and Authority of the New Testament Books*. Wheaton: Crossway, 2012.

Kuhn, Thomas. *The Structure of Scientific Revolutions*. Chicago: University of Chicago Press, 1962.

Kümmel, Werner Georg. *The Theology of the New Testament*. Translated by John E. Steely. Nashville: Abingdon, 1978.

Kuruvilla, Abraham. *Privilege the Text! A Theological Hermeneutic for Preaching*. Chicago: Moody, 2013.

Ladd, George Eldon. *A Theology of the New Testament*. Revised by Donald A. Hagner. Grand Rapids: Eerdmans, 1993. First published in 1974.

Lakoff, George, and Mark Johnson. *Metaphors We Live By*. Chicago: University of Chicago Press, 1980.

Lee, Jae Hyun. *Paul's Gospel in Romans: A Discourse Analysis of Rom 1.16–8.39*. LBS 3. Leiden: Brill, 2010.

Lewis, Gordon R., and Bruce A. Demarest. *Integrative Theology*. 3 vols. Grand Rapids: Zondervan, 2014.

Liefeld, Walter L. *New Testament Exposition: From Text to Sermon*. Grand Rapids: Zondervan, 1984.

Lindbeck, George A. *The Nature of Doctrine: Religion and Theology in a Postliberal Age*. Philadelphia: Westminster, 1984.

Lloyd-Jones, D. Martyn. *Revival*. Wheaton: Crossway, 1987.

Longenecker, Richard N. *New Testament Social Ethics for Today*. Grand Rapids: Eerdmans, 1984.

———. *Studies in Paul, Exegetical and Theological*. NTM 2. Sheffield: Sheffield Phoenix, 2004.

Louw, Johannes P., and Eugene A. Nida. *Greek-English Lexicon of the New Testament Based on Semantic Domains*. 2 vols. New York: United Bible Societies, 1988.

Lunde, Jonathan. "An Introduction to Central Questions in the New Testament Use of the Old Testament." In Kaiser, Bock, and Enns, *Three Views*, 13–18.

Lyons, John. *Semantics*. 2 vols. Cambridge: Cambridge University Press, 1977.

Maddox, Marion. "'In the Goofy Parking Lot': Growth Churches as a Novel Religious Form for Late Capitalism." *Social Compass* 59 (2012): 146–58.

Marley, David John. *Pat Robertson: An American Life*. Lanham, MD: Rowman & Littlefield, 2007.

Marsden, George. *Fundamentalism and American Culture*. 2nd ed. New York: Oxford University Press, 2006.

Marshall, I. Howard. *Biblical Inspiration*. Grand Rapids: Eerdmans, 1982.

Martin, Ralph P. "The Christology of the Prison Epistles." In *Contours of Christology in the New Testament*, edited by Richard N. Longenecker, 193–218. Grand Rapids: Eerdmans, 2005.

Mathewson, David L., and Elodie Ballantine Emig. *Intermediate Greek Grammar: Syntax for Students of the New Testament*. Grand Rapids: Baker Academic, 2016.

McClendon, James William. *Ethics*. Vol. 1 of *Systematic Theology*. 2nd ed. Nashville: Abingdon, 2002.

McDermott, Gerald R. "The Emerging Divide in Evangelical Theology." *JETS* 56 (2013): 355–77.

McDonald, Lee Martin. *The Biblical Canon: Its Origin, Transmission, and Authority*. Peabody, MA: Hendrickson, 2007.

McDonald, Lee Martin, and Stanley E. Porter. *Early Christianity and Its Sacred Literature*. Peabody, MA: Hendrickson, 2000.

McKenzie, Steven L., and John Kaltner, eds. *New Meanings for Ancient Texts: Recent Approaches to Biblical Criticisms and Their Applications.* Louisville: Westminster John Knox, 2012.

McKim, Donald K. *The Bible in Theology and Preaching: How Preachers Use Scripture.* Nashville: Abingdon, 1994.

McKnight, Edgar V. *What Is Form Criticism?* GBS. Philadelphia: Fortress, 1969.

McLean, Bradley H. *Biblical Interpretation and Philosophical Hermeneutics.* Cambridge: Cambridge University Press, 2012.

Meeks, M. Douglas. *Origins of the Theology of Hope.* Philadelphia: Fortress, 1974.

Metzger, Bruce M. *The Canon of the New Testament: Its Origin, Development, and Significance.* Oxford: Oxford University Press, 1987.

Milbank, John. *Theology and Social Theory.* Oxford: Blackwell, 1990.

Mitchell, Margaret M. "The Letter of James as a Document of Paulinism?" In *Reading James with New Eyes: Methodological Reassessments of the Letter of James,* edited by Robert L. Webb and John S. Kloppenborg, 75–98. New York: T&T Clark International, 2007.

Moltmann, Jürgen. *Theology of Hope: On the Ground and the Implications of a Christian Eschatology.* London: SCM, 1967.

Moltmann, Jürgen, and M. Douglas Meeks. *Hope for the Church: Moltmann in Dialogue with Practical Theology.* Edited by Theodore Runyon. Nashville: Abingdon, 1979.

Moo, Douglas. "The Problem of *Sensus Plenior.*" In *Hermeneutics, Authority, and Canon,* edited by D. A. Carson and John D. Woodbridge, 179–211. Grand Rapids: Zondervan, 1986.

Morris, Leon. *The Gospel according to John.* NICNT. Grand Rapids: Eerdmans, 1971.

Moyise, Steve. *The Old Testament in the New: An Introduction.* 2nd ed. T&T Clark Approaches to Biblical Studies. London: Bloomsbury T&T Clark, 2015.

Munday, Jeremy. *Introducing Translation Studies: Theories and Applications.* London: Routledge, 2012.

Murray, Iain H. *Revival and Revivalism: The Making and Marring of American Evangelicalism 1750–1858.* London: Banner of Truth, 1994.

Neill, Stephen, and N. T. Wright. *The Interpretation of the New Testament 1861–1986.* Rev. ed. Oxford: Oxford University Press, 1988.

Nida, Eugene A. *Toward a Science of Translating, with Special Reference to Principles and Procedures Involved in Bible Translating.* Leiden: Brill, 1964.

Nida, Eugene A., and Charles R. Taber. *The Theory and Practice of Translation.* Leiden: Brill, 1969.

Nienhuis, David R. *Not by Paul Alone: The Formation of the Catholic Epistle Collection and the Christian Canon.* Waco: Baylor University Press, 2007.

Nineham, Dennis. *The Use and Abuse of the Bible: A Study of the Bible in an Age of Rapid Cultural Change.* London: SPCK, 1976.

Nöth, Winfried. *Handbook of Semiotics.* Bloomington: Indiana University Press, 1995.

Olson, Roger E. *Reformed and Always Reforming: The Postconservative Approach to Evangelical Theology.* Grand Rapids: Baker Academic, 2007.

Osborne, Grant R. *The Hermeneutical Spiral: A Comprehensive Introduction to Biblical Interpretation.* 2nd ed. Downers Grove, IL: InterVarsity, 2006.

Pannenberg, Wolfhart. "What Is Truth?" In vol. 2 of *Basic Questions in Theology*, translated by George H. Kehm, 20–21. Philadelphia: Fortress, 1970.

Parker, D. C. *The Living Text of the Gospels.* Cambridge: Cambridge University Press, 1997.

Peirce, Charles. *Pragmatism as a Principle and Method of Right Thinking: The 1903 Harvard Lectures on Pragmatism.* Edited by Patricia Ann Turrisi. Albany: State University of New York Press, 1997.

Perrin, Norman. *What Is Redaction Criticism?* GBS. Minneapolis: Fortress, 1969.

Petersen, Norman. *Rediscovering Paul: Philemon and the Sociology of Paul's Narrative World.* Philadelphia: Fortress, 1985.

Pitts, Andrew W. *History, Biography and the Genre of Luke-Acts: An Exploration of Literary Divergence in Greek Narrative Discourse.* Biblical Interpretation Series 177. Leiden: Brill, 2019.

Porter, Stanley E. *The Apostle Paul: His Life, Thought, and Letters.* Grand Rapids: Eerdmans, 2016.

———. "The Authority of the Bible as a Hermeneutical Issue." *EvQ* 86, no. 4 (2014): 303–24.

———, ed. *Dictionary of Biblical Criticism and Interpretation.* London: Routledge, 2007.

———. "Hermeneutics, Biblical Interpretation, and Theology: Hunch, Holy Spirit, or Hard Work?" In *Beyond the Bible: Moving from Scripture to Theology*, by I. Howard Marshall, with Kevin J. Vanhoozer and Stanley E. Porter, 97–127. Grand Rapids: Baker Academic, 2004.

———. *How We Got the New Testament: Text, Transmission, Translation.* Grand Rapids: Baker Academic, 2013.

———. *Idioms of the Greek New Testament.* 2nd ed. BLG 2. Sheffield: Sheffield Academic, 1994.

———. *Jesus as the Divine Son: Five Gospel Studies.* Manuscript in preparation.

———. *The Letter to the Romans: A Linguistic and Literary Commentary.* NTM 37. Sheffield: Sheffield Phoenix, 2015.

———. *Linguistic Analysis of the Greek New Testament: Studies in Tools, Methods, and Practice.* Grand Rapids: Baker Academic, 2016.

———. "Literary Approaches to the New Testament: From Formalism to Deconstruction and Back." In *Approaches to New Testament Study*, edited by Stanley E. Porter and David Tombs, 77–128. Sheffield: Sheffield Academic, 1995.

———. "A Newer Perspective on Paul: Romans 1–8 through the Eyes of Literary Analysis." In *The Bible in Human Society: Essays in Honour of John Rogerson*, edited by M. Daniel Carroll R., David J. A. Clines, and Philip R. Davies, 366–92. JSOTSup 200. Sheffield: Sheffield Academic, 1995.

———. *New Testament Theology and the Greek Language: A Linguistic Reconceptualization*. Cambridge: Cambridge University Press, 2022.

———. *The Pastoral Epistles: A Commentary on the Greek Text*. Grand Rapids: Baker Academic, forthcoming.

———. *The Paul of Acts: Essays in Literary Criticism, Rhetoric, and Theology*. WUNT 115. Tübingen: Mohr Siebeck, 1999. Reprint, *Paul in Acts*. Peabody, MA: Hendrickson, 2001.

———. "Paul, Virtues, Vices, and Household Codes." In vol. 2 of *Paul in the Greco-Roman World: A Handbook*, edited by J. Paul Sampley, 369–90. 2nd ed. London: Bloomsbury, 2016.

———. "Pillars of Worship." *MJTM* 12 (2010): 125–31.

———. "Reframing Social Justice in the Pauline Letters." In *The Bible and Social Justice: Old Testament and New Testament Foundations for the Church's Urgent Call*, edited by Cynthia Long Westfall and Bryan R. Dyer, 125–51. MNTS. Eugene, OR: Pickwick, 2015.

———. *Sacred Tradition in the New Testament: Tracing Old Testament Themes in the Gospels and Epistles*. Grand Rapids: Baker Academic, 2016.

———. *Verbal Aspect in the Greek of the New Testament, with Reference to Tense and Mood*. SBG 1. New York: Peter Lang, 1989.

———. "What Exactly Is Theological Interpretation of Scripture, and Is It Hermeneutically Robust Enough for the Task to Which It Has Been Appointed?" In *Horizons in Hermeneutics: A Festschrift in Honor of Anthony C. Thiselton*, edited by Stanley E. Porter and Matthew R. Malcolm, 234–67. Grand Rapids: Eerdmans, 2013.

———. "Where Have All the Greek Grammarians Gone? And Why Should Anyone Care?" *BAGL* 9 (2020): 5–38.

Porter, Stanley E., and Sean A. Adams, eds. *Pillars in the History of Biblical Interpretation*. Vol. 1, *Prevailing Methods before 1980*. MBSS 2. Eugene, OR: Pickwick, 2016.

———, eds. *Pillars in the History of Biblical Interpretation*. Vol. 2, *Prevailing Methods after 1980*. MBSS 2. Eugene, OR: Pickwick, 2016.

Porter, Stanley E., and Zachary K. Dawson, eds. *Pillars in the History of Biblical Interpretation*. Vol. 3, *Further Essays on Prevailing Methods*. MBSS 6. Eugene, OR: Pickwick, 2021.

Porter, Stanley E., and Bryan R. Dyer, eds. *The Synoptic Problem: Four Views*. Grand Rapids: Baker Academic, 2016.

Porter, Stanley E., and Matthew R. Malcolm, eds. *The Future of Biblical Interpretation: Responsible Plurality in Biblical Hermeneutics*. Downers Grove, IL: InterVarsity, 2013.

Porter, Stanley E., and Jason C. Robinson. *Active Hermeneutics: Seeking Understanding in an Age of Objectivism*. London: Routledge, 2021.

———. *Hermeneutics: An Introduction to Interpretive Theory*. Grand Rapids: Eerdmans, 2011.

Porter, Stanley E., and Beth M. Stovell, eds. *Biblical Hermeneutics: Five Views*. Spectrum Multiview Books. Downers Grove, IL: InterVarsity, 2012.

Porter, Stanley E., and Steven M. Studebaker, eds. *Evangelical Theological Method: Five Views*. Spectrum Multiview Books. Downers Grove, IL: IVP Academic, 2018.

———. "Method in Systematic Theology: An Introduction." In Porter and Studebaker, *Evangelical Theological Method*, 1–28.

Pym, Anthony. *Exploring Translation Theories*. London: Routledge, 2010.

Quicke, Michael J. *360-Degree Preaching: Hearing, Speaking, and Living the Word*. Grand Rapids: Baker Books, 2003.

Rapske, Brian. *Paul in Roman Custody*. Vol. 3 of *The Book of Acts in Its First-Century Setting*. Grand Rapids: Eerdmans, 1994.

Rauschenbusch, Walter. *Christianity and the Social Crisis*. New York: Macmillan, 1910.

Reid, Daniel G., ed. *The IVP Dictionary of the New Testament: A One-Volume Compendium of Contemporary Biblical Scholarship*. Downers Grove, IL: InterVarsity, 2004.

Reventlow, Henning Graf. *History of Biblical Interpretation*. 4 vols. Translated by Leo G. Perdue and James O. Duke. Atlanta: SBL, 2009–10.

Richardson, Kurt A. "The Antiochene School." In Porter, *Dictionary of Biblical Criticism and Interpretation*, 14–16.

Robinson, Haddon W. *Biblical Preaching: The Development and Delivery of Expository Messages*. Grand Rapids: Baker Academic, 2001.

Rogers, Jack B., and Donald K. McKim. *The Authority and Interpretation of the Bible: An Historical Approach*. New York: Harper & Row, 1979.

Ruhl, Charles. *On Monosemy: A Study in Linguistic Semantics*. New York: SUNY Press, 1989.

Runia, Klaas. *The Sermon under Attack*. Exeter: Paternoster, 1983.

Saussure, Ferdinand de. *Course in General Linguistics*. Edited by Charles Bally and Albert Sechehaye. Translated by Wade Baskin. London: Collins, 1959.

Scheidel, Walter. "Progress and Problems in Roman Demography." In *Debating Roman Demography*, edited by Walter Scheidel, 1–82. Leiden: Brill, 2001.

Schemm, Peter R., Jr. "Kevin Giles's *The Trinity and Subordinationism*: A Review Article." *JBMW* 7 (2002): 67–78.

Schleiermacher, Friedrich E. *Brief Outline of Theology as a Field of Study*. 3rd ed. Translated by Terrence N. Tice. Louisville: Westminster John Knox, 2011.

———. *On Religion: Speeches to Its Cultured Despisers*. Cambridge Texts in the History of Philosophy. Cambridge: Cambridge University Press, 1996.

Schnelle, Udo. *Theology of the New Testament*. Translated by M. Eugene Boring. Grand Rapids: Baker Academic, 2009.

Scott, Bernard Brandon. *Hear Then the Parable: A Commentary on the Parables of Jesus*. Minneapolis: Fortress, 1989.

Senior, Donald. *What Are They Saying about Matthew?* Rev. and exp. ed. New York: Paulist Press, 1996.

Shank, Michael H. "That the Medieval Christian Church Suppressed the Growth of Science." In *Galileo Goes to Jail and Other Myths about Science and Religion*, edited by Ronald L. Numbers, 19–27. Cambridge, MA: Harvard University Press, 2009.

Shuler, Philip L. *A Genre for the Gospels: The Biographical Character of Matthew*. Philadelphia: Fortress, 1982.

Silva, Moisés. *Biblical Words and Their Meaning: An Introduction to Lexical Semantics*. Grand Rapids: Zondervan, 1983.

Smith, James K. A. *The Fall of Interpretation: Philosophical Foundations for a Creational Hermeneutic*. 2nd ed. Grand Rapids: Baker Academic, 2012.

Snodgrass, Klyne. "From Allegorizing to Allegorizing: A History of the Interpretation of the Parables of Jesus." In *The Challenge of Jesus' Parables*, edited by Richard N. Longenecker, 3–29. Grand Rapids: Eerdmans, 2000.

———. *Stories with Intent: A Comprehensive Guide to the Parables of Jesus*. 2nd ed. Grand Rapids: Eerdmans, 2018.

Spencer, F. Scott. "The Literary/Postmodern View." In Porter and Stovell, *Biblical Hermeneutics*, 48–68.

Stein, Robert H. *An Introduction to the Parables of Jesus*. Philadelphia: Westminster, 1981.

Sterling, Gregory E. *Historiography and Self-Definition: Josephos, Luke-Acts, and Apologetic Historiography*. NovTSup 64. Leiden: Brill, 1992.

Stevenson, Geoffrey, ed. *The Future of Preaching*. London: SCM, 2010.

Stott, John R. W. *Between Two Worlds: The Art of Preaching in the Twentieth Century*. Grand Rapids: Eerdmans, 1994.

Stout, Harry S. *The Divine Dramatist: George Whitefield and the Rise of Modern Evangelicalism*. Grand Rapids: Eerdmans, 1991.

Stuart, Douglas. *Old Testament Exegesis: A Handbook for Students and Pastors*. 4th ed. Louisville: Westminster John Knox, 2009.

Talbert, Charles H. *What Is a Gospel? The Genre of the Canonical Gospels*. Philadelphia: Fortress, 1977.

Thiselton, Anthony C. *Hermeneutics: An Introduction*. Grand Rapids: Eerdmans, 2009.

———. *The Hermeneutics of Doctrine*. Grand Rapids: Eerdmans, 2007.

———. *New Horizons in Hermeneutics: The Theory and Practice of Transforming Biblical Reading*. Grand Rapids: Zondervan, 1992.

———. "Reader-Response Hermeneutics, Action Models, and the Parables of Jesus." In *The Responsibility of Hermeneutics*, by Roger Lundin, Anthony C. Thiselton, and Clarence Walhout, 79–113. Grand Rapids: Eerdmans, 1985.

———. "Semantics and New Testament Interpretation." In *New Testament Interpretation: Essays on Principles and Methods*, edited by I. Howard Marshall, 75–104. Grand Rapids: Eerdmans, 1977.

———. *The Two Horizons: New Testament Hermeneutics and Philosophical Description with Special Reference to Heidegger, Bultmann, Gadamer, and Wittgenstein*. Grand Rapids: Eerdmans, 1980.

Tillich, Paul. *Systematic Theology*. 3 vols. Chicago: University of Chicago Press, 1951.

Tracy, David. *Blessed Rage for Order: The New Pluralism in Theology*. New York: Seabury, 1975.

Tucker, Gene M. *Form Criticism of the Old Testament*. GBS. Philadelphia: Fortress, 1971.

Turbayne, Colin M. *The Myth of Metaphor*. Columbia: University of South Carolina Press, 1970.

van den Hoek, A. "Allegorical Interpretation." In Porter, *Dictionary of Biblical Criticism and Interpretation*, 9–12.

van der Merwe, Christo H. J., Jacobus A. Naudé, and Jan H. Kroeze. *Biblical Hebrew Reference Grammar*. 2nd ed. London: T&T Clark, 2017.

Vanhoozer, Kevin J. *The Drama of Doctrine: A Canonical-Linguistic Approach to Christian Theology*. Louisville: Westminster John Knox, 2005.

Volf, Miroslav. *The End of Memory: Remembering Rightly in a Violent World*. Grand Rapids: Eerdmans, 2006.

———. *Exclusion and Embrace: A Theological Exploration of Identity, Otherness, and Reconciliation*. Nashville: Abingdon, 1996.

von Rad, Gerhard. *Biblical Interpretations in Preaching*. Translated by John E. Steely. Nashville: Abingdon, 1977.

Wakefield, Andrew H. *Where to Live: The Hermeneutical Significance of Paul's Citations from Scripture in Galatians 3:1–14*. Atlanta: SBL, 2003.

Wall, Robert W. "Canonical Criticism." In *A Handbook to the Exegesis of the New Testament*, edited by Stanley E. Porter, 291–312. Leiden: Brill, 1997.

Ward, Graham. *Cities of God*. New York: Routledge, 2003.

Warfield, Benjamin B. "The Idea of Systematic Theology." *PRR* 7 (1896): 243–71.

Watson, Francis. "The Bible." In Webster, *Cambridge Companion to Karl Barth*, 57–71.

———. *Paul and the Hermeneutics of Faith*. London: T&T Clark, 2004.

Webster, John, ed. *The Cambridge Companion to Karl Barth*. Cambridge: Cambridge University Press, 2000.

Wellek, René, and Austin Warren. *Theory of Literature*. New York: Harcourt, Brace, 1948.

Westphal, Merold. *Whose Community? Which Interpretation? Philosophical Hermeneutics for the Church*. The Church and Postmodern Culture. Grand Rapids: Baker Academic, 2009.

White, James F. *Introduction to Christian Worship*. 3rd ed. Nashville: Abingdon, 2000.

White, R. E. O. *A Guide to Preaching*. Grand Rapids: Eerdmans, 1973.

Wiles, Gordon P. *Paul's Intercessory Prayers: The Significance of the Intercessory Prayer Passages in the Letters of Paul*. SNTSMS 24. Cambridge: Cambridge University Press, 1974.

Wimsatt, W. K. *Day of the Leopards: Essays in Defense of Poems*. New Haven: Yale University Press, 1976.

Wiseman, Donald. *1 and 2 Kings: An Introduction and Commentary*. Downers Grove, IL: InterVarsity, 1993.

Woodbridge, John D. *Biblical Authority: A Critique of the Rogers/McKim Proposal*. Grand Rapids: Zondervan, 1982.

Worth, Roland H., Jr. *The Sermon on the Mount: Its Old Testament Roots*. New York: Paulist Press, 1997.

Wright, Adam Z. *Of Conflict and Concealment: The Gospel of Mark as Tragedy*. MBSS. Eugene, OR: Pickwick, 2020.

Wright, N. T. *The Last Word: Beyond the Bible Wars to a New Understanding of the Authority of Scripture*. New York: HarperCollins, 2005.

Yamasaki, Gary. *Perspective Criticism: Point of View and Evaluative Guidance in Biblical Narrative*. Eugene, OR: Cascade Books, 2012.

Yarchin, William, ed. *History of Biblical Interpretation: A Reader*. Peabody, MA: Hendrickson, 2004.

Young, Frances. "Alexandrian and Antiochene Exegesis." In *A History of Biblical Interpretation: The Ancient Period*, edited by Alan Hauser and Duane Watson, 334–54. Grand Rapids: Eerdmans, 2003.

Index of Modern Authors

Index of Ancient Sources